WEAPONS & EQUI
OF THE
NAPOLEONIC
WARS
Philip J. Haythornthwaite

WEAPONS & EQUIPMENT
OF THE
NAPOLEONIC WARS
Philip J. Haythornthwaite

ARMS AND
ARMOUR

War: which no man could behold without raising his voice in thanksgiving to the Author of all good, that the home of his childhood had been preserved from such fearful visitations ...

Captain Sir John Kincaid

DEDICATION
To my Parents

ILLUSTRATIONS
Drawings devised by John Mollo and drawn by Peter Sarson and Tony Bryan. Other illustrations from the Author's Collection.

Cover illustration: *The 74th Highlanders at the Battle of Assoigne, India, 1803,* by David Rowlands. Reproduced by courtesy of the artist.

ARMS AND ARMOUR
An imprint of the Cassell Group
Wellington House, 125 Strand, London WC2R 0BB

Copyright © Philip J. Haythornthwaite 1979, 1996

First published 1979 by Blandford Press
This revised edition 1996 by Arms and Armour

First paperback edition 1998

ISBN 1-85409-495-5

British Library Cataloguing-in-Publication Data
A catalogue record for this book is available from
the British Library.

Distributed in the USA by Sterling Publishing Co. Inc.,
387 Park Avenue South, New York, NY 10016-8810

Printed and bound in Great Britain

CONTENTS

Fig. 1.   The Emperor Napoleon. Print after Meissonier.

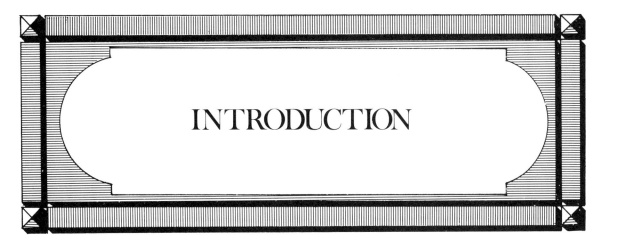

INTRODUCTION

Weapons and Equipment of the Napoleonic Wars was published originally in 1979. This new edition reproduces the main text without alteration, but the opportunity has been taken to provide an extended bibliography, and a number of new illustrations.

Any 'general' work on the Napoleonic Wars must, from the volume of material to be considered, include some generalizations and broad assertions which, though representing the basic facts, were not universally true. Similarly, some areas – particularly regarding the tactics and capabilities of individual commanders – are still in dispute; even such apparently technical details as ranges and capabilities of fieldpieces, for example, depend upon contemporary statistics which are sometimes at variance. It should be remembered that some 'period' sources include 'eyewitness' accounts written in some cases more than thirty years after the event from memories conceivably clouded by the lapse in time, works produced in haste after the events described and thus lacking in a balanced view, and others which exhibit bias, either intentional or otherwise.

The question of the amount of reliability which can be placed upon 'contemporary' material is illustrated, albeit in its most extreme case, by a work published in 1819 and frequently reprinted. In *Historic Doubts Relative to Napoleon Bonaparte* by Richard Whately, Archbishop of Dublin, the theory was argued that Napoleon *never existed*, but was rather a composite image of the deeds of many generals, his name originating from the Greek 'Lion of the Forest' and from 'Buona Parte', 'originally a sort of cant term applied to the "good [i.e. the bravest, or most patriotic] part" of the French army, collectively'.[1] There may have been some validity in arguing that, for most people, there was no *proof* that he ever existed in the sense of personal knowledge of the fact, but the comment by *Chambers' Edinburgh Journal* (17 July 1847) that it was a 'curious' publication which took a 'strange line of argument' was surely valid. While such fanciful theories may be dismissed immediately (indeed, even this work never seriously intended to suggest that Napoleon *was* actually a fiction), the reader will find many other discrepancies between contemporary works, for, in the words of the Duke of Wellington, 'As soon as an accident happens, every man who can write, and who has a friend who can read, sits down to write his account of what he does not know, and his comments on what he does not understand.'[2]

Although this book is concerned primarily with the weaponry and equipment of the Napoleonic Wars, as the subjects of tactics, strategy and weapons-performance were inter-related some attention is paid to the first, but primarily only in relation to the performance and utilization of weapons and equipment. For more exhaustive treatment of the methods and concepts of the strategy and tactics of the era, reference should be made to volumes listed in the bibliography.

In the following pages, considerable mention is made of 'weapon effectiveness', i.e. killing-power. Although this consideration is a historical necessity, and at the time was a vital factor in the military trade, it is an irony of mankind that the weapons considered 'best' should be those with the greatest facility for carrying away mankind itself. In considering impersonal descriptions of tactical ploys, and even more impersonal statistics regarding the victims of those tactics, it should never be forgotten that each statistic represents a human tragedy, a fact which apparently escaped some of the generals of the period. How apt was Wellington's comment that, next to a battle lost, the greatest sorrow was a battle won.

1. *Historic Doubts*, pp. 50–51.
2. Wellington to Robert Craufurd, 23 July 1810; *Wellington's Dispatches* VI, p. 287.

INFANTRY WEAPONS & TACTICS

THE INFANTRY

The composition of infantry units in all armies was basically similar. The principal tactical formation was the battalion, of which a 'regiment' might contain one or several, each battalion being a separate entity. The battalion comprised a number of companies, each containing perhaps a hundred men with officers, N.C.O.s and musicians attached. Each battalion usually consisted of a number of 'centre' companies and two 'flank' companies, the terms indicating the position occupied by the company when the battalion was formed in line. In theory the 'flank' companies, guarding the most vulnerable part of the line, were the battalion élite, the senior flank company usually styled 'grenadiers', supposedly the bravest and tallest of the regiment, their title a survival of the privileged position of those who threw hand-grenades. The junior flank company consisted of light infantry, small, agile sharpshooters adept at skirmishing and scouting; in French and satellite armies they were termed 'voltigeurs' (literally, 'vaulters'). The 'centre' companies had a variety of names, 'fusilier' being most common (i.e. one who carried a fusil or musket); in Britain the term 'battalion company' was used. These terms were common throughout Europe: for example, 'fucilieri', 'granatieri' and 'volteggiatori' in Italy, 'fusileros', 'granaderos' and 'cazadores' in Spain, the latter, like the Portuguese 'caçadore', equating with 'chasseur', for which see below.

Battalion-establishments varied greatly between armies and dates, but some examples are given below. Active service usually rendered official establishments correct only on paper.

Prior to the Revolution, French infantry was organized in two-battalion regiments, each battalion of four fusilier and one flank company, grenadiers in one battalion and light infantry in the other. An entire re-organization was needed during the Revolutionary Wars to leaven the many untrained volunteer units with veterans, so the 'amalgame' was devised, put into effect from January 1794, which established 'demi-brigades' of three battalions each, one regular and two volunteer, the 2nd or 'centre' battalion being composed of regulars. Each demi-brigade battalion initially comprised three companies of 330 men each, later increased to nine of between 150 and 200 men each, one company being styled grenadiers; on service it was rare for a demi-brigade to have above about 2,500 men.

In September 1803 the demi-brigades were re-titled 'regiments' (the term demi-brigade thereafter indicating provisional groupings of battalions), and from 1805–08 a further re-organization caused each regiment to comprise four battalions of six companies each, four fusilier, one grenadier and one voltigeur, the latter a new addition. In addition to the four 'combat battalions' ('bataillons de guerre'), of which the fourth was often detached to form composite provisional regiments, there was a depôt battalion to provide drafts and train recruits.

A Decree of February 1808 regulated organization, each regiment having the following staff: colonel, major, four 'chefs de bataillon', five adjutants, quartermaster, paymaster, surgeon-major, four assistant-surgeons, five assistant-adjutants, ten sergeant-majors, drum-major, corporal-drummer, bandmaster, seven musicians, four master-craftsmen, eagle-bearer (a subaltern of ten years' service) and two eagle-escorts (N.C.O.s whose illiteracy prevented further advancement). Company establishment was: captain, lieutenant, sub-lieutenant, sergeant-major, four sergeants, quartermaster-corporal, eight corporals, two drummers (hornists for voltigeurs) and 121 privates. Regimental strength was therefore 3,970 (108 officers), with four pioneers per battalion (grenadiers) and a pioneer-corporal per regiment.

In line, the grenadiers occupied the right flank and the voltigeurs the left; 'when the six companies are present with the battalion it will always march and act by divisions. When the grenadiers and the light infantry are absent . . . it will always manoeuvre and march by platoon. Two companies will form a division; each company will form a platoon; each half company a section.' This illustrates how the terms 'division', 'platoon', etc. referred to tactical formations, not sub-units of the battalion.[3]

British battalions comprised ten companies (one grenadier, one light), with a theoretical establishment of thirty-five officers and 1,000 rank and file, though this strength was hardly ever seen in the field. A regiment's '1st Battalion' on campaign would initially have a greater strength than the 2nd Battalion, having filled its ranks with fit men drawn from the 2nd, which had to leave behind not only its own ineffective personnel but those of the 1st Battalion as well. Statistics for Wellington's infantry in 1811 show how (as in *all* armies) 'actual' strength often bore no relation to 'establishment'. Of forty-six battalions, only nine had more than 700 men (two of which were Guards with a higher initial establishment); sixteen had between 500 and 700, and ten from 400 to 500.

Eleven had less than 400; the average was no more than 550. The strongest (1/43rd) had 1,005 and the weakest (2/38th) but 263.[4]

Some German armies used the term 'musketeer' for the centre companies and 'fusilier' for light infantry; thus in 1807 a Prussian regiment comprised two musketeer battalions, a light battalion, and two grenadier companies. By December 1808 each battalion comprised four companies, each of five officers, thirty-two N.C.O.s, 115 privates, three musicians and a medical orderly, the 'paper' strength (632) increased in war-time by about fifty men per company. The three regimental battalions usually operated together, with the grenadiers detached and formed into composite grenadier battalions. Austrian regiments in 1805 comprised four fusilier and one grenadier battalion, each of four companies, with 800 men per fusilier battalion and 600 per grenadier. Russian infantry underwent several changes of organization; in 1805 all line regiments had an establishment of 2,256 men, both 'musketeer' and élite 'grenadier' regiments, the former consisting of three battalions, including one of grenadiers. By 1812, each musketeer battalion comprised four companies, including one of grenadiers, divided into two platoons: grenadiers proper who held the right flank, and 'Jägers' on the left.

Organization of other armies often followed that of one of the major powers; exceptions included Spain which in 1807 had three-battalion regiments of four companies per battalion, each company unwieldy with 188 men and only three officers, and Portugal, which in 1809 had two-battalion regiments, each battalion of 770 men in seven companies (actual strength fluctuated greatly; instead of 1,550 per regiment the September 1809 returns vary from the 11th Regiment's 1,498 men to the 21st's 193!).

Light infantry regiments acted like the light companies of the line, adept at skirmishing, though in practice many differed little from their line colleagues except in the prestige accorded to light infantry. French light regiments were organized like the line, the original 'demi-brigades légère' formed around regular 'chasseur' battalions. (The latter term – meaning 'hunter' – was commonly adopted by light infantry and cavalry to symbolize their fast-moving rôle); instead of fusiliers and grenadiers the terms 'chasseur' and 'carabinier' were used in French regiments. British light infantry units were classed as part of the line, with identical establishments. In 1807 Spanish light infantry were single-battalion corps of 1,200 men each; Portuguese 'caçadore' battalions consisted of 770 men in five companies, including one of 'atiradores' (sharpshooters).

German light infantry were usually styled 'Jäger' (the equivalent of 'chasseur'), often known in English as 'rifles' due to the predominance of rifled muskets. These units were often small; from 1808 Prussian 'Jäger' and 'Schützen' (sharpshooter) battalions had a complement of officers and N.C.O.s like the line but only eighty-eight men and two buglers per company, a total battalion strength of 429. Volunteer Jäger companies were often attached to line regiments on campaign. Austria possessed similar Jäger corps, plus 'Grenz' (frontier) battalions of Croatian light infantry. Russian Jäger battalions in 1812 consisted of four companies, one of which, styled 'Jäger-grenadiers', comprised a platoon of grenadiers and one of 'carabiniers', an imitation of the flank-company system of the line. The two British 'rifle' corps were the 60th and 95th, both multi-battalion regiments and an experienced élite.

Flank companies were sometimes detached to form composite élite battalions; most armies at some time used this method of providing a veteran reserve or provisional light corps by drawing personnel from a number of line battalions.

Infantry tactics were governed by weapon-performance and the tactical developments of the eighteenth century. Only by manoeuvring in tightly-packed masses could discipline be maintained, volley-fire be effective, and infantry reasonably safe against cavalry. The tenets of infantry tactics utilized two basic formations: line and column.

Relying upon disciplined firepower rather than the impetus of charge, the line had emerged in the eighteenth century as the predominant formation; without the disciplined fire of a three or four-deep line no manoeuvre

had much chance of success. Though the French drill-book 'Réglement d'Infanterie' (1791) clung to the line (though providing for a rapid advance in column), the armies of the Revolution, including large numbers of untrained conscripts, lacked the discipline and cohesion to manoeuvre in a conventional manner. So a new tactic was devised: the attack in column. First masking the entire French line with hordes of skirmishers to occupy and absorb the fire of the enemy, densely-packed columns of troops were launched at specific points on the enemy line. Expensive though such column-attacks were, they enabled the French to use their levies to bludgeon a hole in the opposing line. Thus the untrained masses of the Revolution were able to overthrow the most professional armies in Europe by sheer weight of numbers. The organization of the demi-brigade also allowed the centre (regular) battalion to operate in line, and the two flank (conscript) battalions in column, a compromise which employed both conventional firepower and the 'horde' tactic of the untrained.

This manoeuvre was taken a stage further. The column's main disadvantage was that, excepting the first two or three ranks, no muskets could be fired. Realizing the need for maximum firepower, Napoleon instituted the 'ordre mixte' as earlier recommended by General Guibert; like the demi-brigade formation noted above, columns (from battalion to divisional level) were linked by units placed in line, thus increasing the overall firepower whilst maintaining the impetus of the column.

Fig. 2. Overleaf: *Infantry formations. A. A British battalion in close order; B. A French regiment in column of divisions, three battalions to a regiment; C and D. Alternative formations for single battalion formations after the 1809 reorganization; E. 'L'Ordre Mixte'. showing a three battalion regiment deployed partly in line and partly in column; F. A Prussian four company battalion (1812) moving from columns into line; G. A Prussian brigade of two regiments deployed for attack (1812); H. A seven company battalion moving from column into line; J. An eight company battalion forming square from line.*

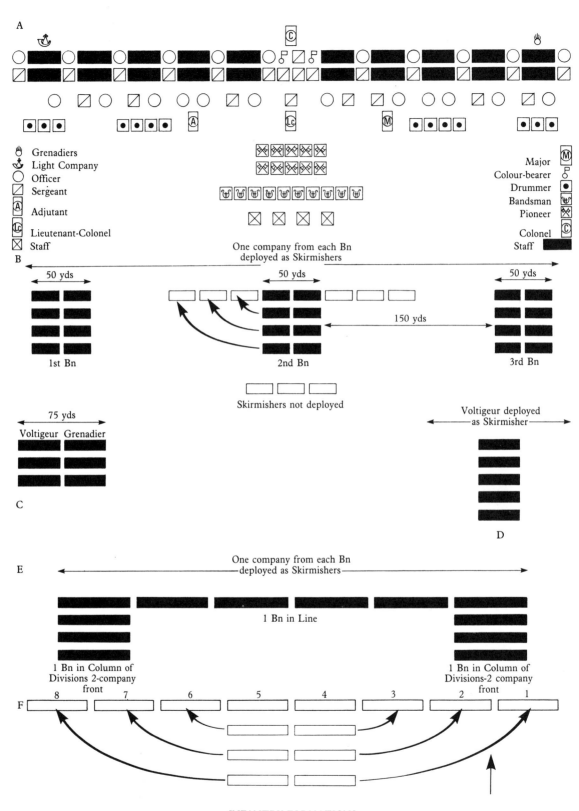

A

👐 Grenadiers
⚓ Light Company
○ Officer
◿ Sergeant
Ⓐ Adjutant
ⓁⒸ Lieutenant-Colonel
⊠ Staff

Major Ⓜ
Colour-bearer 🎺
Drummer ●
Bandsman 🎺
Pioneer ⊠

Colonel Ⓒ
Staff ■

One company from each Bn
deployed as Skirmishers

B

50 yds

50 yds

50 yds

150 yds

1st Bn

2nd Bn

3rd Bn

Skirmishers not deployed

Voltigeur deployed
as Skirmisher

75 yds

Voltigeur Grenadier

C

D

One company from each Bn
deployed as Skirmishers

E

1 Bn in Line

1 Bn in Column of
Divisions 2-company
front

1 Bn in Column of
Divisions-2 company
front

F 8 7 6 5 4 3 2 1

INFANTRY FORMATIONS

6

G

Skirmishers from Fusilier Battalions
— deployed —

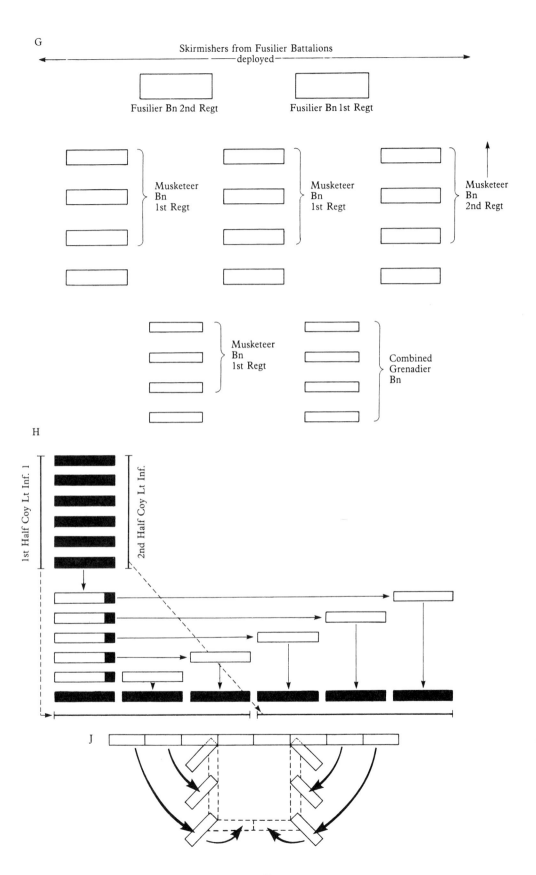

Fusilier Bn 2nd Regt   Fusilier Bn 1st Regt

Musketeer Bn 1st Regt

Musketeer Bn 1st Regt

Musketeer Bn 2nd Regt

Musketeer Bn 1st Regt

Combined Grenadier Bn

H

1st Half Coy Lt Inf. 1

2nd Half Coy Lt Inf.

J

7

The subject of Napoleonic tactics is too complex to be covered in any depth, but basic facts are noted below. The skirmish-cloud which preceded an advance would be drawn from the voltigeur companies of the battalions participating, or even entire regiments deployed in open order. Behind them, a battalion would normally advance in 'column of divisions', a two-company frontage, four companies deep (for a nine-company regiment). Every company was deployed in three ranks with about a yard between; so that a 'battalion column' had a 50-yard front and a depth of about 21 yards (twelve ranks). With the later six-company French establishment, a battalion column consisted of three 'divisions', with a 75-yard front and 15-yard depth (nine ranks). When the voltigeurs were deployed a 'column of companies' was often used, one company behind the other. If morale was good the grenadiers would lead the advance; if not they would be placed at the rear to encourage the others.

Large attacks were mounted by a series of battalion columns in line or echelon, with at least 150 yards between to enable each battalion to deploy into line and the skirmish-screen to retire just before the attack engaged the enemy. Battalion columns could be drawn into checkerboard lines to allow cavalry and artillery to manoeuvre between, the latter ideally accompanying the advance to bombard the 'target' section of the enemy line. The system was so flexible as to allow its variation according to terrain. The 'ordre mixte' was equally flexible, the column allowing both rapid movement and easy change of formation without the time-consuming intervals needed to re-align linear formations. Huge divisional columns, employed when the quality of the infantry began to deteriorate, were often less effective.

With trained infantry, the column-attack was intended to deploy into line immediately before contact. Whether the frequent failure to do so was by design or not is uncertain; some generals may have believed that the old 'sledgehammer' tactic, having worked with the conscripts of the Revolution, might work again. However, it appears that many column-attacks *did* attempt to deploy, but too late before actual contact with the enemy. By his judicious placement of troops on the reverse slope of a hill, Wellington not only protected them from enemy fire but rendered the French commanders incapable of knowing *when* to deploy into line, their target being concealed from view. Against armies not employing the 'reverse slope' tactic, however, the French column-attack was potentially invincible; indeed the *sight* of an advance was enough to dishearten most troops; as Wellington said, 'I suspect all the continental armies are half-beaten before the battle begins;'[5] but against a line of uncowed troops, willing even to throw forward its wings to envelop the column, the French system could hardly have been expected to succeed against concentrated musketry.

The line was commonly formed of three ranks, the troops packed together but not so tightly as to affect loading: the British instructions specified that:

'Each soldier ... must just feel with his elbow the touch of the neighbour to whom he dresses; nor in any situation of movement in front must he ever relinquish such touch ... each man will then occupy a space of 22 inches ... There are two distances of ranks, open and close; when they are open they are three paces asunder; when they are close they are one pace; and when the body is halted and ready to fire they are still closer locked up ... Open order is only an occasional exception made in situations of parade....'[6]

The depth of line caused a great controversy, most nations favouring three-deep; despite the successful use of the two-deep line in America, Dundas' 'Rules and Regulations' (1792) defended the three-deep system, claiming 'In no service is the fire and consistency of the third rank given up...,'[7] but in fact the third was *not* as effective as the other two; so the two-deep line was used increasingly, given tacit official approval 'even at reviews' in 1801.[8] Compared to a column or even a three-deep line its power was crushing. For example, a French division of 5,000 men advancing on a two-company front could only bring 340 muskets to bear; but 500 men in a two-deep line could fire between six and ten shots per yard per minute which, directed at a small, dense target like the head of a column, was lethal. Against an

Fig. 3.   British squares resist French cavalry at Waterloo. Print by R. Reeve after William Heath.

equally-strong three-deep line it overlapped; in one of the few combats between two- and three-deep lines, at Maida, the outnumbered two-rank British inflicted 2,000 casualties on the three-rank French, suffering only 320 casualties in the process. A major disadvantage of the two-deep line, however, was the 'shrinkage' caused by the movement of men towards the centre to fill gaps made by casualties, there being no third rank to keep the line intact. Its effectiveness also depended upon: a) that it should not be exposed to the enemy until the last moment (i.e. use of reverse slope); b) it should be screened by light infantry to keep the French skirmishers back; and c) its flanks should be covered by cavalry or the terrain to protect against flank-attacks. Against a rear-attack the second rank could 'about-face' and fight back-to-back, as did the British 28th at Alexandria. Despite the obvious advantages of the two-deep line and use of reverse slope, its benefits seem to have escaped all commanders except Wellington.

Under normal circumstances, infantry in line were helpless against cavalry and could be massacred, as happened at Albuera. Their only protection was the square, a bristling hedge of bayonets impenetrable in all but extreme cases as the cavalry (unless armed with lances) could not reach the infantry over their bayonets and their horses would not charge the fearsome sight. When squares *were* broken by cavalry, as at Garcia Hernandez, the infantry were either tired, disheartened or inexperienced, or the side of the square was crushed by a falling horse. But if horse artillery accompanied the cavalry, the square could be annihilated by canister.

The square, almost invariably hollow with sides four-deep (two-deep when guarding baggage), needed several hundred men to make it practicable: at Salamanca the British 53rd, 245 strong, were forced to retire in line before cavalry, 'the ranks too much thinn'd to attempt a square.'[9] Normally of battalion-size, a square could be formed by two, or even a brigade; 'battalion guns', usually two field-pieces, would be sited at opposite corners of the square. To form square quickly demanded some precision, any fault in timing revealing a gap into which cavalry could rush (this

9

Fig. 4. The raising of the siege of Thionville, 16 October 1792. French infantry in foreground routing Hungarian infantry. After Hippolyte Lecomte.

happened with the British 42nd at Quatre Bras; they closed the square and killed the French cavalry trapped inside). Squares could be formed from line upon any company or from column; with a ten-company battalion the 'square' was often oblong, three companies on two opposite sides and two on the others. When a unit was completely scattered, any officer or N.C.O. could cry 'Form Rallying Square', whereupon any men nearby would run to him, the first two joining his right and left, the next three in front and a further three behind, all facing outwards. By the time about eighty had run up a solid, tightly-packed mass would have been formed, incapable of offence but impervious to cavalry.

Deploying was usually carried out beyond enemy musket-range and at the halt; when Packenham deployed the British 3rd Division at Salamanca on the move, officers dressing ranks as they marched, it was manoeuvre not included in the drill-books!

Other nations did not profit from the example of British success over French column; the Prussian 'Manoeuvre Regulations' of 1812 were apparently inspired by the 1791 French drill and the 'Napoleonic' Westphalian system. Each Prussian company comprised two 'Zügen' (platoons), numbered one to eight within the battalion. Each 'Züg' had a place in the firing-line and was formed three-deep; for column a 'Zügkolonne' of one-Züg frontage was used, or a double-Züg column with double-Züg frontage, four Zügen deep. For larger formations, a common version consisted of three battalion-columns with fusiliers deployed as skirmishers, with one musketeer and the combined grenadier battalion in reserve. Other defeated nations similarly copied the French system; for example, Austria's revised drill-book provided for skirmishers, but limited in number and not as enthusiastic as the French whom they were intended to emulate.

The Russian 'Military Code' (1796) recommended the three-rank line, with the platoon column (four platoons per company) the basis of all evolutions. Firing was by 'rolling volley', the four platoons of each company firing in succession. Suvorov dismissed the 1796 Code as a 'rat-eaten parchment found in the corner of an old castle,'[10] and emphasized instead the mass-attack with the bayonet. This obsession with the bayonet reached a peak in 1812, when virtually all infantry at Borodino was arrayed in French-style battalion columns. Russian manoeuvres were criticized in the earlier years by observers from other armies: 'They are absolutely useless for anything that has to do with manoeuvre, and in this respect an ordinary French soldier is worth more than all the officers of the Russian army put together ... their gallantry goes for nothing because they do not know how to direct it ... they charge with the bayonet ... but they are so clumsy that they never manage to catch anyone.'[11] Even the battalion columns at Borodino were not a success, presenting a superb target for the French artillery and resulting in heavy casualties. Later in the 1812 campaign the Russians arrayed their infantry in longer, thinner lines and less densely-packed, thus negating much of the French artillery fire.

Effective light infantry tactics demanded specialist training and a high *esprit de corps*; for this reason it was preferable to have light troops gathered in companies, instead of a number of men in every company trained as skirmishers, 'otherwise you may lose ... the services of both; because the active may be of no use, being kept back by their sluggish companions; and unless they are previously divided into separate bodies, you cannot distinguish and separate them when wanted.'[12] Nevertheless, Russia continued this practice until 1810, the Jäger platoon

spread as an extra rank at the rear of the battalion, where their supposed specialist skills were useless (in effect, the smallest men were automatically posted to the Jägers, until Barclay de Tolly improved training and made 'élite' status a matter of reward). A few British colonels trained perhaps fifteen to twenty men per company to act as 'flankers' to support the light company, but the practice was short-lived and Oman found only one reference to its use in action, at Maida.[13]

Ideally, a detachment of light infantry should have been attached to every larger formation; French divisions and even brigades often contained at least one light infantry battalion in addition to regimental light companies. Though the British light infantry in the Peninsula were collected into one brigade (later Division), each division had light infantry units attached, either British rifle companies or Portuguese caçadore regiments.

Skirmishing, in which the light infantryman operated as an individual, required a degree of intelligence above that of the automatic drill of the line. In skirmish order the men were rarely widely-spaced (in British service 'open order' signified two feet between files, 'extended order' two paces), though in combat frequently adopted a much more 'individual' rôle. Light troops generally worked in pairs, so that one would always have a loaded musket, and all movements executed in 'quick time', 'each firing as quick as he can, consistent with loading properly....'[14] Two basic methods of movement were practised: either formed in two lines, the rear rank advancing directly through the gaps in the front rank; or, when 'covering' each other, '... as soon as the front rank man has fired, he is to slip to the left of the rear man, who will make a short pace forward, and put himself in the other's place, whom he is to protect while loading. When the first man returns his ramrod, he will give his comrade the word *ready*, after which, and not before, he may fire, and immediately change places as before.'[15]

When advancing the same drill was used, save that the rear man would move around his comrade and six paces in front; when retiring the front man would do likewise but withdraw twelve paces. Naturally, terrain-

Fig. 5. The combination of British musketry and controlled bayonet-charges repel a French attack at Busaco. Print after Major T. S. St. Clair.

features used as cover usually threw these drill-book manoeuvres completely out of time.

The essence of light infantry tactics is given in the British *Volunteer Manual* (1803):

'Vigilance, activity, and intelligence, are particularly requisite ... The first is to guard against surprise ... Rapidity of movement ... establishes their own security, at the same time that it renders them the terror of the enemy ... Being unincumbered [sic] they can change their situation without difficulty ... and they can appear suddenly upon points where they are least expected, and the most to be dreaded. The intelligence chiefly required in a light infantry man is, that he should know how to take advantage of every circumstance of ground which can enable him to harass and annoy an enemy, without exposing himself ... In some situations they must conceal themselves by stooping, in others they must kneel, or lie flat upon the ground ... Light infantry must know how to gain upon an enemy along hedges, through

corn fields, amongst gardens and ditches, almost without being perceived ... Light infantry ought to be perfectly aware that they have little to apprehend in any situation from artillery, and that in close country they are greatly an over-match for cavalry. They may pick off the men employed at the guns, and likewise gall the dragoons by their fire, without risk to themselves ... Against regular infantry formed ... in close order ... they must hover continually in every quarter. If the regulars advance rapidly upon them, the light troops must recede; and when the enemy is exhausted ... they must again line the hedges and ditches round him ... light infantry can be opposed no otherwise than by men acting in the same manner with themselves. These they must endeavour to outwit; to lead them into an ambuscade; and to bring, by a pretended retreat, into places where they can be acted against by cavalry, or cut off ... and overpowered...

'... light troops should all be expert marksmen. To fire seldom and always with effect

Fig. 6. An infantry firing-line: French grenadiers in Spain. Engraving after H. Bellangé.

should be their chief study ... Noise and smoke is not sufficient to stop the advance of soldiers accustomed to war: they are to be checked only by seeing their comrades fall. ...'[16]

Amongst the traditionalists, these facts were not always evident; thus, despite experience during the American War of Independence, British light infantry skill had fallen into such disrepair that German mercenaries had to be used until Sir John Moore re-established and perfected light infantry training at Shorncliffe. Despite the widespread use of French 'tirailleur' (sharpshooter) screens, they rarely used more than regimental voltigeur companies in this rôle in the Peninsular War: 1,000 or 1,200 men per division employed as skirmishers. Conversely, an Anglo-Portuguese division would send out both regimental light companies and attached caçadore or rifle detachments, about 1,200 to 1,500 per 5,000 or 5,500 men, so that the resulting skirmish-line was so substantial that on occasion the French

believed it to be the main line! Accurate skirmish-fire, even though it did not kill, inevitably damaged morale:

'... though the enemy fired at be not wounded, yet the ball passes so close to him as to intimidate, and prove to him how skilful [sic] an opponent he is engaged with ... when a corps of ... good marksmen engage an enemy ... and never pull a trigger without deliberate and positive good aim, provided that they are not fortunate enough to kill, they are sure to intimidate. ...'[17]

THE MUSKET

The very basis of Napoleonic warfare was its simplest factor – the private soldier and his musket.

The musket of the Napoleonic Wars was a 'smoothbore' (i.e. lacking 'rifling' to impart a spin on the projectile) and operated on the flintlock system. The 'lock' consisted of three main parts. The hammer (or cock) comprised

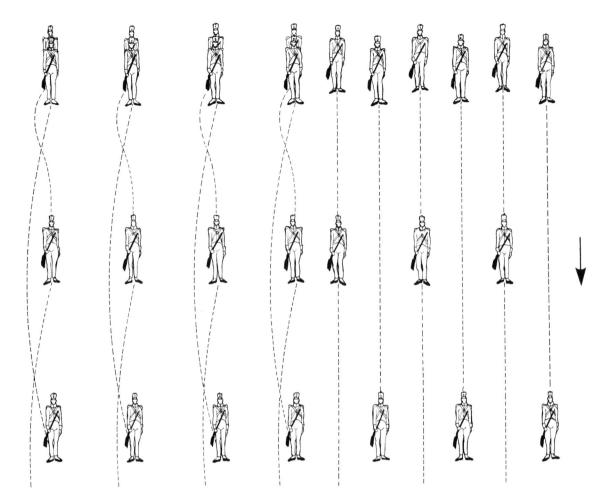

Fig. 7. British Light Infantry Exercise. Left: *Four files firing advancing in extended order, covering each other.* Right: *A rank of six men advancing firing in ordinary extended order.*

a pair of steel jaws, closed by a screw, holding a shaped piece of flint; its position was on the 'lockplate' on the right-hand side of the musket, level with the trigger which was connected internally to the hammer. The third element was the 'frizzen', a hinged steel plate covering the 'priming-pan', the latter a small depression on the lockplate, connected to the inside of the barrel by a 'touch-hole'. (The frizzen was also known as the 'steel' or 'hammer', when the flint-holder was termed the 'cock'.)

To fire the musket, the charge of gunpowder and the ball it propelled were inserted into the barrel via the muzzle (hence 'muzzle-loading') and the hammer drawn back on to 'half-cock', which allowed a small amount of powder to be poured into the priming-pan and the frizzen pulled upright, closing the pan-cover. The hammer was then drawn back an extra notch on to 'full-cock', at which stage pressure on the trigger would send the hammer and flint crashing on to the frizzen and, in forcing it backwards, striking a shower of sparks which ignited the powder in the pan. As this powder ignited with a flash, the spark passed into the barrel via the touch-hole and ignited the main charge, which exploded with an even greater cloud of smoke and sent the ball on its uneven course. A 'misfire' occurred when the spark did not pass through the touch-hole, despite a 'flash in the pan'; thus

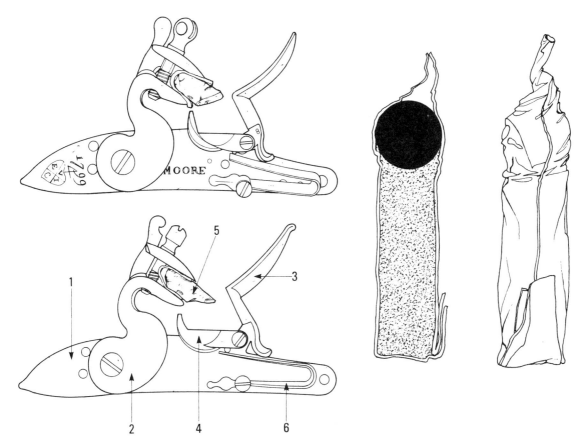

Fig. 8. Left: *Flintlock mechanism. 1. Lockplate; 2. Cock; 3. Hammer (or Steel or Frizzen); 4. Pan; 5. Flint held in jaws of the Cock; 6. Spring.* Right: *Paper musket cartridge showing the position of the ball and charge of powder.*

'hanging fire', the musket had to be unloaded carefully or a second ignition attempted. Recoil was fierce, the repeated kick so bruising the right shoulder that a soldier might be incapacitated after a long action. Idle soldiers remedied the recoil by using a reduced charge, thus drastically reducing the range of the musket.

Most muskets used a 'prepared' cartridge, a waxed or greased paper tube containing both gunpowder and ball. The ball, a lead sphere about an ounce in weight, was a fearsome weapon despite its many shortcomings. Flattening on impact, it could produce horrific injuries; though a 'spent ball', one striking the target at extreme range, might produce a bruise at worst. Without a prepared charge, the musketeer had to resort to loose ball and a powder-flask, from which a measured charge could be poured into the muzzle. This method was regularly used with the rifle, often with an additional flask of finely-ground 'priming powder'. Prepared cartridges were almost universal in combat, a unit's firepower dictated by the amount which could be carried on the person due to

Fig. 9. Overleaf: *British Manual and Platoon Exercise. 1. Shoulder Arms; 2. Order Arms; 3. Support Arms; 4. Fix Bayonets; 5. Port Arms; 6. Charge Bayonets; 7. Handle Cartridge, first movement; 8. Handle Cartridge, second movement; 9. Prime; 10. Load; 11. Draw Ramrods; 12. Ram Down Cartridge; 13. Withdraw Ramrods; 14. Return Ramrods; 15. Make Ready; 16. Present Fire; 17, 18. Make Ready Present Fire in three ranks.*

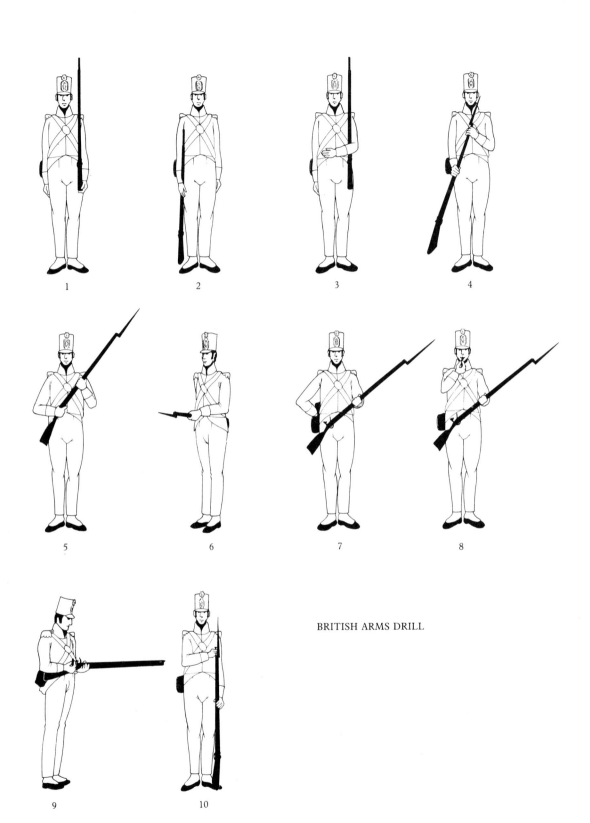

1   2   3   4

5   6   7   8

BRITISH ARMS DRILL

9   10

16

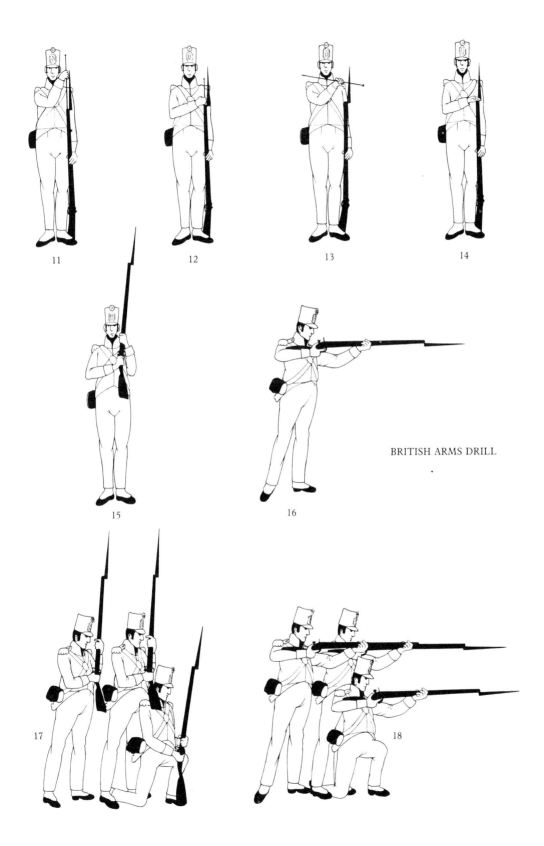

11

12

13

14

15

16

BRITISH ARMS DRILL

17

18

unreliable supply arrangements; in addition to the forty or sixty cartridges in his cartridge-box, before action a soldier might receive an extra ammunition-container or 'magazine', or a handful of loose cartridges to put in his pockets. The musket-ball varied between armies; Britain used a standard No. 11 bore (0.76 in. calibre) and a ball of No. 14 bore (0.71 in. in diameter); the difference between barrel-bore and ball-diameter was therefore 1/20th of an inch, this 'windage' facilitating loading. France used a smaller calibre (0.70 in.) and consequently a lighter ball (twenty-two to the pound against the British fourteen); the difference in efficiency was negligible, the French ball possibly having longer range and the British volley more 'weight'. Whereas French musket-balls could be used by the British (Wellington noting in 1813 that 'I have been obliged to use the French ammunition, of a smaller calibre than ours ...'),[18] the French were unable to use captured British ammunition. Several calibres existed within every army (musket-bore, carbine- and pistol-bore, etc.) – Russia had twenty-eight different calibres in 1812. In an emergency smoothbore firearms could use a wide range of projectiles – pebbles, buttons and one recorded instance of a cut-throat razor. Contemporary press reports list even more bizarre projectiles: a man shot through 'most fatal' with a wooden ruler,[19] and two people wounded, one fatally, by the discharge of a gun 'loaded only with powder and a piece of chewed tobacco',[20] for example.

Musket-drill (or 'Manual Exercise') varied between armies, but followed the same basic movements. The long and complicated drill not only turned the soldier into an automaton but ensured that a trained battalion would load and fire like second-nature, despite whatever carnage was around them. For drill, a 'fugel-man' could be used, a chosen soldier standing some way ahead of the main body, from whom the others would 'take their time'.

The following drill was followed in loading the musket. The musket would be held horizontally in the left hand, the soldier reaching behind him with the right hand to the cartridge-box, slung over the left shoulder and resting on the rear of the right hip. Extracting a cartridge, the soldier transferred it to his mouth, biting off the end of the paper tube (hence the raging thirst, caused by gunpowder in the mouth, which afflicted soldiers in combat) and, with the hammer on half-cock and the priming-pan uncovered, a small amount of powder was tipped into the pan and the cover closed. The musket-butt was then grounded and the remainder of the cartridge – paper, powder and ball – pushed into the muzzle. The ramrod was then drawn from its retaining tubes on the underside of the musket, reversed so that the 'button'-end pointed downwards, and inserted in the muzzle, ramming the cartridge to the bottom of the barrel. The ramrod was then replaced, the musket lifted to the 'shoulder arms' position and the hammer moved on to 'full cock'. The musket was fired by bringing the butt to the right shoulder, the soldier often leaning forward and taking his weight on the left foot, not always deliberately 'aiming' but simply pointing the gun in the appropriate general direction.

The procedure for firing could be varied; with an unobscured target, an entire battalion could fire a massive initial volley, after which firing was usually by sub-units or (in the early period) by ranks, rank-fire producing a continuous fusillade along the whole frontage of the unit. The rate of fire depended upon many variables, the proficiency of the individual being paramount. Firing independently an experienced soldier could discharge five shots a minute, falling to two or three in controlled volley. Even this rate could not be sustained for long, fatigue taking its toll, burnt powder blocking the touch-hole and flint becoming worn. Light rain had little effect providing the priming-pan was closed quickly or shielded from the wet, but heavy rain would render the musket useless, soaking the cartridge even on the short distance between cartridge-box and muzzle. Hughes (*Firepower*) estimates that a battalion of 500 men, formed in two ranks at 22 inches per file (a frontage of about 150 yards) could fire between 1,000 and 1,500 bullets per minute: in effect, six to ten shots per yard per minute.

'Short-cuts' to increase the rate of fire invariably increased the misfire rate as well, which in dry weather might be as high as

15 per cent. rising to a quarter in wet. Such short-cuts included the ramming of the whole cartridge down the barrel with sufficient force to shake enough powder through the touch-hole and into the pan, thus removing the 'prime' stage of the loading-drill; the same except that the butt was banged on the ground to shake the powder through to the pan; the load could be 'running ball' without the cartridge-paper wadding, so that the ball would roll out when the muzzle was lowered (a load often used by sentries); or by sticking the ramrod into the ground, thus eliminating the frequent drawing and replacing of the ramrod, a practice not encouraged due to the chance of a rapid change of position which might result in leaving the ramrod behind.

The real shortcomings of the smoothbore musket were in range and accuracy, for in aiming at an individual at all but the closest ranges it was wildly inaccurate. Before considering the mass of contemporary statistics which indicate both the theoretical and actual performance of the musket, it must be remembered that in the context of Napoleonic warfare it was not *necessary* for a musket to hit an individual target, tactics demanding that it should simply score a hit anywhere on a mass of men many times larger than the proverbial barn door. Ironically, it was the very inaccuracy of the musket which helped formulate those tactics, but it is uncertain how quickly tactics would have changed even if a more accurate firearm had been developed during the period in question.

Col. George Hanger, an expert marksman and noted advocate of the light infantry tactic, made frequent reference to the poor performance of the musket. His *To All Sportsmen* (1814) claimed that:

'A soldier's musket, if not exceedingly ill-bored (as many are), will strike the figure of a man at 80 yards; it may even at a hundred; but a soldier must be very unfortunate indeed who shall be wounded by a common musket at 150 yards, provided his antagonist aims at him; and as to firing at a man at 200 yards with a common musket, you may as well fire at the moon and have the same hope of hitting your object. I do maintain and will prove ... that no man was ever killed at 200 yards, by a common musket, by the person who aimed at him.'[21]

In *Reflections on the Menaced Invasion*, Hanger passes an opinion on the actual, not theoretical, performance of the musket. Taking a hypothetical case of 1,000 men firing sixty rounds at a similar-sized enemy unit, he estimated that 300 casualties would be caused, a rate of one hit per 200 shots, not because men firing 'at the word of command' were unable to take aim but because the muskets were either crooked or 'bent in soldering the loops on'.[22] More significant in actual fact was the 'windage', for though the difference in diameter of bore and ball facilitated loading and thus increased the rate of fire, it prevented any long-range accuracy.

British tests in 1841 established the range of the 'Brown Bess' musket at between 100 and 700 yards (according to elevation), though at *every* elevation there could be between 100 and 300 yards variance. At 150 yards a target twice as high and twice as broad as a man was hit three times out of four; at any greater range it was not hit at all. At 250 yards ten shots were fired at a target twice as wide again but not one hit was registered. Müller, author of *Elements of the Science of War* gave the following results of trials against a target representing a line of cavalry, including a variation between 'well trained men' and 'ordinary soldiers':[23]

Range	hits by 'trained' men	and 'ordinary'
100 yards	53%	40%
200 ,,	30%	18%
300 ,,	23%	15%

Picard, in *La Campagne de 1800 en Allemagne*,[24] indicates the error of a French musket fired from a rest at 150 metres (164 yards) to be 75 cm. in height and 60 cm. laterally, and gives the following for trained soldiers firing at a target 1.75 metres by 3 metres:

Range	% of hits
75 metres (82 yards)	60
150 ,, (164 ,,)	40
225 ,, (246 ,,)	25
300 ,, (328 ,,)	20

Prussian tests with the 'New Prussian Musket' (the old 0.60 Nothardt re-bored to

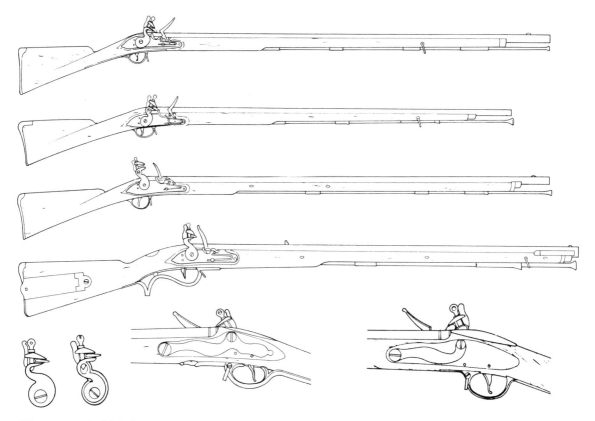

Fig. 10. *British Muskets.* From Top to Bottom: *New Short Land Pattern; India Pattern used in the British service after 1809; New Land Service; Baker Rifle (not drawn to scale with first three muskets).* Bottom Row: *Baker Rifle Cock; Baker Rifle reinforced Cock; Short Land Pattern with flat sideplate; India Pattern with convex sideplate.*

0.72) indicated that a target six feet by 100 feet was hit by two-thirds to three-quarters of shots fired at 100 paces, half at 200, one-quarter at 300 and only 1 per cent. at 600.

In combat not even these results were achieved. Given the misfire-rate (a British test under ideal conditions in 1834 established a misfire-rate of one in $6\frac{1}{2}$) the contemporary theory that to kill a man needed seven times his own weight of shot may not be in-accurate. Roquerol, in *L'Artillerie au début des guerres de la révolution*[25] states that only 0.2 to 0.5 per cent. of bullets were effective. Statistics for Vittoria are provided by the head of the field train department, R. Henegan, in *Seven Years Campaigning*: in this battle the allied infantry began with some 3,000,000 rounds, with a further 1,350,000 distributed during the action. Allowing for only half the replenishment to have been used, these 3,675,000 rounds caused some 8,000 casualties, one hit per 459 shots – and this does *not* include the 6,800 artillery rounds fired: '... at every battle in the Peninsula, except Barossa, the author remarked on the same undue expenditure of ammunition in relation to the small extent of damage done...'.[26]

Müller estimated that 50 per cent. of balls fired at 100 yards hit the target; considering misfire-rate, fatigue and the fact that in combat the target was moving, not stationary as in a controlled test, perhaps 15 per cent. of shots which could have been fired took effect. Further, if the target were a densely-packed mass, it might be expected that some men would be hit more than once. Hughes, calculating the casualties of Talavera, esti-mates that 1,250 to 1,300 French casualties were caused in half an hour by some twenty volleys (30,000 shots) from the British, an effectiveness of about 4 per cent. of the shots ordered to be fired (3 per cent. if thirty volleys were fired).[27]

This would seem to be the average casualty-rate which might be expected at 200 yards under combat conditions, rising to perhaps 5 per cent. or beyond at 100 yards or less. Presuming the quality of the musket to be approximately equal, the decisive factors can be seen to have been the speed at which the musket could be discharged and the number of muskets brought to bear at any one point. Thus the British two-deep line, with every musket capable of simultaneous and effective discharge, was much superior to the three-deep French line and infinitely more so against the column.

A further factor affecting the accuracy of musketry was inexperience of the infantry. In British service, line regiments received thirty rounds ball and seventy blank for practice, per man per year; light infantry fifty and sixty respectively, and riflemen sixty each, the blank to practise firing by volley, but only light infantry receiving tuition in 'firing ball at a mark'.[28] Other nations were even more parsimonious with practice-ammunition: in 1805 Archduke Ferdinand of Austria attempted to train recruits by allowing six live rounds per man, though in Russia from 1810 Barclay de Tolly stressed the importance of firing at a target, designing one in 1811 painted with horizontal stripes to assist in the elevation or depression of the musket according to range. In the heat of battle, inexperienced troops might forget their training and render their muskets useless by firing away the ramrod or loading cartridge after cartridge until the eventual explosion destroyed the barrel. Another factor was revealed by the French Surgeon-General Larrey, ordered in 1813 to investigate almost 3,000 cases of 'self-inflicted' wounds. Though the conscripts in question had hand and forearm injuries, burnt skin and charred sleeves, Larrey discovered that some had been caused by charging uphill with raised muskets, taking the enemy fire on the hands, and the remainder by such lack of experience that the third-rank men had burnt the men in the two forward ranks or simply shot them by mistake!

Among the many national patterns of musket, the British Brown Bess is undoubtedly the most famous, due partly to its nickname, either a term of endearment or a corruption of the German 'Büsche' (gun). Manufacture of the original Brown Bess – the 'Long Land Service' musket with 46-inch barrel – apparently lasted until 1790, despite the development in 1768 of the 'Short Land Service New Pattern' with 42-inch barrel. Upon the outbreak of war supplies of both were found to be so inadequate that large numbers of often poor-quality arms were ordered from foreign gunsmiths, sources which could not supply the requisite number and standard. The Board of Ordnance – faced in 1794 with only 110,000 muskets to equip 250,000 men – therefore 'persuaded' the East India Company to transfer their large arsenal, intended for Company use in India, to the Government; by the end of 1794 no less than 28,920 muskets, 2,680 fusils and carbines, 1,342 brace of pistols and 300 wall-pieces had been ceded to the Ordnance. From 1794 to 1796 Short Land arms were still produced and foreign weapons still bought, but in 1797 Ordnance gunsmiths were ordered to produce only the 'India Pattern'.

Compared to the Short Land Pattern, the India Pattern was of inferior quality, with simplified 'furniture' (fittings) and a 39-inch barrel, easier and quicker to produce. Those purchased directly from the East India Company bore the Company mark – a quartered heart bearing the letters VEIC (United East India Company) and the numeral '4' on the lock. The pattern remained unchanged for the duration of its manufacture (1815) except for the introduction of a reinforced cock in 1809. Between 1804 and 1815 some 1,603,711 India Pattern were produced, including 278,932 in 1812 alone, many being supplied to allied nations (Prussia received 113,000 and Russia 60,000). After the Peace of Amiens a new pattern was introduced but saw only limited service: the New Land Service musket, plainer than the India Pattern and with a 42-inch barrel. From 1803–10 a Light Infantry version with 39-inch barrel and backsight (necessary for aiming at a particular target) was issued to light infantry. Another pattern was the 'Extra Service' musket, in reality a sub-standard weapon produced to use up stocks and barrels previously rejected; in 1814 the Tower armouries contained some 16,672 of these much-inferior weapons.

The 'Duke of Richmond's' musket, probably the finest mass-produced musket in history, was designed by Henry Nock and incorporated his patent 'screwless lock', a simplified mechanism fastened by plugs with all working parts on the *interior* of the lockplate. With 42-inch barrel, the 10-lb musket was designed for efficiency alone, one version having the ramrod sliding into the butt and resting on the interior of the butt-plate. Nock was unable to produce them with alacrity, however, and the project was abandoned in 1798 after only 3,300 had been produced.

The standard French musket was the Model 1777, used with only slight modifications until the 1830s. With a barrel of 113.7 cm. and a weight of about 9¾ lbs, its stock was more slender than the British musket. Though about equal with the Brown Bess in accuracy, the coarse-ground French gunpowder resulted in excessive fouling, requiring the washing of the barrel about every fifty shots; in a prolonged action men might be compelled to urinate down the barrel to clear the fouled powder. Slightly modified in 1800–01, about 2,000,000 of the '*An* IX' and following '*An* XIII' patterns were produced (French equipment-patterns were referred to by the year of first production, the old Republican calendar being retained). Its more common name, 'Charleville', is taken from one of the chief factories of its production. In addition, some 700,000 captured muskets were overhauled and re-issued to French troops during the Napoleonic Wars. A further variation were the muskets issued to the Imperial (originally Consular) Guard, a special pattern being ordered in 1795 from the Versailles factory, the 1777 design with the 1781 overlapping pan on the lockplate, an 'improvement' which made the weapon even more prone to fouling and which was abolished by Napoleon when First Consul. Later 'Guard' muskets were of '*An* IX' pattern, with special brass fittings and an extra-fine stock, the butt with a carved cheek-hollow, with an overall length of 138 cm., and 152 cm. for grenadiers. In 1800 'Master Boutet' of the Versailles factory began to manufacture two such patterns, described as 'infantry' and a shorter version as 'vélite'. Between then and 1813 some 10,000 were delivered to the Grenadiers and Chasseurs à Pied of the Guard, but were essentially the same as the ordinary infantry musket; as General Gassendi wrote in 1809, 'The firearms of the Guard are identical with those of the Line except that they are more highly finished at an extra cost of ten francs.'[29]

A shorter version, the 'Dragoon Musket', was issued not only to dragoons but apparently to foot artillery and marines as well, varying slightly in length, and to the voltigeurs of some infantry units, its shorter length suited to skirmishing. A further pattern was specified by Napoleon for the use of the Grenadiers à Cheval of the Consular Guard, a 'distinguished model, as handsome as possible, the length of a dragoon musket, with a bayonet.'[30] Finally, there existed 'fusils d'honneur', instituted in 1795 by the minister Aubert-Dubayet: finely-made muskets bearing engraved plaques recording details of the brave incidents which led to their presentation to deserving soldiers.

The Prussian 1782-pattern musket, like the Danish 1791-pattern, used the British system of construction, the barrel being secured to the stock by pins or keys rather than the more usual continental method of metal barrel-bands. In 1805 a new Prussian pattern, the 'Nothardt-Gewehr', had a slightly-altered butt and furniture, but not until the 'Neupreussisches Gewehr' of 1809 were barrel-bands introduced. The Austrian 1798-pattern, used until 1828, used similar barrel-bands. In performance, all patterns were approximately equal, with a few exceptions, of which the Russian musket deserves mention. The issued musket was generally so inferior that the 60,000 British muskets they procured were distributed as rewards to deserving soldiers! A contemporary observer, Dr Clarke (who wrote *Travels in Various Countries of Europe* [1810]), reported that the Imperial factory at Tula produced 1,300 muskets a week, but 'the name of musquet is degraded by such things as they produce; it is wonderful that any troops can use them: besides being clumsy and heavy, they miss fire five

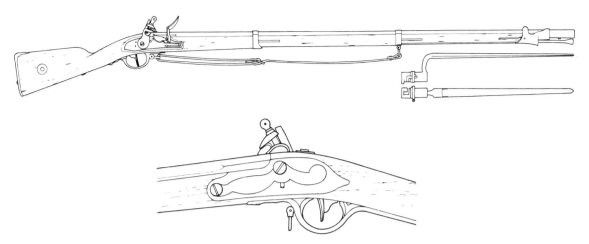

Fig. 11. *French Musket. An XIII pattern.*

times out of six, and are liable to burst whenever they are discharged.' (In reality they were not *so* bad.)

A variation on the standard lock was found in Spain and the Caucasus, where the old 'miquelet' type had been retained, principally for non-regulation weapons. Its hammer was robust, to hold irregularly-shaped lumps of flint, and was ideal for the rugged service required by the guerrillas.

Often found with the 'Catalan stock', an archaically-shaped butt with square-cut end and 'hook' on the underside, it was also favoured by the Asiatic tribesmen of the Russian army. The characteristic feature of regulation Spanish muskets was the straight hammer, instead of the swan- or ring-neck patterns favoured by other nations, though latterly British muskets were used in great numbers by all allied nations.

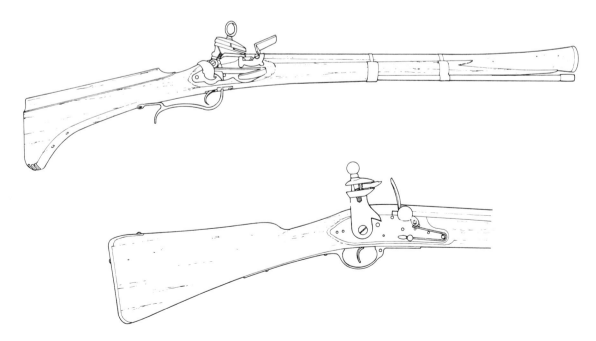

Fig. 12. Above: *Spanish Miquelet lock musketoon.* Below: *Spanish musket, 1804.*

Fig. 13.   Firing from cover: rifle tactics demonstrated by the Duke of Cumberland's Sharpshooters. The officer in the foreground, Charles Random de Berenger, a noted rifle-shot, became infamous from his participation in the Stock Exchange fraud of 1814. Print by Reinagle after Berenger.

THE RIFLE

A 'rifled' barrel has spiral grooving on the interior, which imparts a spin upon the projectile, stabilizing its flight and providing greater accuracy. A muzzle-loading rifle was loaded in the same way as a musket, except that the tighter fit of the ball needed greater pressure to force it down the barrel (occasionally requiring a mallet to drive it home), slowing down the rate of fire to perhaps two shots a minute, even slower when burnt powder clogged the barrel. When prepared cartridges were not used, loose powder and ball and a greased patch below the ball were used, the earlier British rifles including a lidded 'patch box' in the butt; later patterns incorporated cleaning-tools in the butt-box, suggesting an increasing use of prepared cartridges which were carried in any case, for situations demanding more rapid fire.

The rifle was German in origin, the 'military' version originally a privately-owned weapon used by the huntsmen and game-keepers formed into specialist 'Jäger' (sharp-shooter) units. Such hunting rifles were used throughout the Napoleonic Wars, but it is the British 'Baker' rifle which has justly become the most famous arm of its type (the first British 'regulation' rifle was probably the pattern commissioned from Durs Egg in 1796). Rate of fire being secondary to accuracy, riflemen were invariably employed in skirmishing duties where rifles in the hands of trained marksmen could perform prodigies. The inventor Ezekiel Baker recorded a test made personally with one of his guns; firing at a man-sized target at 100 and 200 yards range, he discharged thirty-four and twenty-four shots respectively; *every one* hit the target. Similar accuracy was recorded in action: George Simmons of the

British 95th Regiment claimed to have silenced a French battery at Badajos by a continuous fusillade from 'forty as prime fellows as ever pulled a trigger,'[31] the 95th being the exponents par excellence of the rifle and its tactics. In aiming, due to the removal of the original back-sight of the Baker, the soldier was trained to aim at the enemy's cross-belts up to 200 yards and at his head and shoulders thereafter.

The Baker's 30-inch barrel was admirably suited to skirmishing duties, its calibre varying from 0.615 to 0.70; Baker also produced a rifled cavalry carbine with 20-inch barrel, which in 1803 scored nine hits out of twelve on a target at 200 yards range, against only three hits by Henry Nock's rifled carbine; but it had only limited use. Over 30,000 Baker rifles were produced between 1800 and 1815, equipping not only the British rifle corps (60th and 95th Regts), some militia and volunteers, but foreign units like the Portuguese caçadores as well. Only minor alterations occurred, such as the change from swan-neck hammer to ring-neck. Other types of rifle remained in use: in 1807 for example the 8th Btn King's German Legion complained that their rifles were of three different calibres!

Prussia used several varieties of rifle, the 'Alte Corpsbüsche' and the 1787-pattern rifle both introduced in that year, the former without provision for a bayonet and neither with a patch-box; a new pattern adopted in 1810 had both. The Austrian 1807-pattern Jäger rifle also resembled the 'Baker'. Some German units serving with the French carried rifles, but the weapon never found favour in France, being issued only to selected officers and N.C.O.s of voltigeur companies and a few rifled carbines to Guard cavalry, but all were withdrawn by Napoleon in 1807. Russia used no less than eleven patterns of rifle, twelve being issued to the best shots of each Jäger company and sixteen per squadron of cuirassiers and dragoons.

The original rifle-bayonet was a hunting-knife or 'Hirschfänger', of 'socket' variety or fitting on to the side of the barrel by a clip. A 'sword-bayonet' – a straight-bladed sword with stirrup-hilt bearing a bayonet-fitting – was originally designed for the Baker, soon replaced by a version with curved knuckle-bow. Due to the large number of different rifles, many patterns of bayonet were in use, including such obscure items as the 'long cutting Bayonet' designed by James Sadler for his 'Patent gun',[32] and the 'Rifle-barrelled Gun of a new construction' used by the London and Westminster Light Horse, 'their Broad Swords are so contrived as to serve occasionally as Bayonets'.[33]

Unlike the musket, the rifle could be loaded and fired with ease in the prone position, the firer lying on his breast and supporting the barrel on a rock or his shako; other positions included sitting down, with elbows braced on the knees, or as Capt. Henry Beaufroy wrote under his pseudonym of 'A Corporal of Riflemen' in *Scloppetaria*: '. . . to fire laying on the back, the sling must be sufficiently loosened to let it be passed on the ball of the right foot, and as the leg is kept stiff, so, on the contrary, the butt is pulled towards the breast, the head is raised up, till the front sight is brought into the notch in the usual way . . . the position is not only awkward but painful. . . .'[34]

THE FUSIL

The term 'fusil' can be confusing, describing in French an ordinary musket – hence 'fusilier'. In English, however, it described a light musket, styled after a fowling-piece. Originally 'fusee' or 'fuzee' (a name also applied to a grenade-fuze), a derivation of the Italian 'fucile', a flint, it was adopted in the late seventeenth century by regiments raised for escorting the train of artillery, the close proximity of gunpowder preventing employment of the matchlock musket with its burning fuse. Troops armed with the fusil were termed 'fuzileers', but though three British regiments bore this title during the Napoleonic Wars they carried ordinary muskets.

The true fusil saw limited use in the Napoleonic Wars, favoured for its lightness by some cavalry and light infantry. In 1797 Britain approved the recruitment of 'Healthy lads under 16 years of Age who are likely to grow . . . taken as low as Five Feet One Inch';[35] the light fusil was found to be an ideal weapon until they grew sufficiently to handle the ordinary musket.

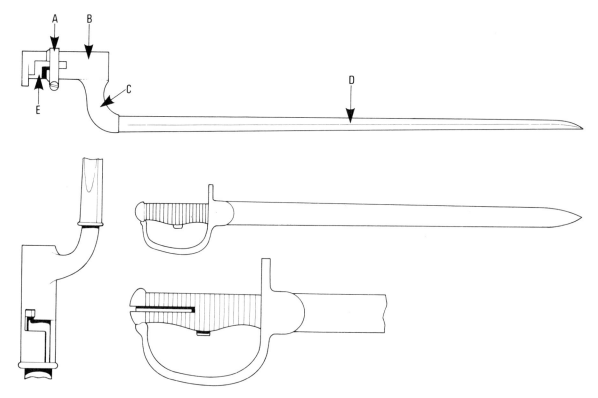

Fig. 14. Above: *Parts of the Bayonet (with locking ring). A. Locking Ring; B. Socket; C. Shoulder; D. Blade; E. Zig-Zag in Socket.* Below Left. *British Socket Bayonet 1800.* Below Right: *Two views of the sword bayonet for the Baker Rifle.*

THE BAYONET

Combining the offensive firepower of the musket with the defensive qualities of the pike, the bayonet was regarded as indispensable by every army, but its actual effectiveness should be considered carefully.

The commonest bayonet consisted of a triangular-sectioned blade about fifteen inches in length, attached to a cylindrical socket which fitted the end of the musket-barrel; though a fixed bayonet might reduce the rate of fire due to the possibility of the soldier impaling himself whilst ramming the cartridge, it was a great improvement on the earlier 'plug' bayonet which fitted *into* the muzzle, thus preventing fire whilst fixed. Socket-bayonets were usually held in place by a right-angled slot passing over the foresight of the musket, very insecure unless a locking-ring was incorporated as on French bayonets

from 1763. Though the bayonet for Nock's 'Richmond' musket had this valuable feature, not until 1853 was a locking-ring added to ordinary British bayonets. As late as 1843 British troops were resorting to string and wire to prevent their bayonets being wrenched off by the enemy! A few bayonets were attached to the side of the barrel by spring-clips, usually German rifle-bayonets and Baker's sword-bayonet. Very few socket-bayonets (none of regulation pattern) were equipped with handguards.

To avoid the heavy casualties of a prolonged fire-fight, many experts advocated immediate shock-action by the bayonet-charge; indeed, the bayonet-charge was claimed as a proud tradition by many nations. But to charge an unshaken body of troops with muskets ready to fire, with any hope of success, demanded very fine troops indeed, so that almost all bayonet-charges actually made were upon an enemy with shaken morale or already disorganized by a raking of musketry, when the mere sight of a yelling mass of men advancing with level bayonets would be sufficient to turn them to rout. The few instances when prolonged bayonet-fights *did* occur, such as the French storm of the 'Bagration flèches' at Borodino, have passed into legend.

General Bugeaud wrote of being on the receiving-end of a British bayonet-charge in the Peninsula, most effective when countercharging a disorganized attacker: the advancing French column would become disorganized by its headlong dash and demoralized by the immobile red wall awaiting them; the French would waver as the British line shouldered arms and 'concentrated volleys swept our ranks; decimated, we turned round to recover our equilibrium; then three deafening cheers broke the silence of our opponents; at the third they were on us, pushing our disorganized flight ...'.[36] This view, that the bayonet was primarily used to finish an action already virtually decided by musketry, is supported by a Peninsula surgeon: '... opposing regiments when formed in line and charging with fixed bayonets, *never* meet and struggle hand to hand and foot to foot; and this for the best possible reason, that one side turns and runs away as soon as the other comes close enough to do mischief'.[37] Thus, the fear of the bayonet, rather than the bayonet itself, was the deciding factor.

It is also interesting to note the analysis of one of the few hand-to-hand fights, between French and Austrians, compiled by Surgeon-General Larrey; he found only five bayonet-wounds against 119 by musket-balls.[38] This is perhaps not surprising, given the frequent ill-temper of some bayonets; after the Battle of the Pyramids, for example, a favourite pastime among French troops was to drag dead mamelukes out of the Nile with bayonets easily bent to resemble fish-hooks!

REGIMENTAL WEAPONS

An example of the diversity of weapons to be found within the same unit is illustrated by a list of those belonging to the French 14th Line in 1808–09. It is slightly confusing due to the use of the French term 'fusil' and 'mousqueton' which probably equate with the English terms 'musket' and 'fusil' respectively. 'Fusils de Dragons' signifies short Dragoon muskets, 'sabres' the officers' version, and 'sabres-briquet' the short, other ranks' sword. Excepting the latter, all terms are translated below:[39]

Rank	Number	Weapons
Officers	134	Nine rifled carbines (for voltigeurs), 38 sabres, 96 'epées'.
Sergeant-Majors	27	Three rifled carbines (voltigeurs), 24 muskets, 27 sabres.
Sergeants	108	Twelve rifled carbines (voltigeurs), 96 muskets, 108 sabres-briquet.
'Fourriers'	27	Three rifled carbines (voltigeurs), 24 muskets, 27 sabres-briquet.
Corporals	216	24 Dragoon muskets (voltigeurs), 192 muskets, 216 sabres-briquet.
Pioneers	13	13 fusils, 13 sabres.
Grenadiers	167	167 muskets, 167 sabres-briquet.
Voltigeurs	241	241 Dragoon muskets.
Fusiliers	2,307	12 fusils, 2,295 muskets (the fusils perhaps for extra musicians appearing on the roll as privates, or for men detailed to guard the regimental baggage).
Drummers and 'Cornets'	54	54 fusils, 54 sabres-briquet.

It was very common to find officially-superseded weapons still in use; for example, at the end of the Empire, the French hussars were supposedly armed with '*An* IX' carbines and '*An* XIII' pistols; but some of the 1786 carbine and 1763 pistol were also *still* in use.

OTHER FIREARMS

The bell-mouthed 'blunderbuss' (a derivation of the Dutch/German 'thunder-gun'), popularly thought to fire a mixture of nails and scrap-iron, was little-used as an 'issue' weapon. Austria had issued the 'trombone' or blunderbuss to cuirassiers in 1760, firing a charge of twelve small balls, and 'Austrian Blunderbusses' was the description given to the hundred 'musketoons' issued to the 'flankers' of the British 23rd Light Dragoons in 1781. Between 1801 and 1813, seventy-three blunderbusses were supplied by the Versailles factory to the mamelukes of the French Imperial Guard, but despite wider use for 'sea service' the blunderbuss was only otherwise used by the Spanish guerrillas, with whom it *did* use peculiar ammunition: Marbot was hit by a jimped-edged flat lead bullet about the size of a half-crown, calculated to cause frightful injury.

A few double- or multi-barrelled firearms saw service, Henry Nock producing a combination weapon in 1787 with two 'screwless' locks, a 39-inch smoothbore barrel and a 20-inch rifled barrel directly above. Britain never adopted the weapon but Austria had a similar type, eventually withdrawn because of weight and inconvenience. 'Volley guns' were principally a naval weapon, being muskets with a number of barrels, Nock producing some 655 seven-barrelled guns firing small shot ($46\frac{1}{2}$ shots to the lb),[40] never popular due to the danger of starting fires with the excessive 'flash'. Double-barrelled pistols were more widely used, both privately-purchased with side-by-side or over-and-under barrels, and 'issue' weapons. The British Royal Horse Artillery received eighty in 1793, one barrel rifled and with a 'shifting' (i.e. detachable) butt, probably styled on the double-barrelled pistols made for the Norfolk Rangers in 1783 and used by some yeomanry

corps in the Napoleonic Wars. The R.H.A. version with small butt and great weight (7 lb 2 oz) made the use of the shoulder-stock essential.

The 'wall piece', popular in the eighteenth century, was half-musket and half-artillery, resembling a giant musket mounted on a swivel and used in a static rôle, mounted upon a fortress-wall or aboard ship. Barrel-length ranged from 4 ft 6 ins to 7 ft, and the ball usually weighed from $6\frac{3}{4}$ to the lb. Though their use decreased towards the end of the eighteenth century some 300 were ceded to the British Government by the East India Company in 1794. Range was about 800 yards. Marshal Saxe proposed a mobile wall-piece in the form of the Amusette, mounted on wheels for use in the field, a test in Dublin in 1761 firing a half-pound ball 800 yards. Though never widely-adopted, Adye gives statistics for one-pounder 'Amuzettes' of five, six and seven-feet length.

INFANTRY SWORDS

The infantry sword acted as a combined weapon and symbol of rank for officers, among whom it was common practice for 'battalion' companies to have straight-bladed swords, and light infantry curved cavalry-style sabres. The first British regulation sword was the 1786-pattern 'spadroon', an elegant straight-bladed weapon with single-bar guard giving hardly any protection. It was replaced by the 1796-pattern which included two kidney-shaped shell-guards, giving better protection but still not intended for protracted combat. General Mercer thought that 'Nothing could be more useless or more ridiculous ... a perfect encumbrance. In the foot artillery ... we generally wore dirks instead...'.[41] The curved 'flank' company sabre appeared (unofficially) in the 1790s, the guard often embossed with appropriate grenade or bugle-horn badges. It was made official by the 1803 pattern, but remained unpopular, contemporary writers referring to it by such disparaging names as 'reaping-hook', 'better calculated to shave a lady's-maid than a Frenchman's head' according to Kincaid! In British service there also existed

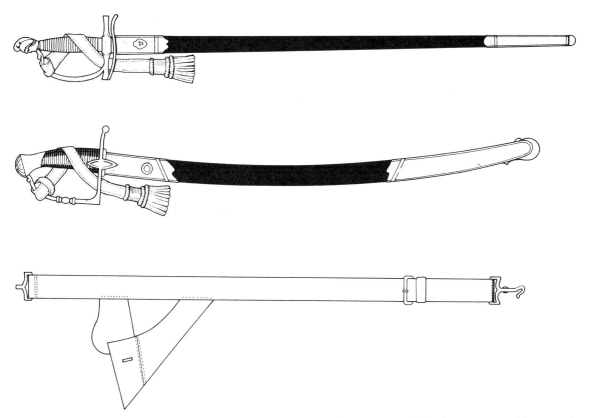

Fig. 15. French swords. Above: *Fusilier company officer.* Below: *Flank company officer; waist belt and sword frog.*

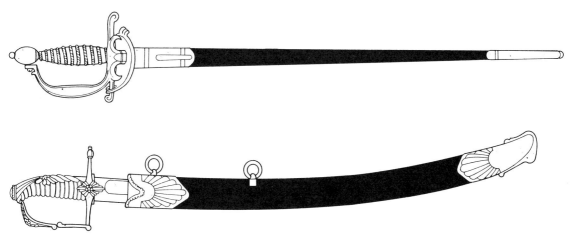

Fig. 16. Above: *Austrian infantry officers' sword, 1798.* Below: *Hungarian infantry officers' sabre, 1811.*

a number of regimental patterns, and the basket-hilted broadsword carried by Highland regiments, sometimes heirlooms of great antiquity. Few British 'other ranks' carried the sword, basically sergeants and musicians, their weapons being as the short-bladed,

curved foot artillery sabre was described in 1819: 'very inefficient ... for any purpose.'[42]

French infantry officers carried straight-bladed 'epées' for 'centre' companies and curved sabres for 'élites', often varied in pattern with unofficial types carried at the

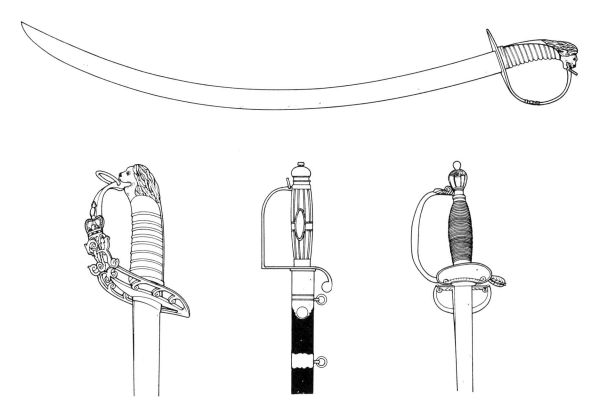

Fig. 17. British swords. Above: *Flank company officers' sabre, 1803.* Below, left to right: *Hilt of the Flank company sabre; Officers' spadroon, c. 1795; Battalion company officers' sword, 1796.*

owner's whim (as in every army). French N.C.O.s, grenadiers and voltigeurs generally carried sabres (the issue varied between regiments), the short sword originally the 1767-pattern with slightly-curved blade and stirrup-hilt, replaced by the 'An IX' and 'An XI' models with slightly more curved blade and curved knucklebow. This pattern was carried by a number of armies in slightly different forms, Prussia using so many captured French swords that in 1818 the 'New Prussian sabre' was styled on the pattern. Prussian officers carried a straight-bladed 'Degen' sword, Fusilier officers (and many musketeer officers as well) having curved sabres. The Russian 'other ranks'' sword differed from most by virtue of its straight blade, though there is evidence again that captured French weapons were also used.

Austrian infantry officers carried straight-bladed swords, grenadier and Jäger officers having curved sabres, the pattern fluctuating with the preference of the owner, only the loosest regulations being implemented. Even

when, in 1811, a pattern was specified for Hungarian regiments, officers were allowed to choose a plain or decorated version according to taste. The grenadier sabre carried by Austrian other ranks changed little, the 1777, 1802 and 1809 patterns resembling the French; but until 1798 Austrian fusiliers carried a typically-German sabre with quillons but no guard, similar to the straight-bladed Prussian 'faschinenmesser' carried by fusiliers. Pioneer and artillery swords were often similar in that they had no knucklebow; for example, the French artillery used the 1771-pattern 'glaive' with eagle-head pommel and leaf-shaped blade until about 1812. Pioneer sabres were designed to act as wood-choppers and often saws as well, with a serrated rear edge.

Among sword-fittings was the ubiquitous sword-knot, a loop of leather or woven material fastened around the guard and ending in a tassel or 'acorn'. Though used as decoration its real function was to loop around the owner's wrist so that even if the

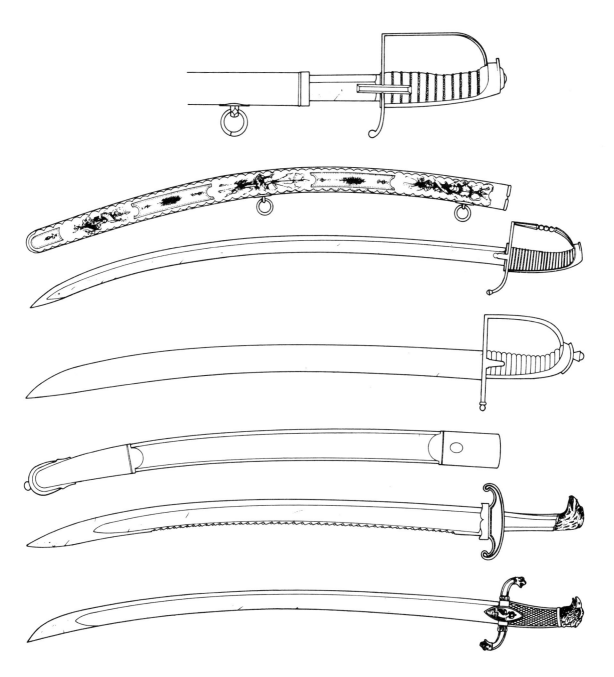

Fig. 18. French swords and sabres. Top to Bottom: *French Drum-Major's sword c. 1810; French Pioneers' sabre (Imperial Guard); French Grenadiers' sabre, 1790; Light Cavalry sabres. (Not to constant scale.)*

sword were knocked from the hand it would not be lost. France used another fitting in the form of a woollen pompom or 'cravat', circling the blade where it joined the hilt, to provide a cushion between hilt and the top of the scabbard to prevent the sword from becoming jammed.

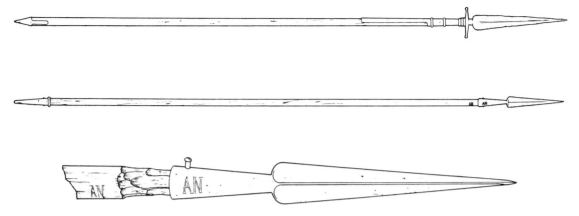

Fig. 19. Above: *British infantry Sergeant's spontoon, c. 1810.* Below: *French Pike, An IV Pattern; detail of head.*

PIKES

The pike was the infantry version of the lance, never extensively used in the Napoleonic Wars, but an easily-produced emergency weapon; thousands of 8- to 10-foot pikes were produced by France in 1792–3, and similarly by Prussia in 1813 for the Landwehr, being replaced as soon as possible by firearms. It was generally only carried by 'second-line' troops – the Russian 'opolchenie' (militia) and, in the guise of sharpened vine-poles, by the Portuguese 'ordenança'. Otherwise, pole-arms were marks of rank, sergeants of British regiments carrying the halberd (pole-axe) at least until 1792, when gradually replaced by the 'spontoon' or half-pike, a nine-foot spear with a cross-bar below the head to prevent over-penetration. Useful for dressing ranks and 'marking', it deprived a battalion of a quantity of trained men who would otherwise have carried muskets and was even dangerous to the owner, Sergt Cooper noting a sergeant who ran himself through by falling upon the blunt butt-end! Many armies equipped their colour-parties with pikes and halberds of various kinds, more for 'esprit de corps' than utility.

ARCHERY

Incredibly, the employment of the longbow was considered seriously as late as 1792 when Lt-Col. Lee of the British 44th urged the replacement of the musket. His arguments were valid: the accuracy of the longbow was no worse, the rate of fire four to six times as great, the bow caused no smoke to obscure the target, a 'hail' of arrows shattered enemy morale more than a volley of musketry, any kind of hit put a man *hors de combat* at least until the arrow was extracted, and archery tackle was much cheaper. But the longbow was rendered ineffective by strong wind, an archer needed more space around him than a musketeer, and the prime objection: a conscript could be trained to use a musket in a matter of hours, whereas a proficient longbowman needed years of training and development of physique. Nevertheless, if Henry V's 'yew hedge' *had* been transported into the Napoleonic age it would certainly have out-shot any troops it met.

The actual use of archery in Napoleonic warfare was restricted to the Asiatic light cavalry employed by Russia, bashkirs and kalmuks. Dressed like refugees from the Dark Ages in mail-coats and armed with 'compo-

Fig. 20A.   French infantry advance in column. Print after Raffet.

Fig. 20B.   The appearance of troops in line is shown graphically in this view of Quatre Bras. Print by T. Sutherland after William Heath.

site' bows, they were regarded with derision by the French, who nicknamed them 'les Amours', a reference to their cupid-like weapon. Their only tactic was a wild charge, 'helter-skelter like a flock of sheep', with a volley of arrows at the end; contemporary observers like Marbot wondered why they were employed at all, claiming that they only served to consume supplies needed by more useful troops. Marbot claimed he knew of only one man killed by 'this ridiculous weapon', though he himself was wounded by a four-foot bashkir arrow.

3. Quoted in Rogers, *Napoleon's Army*, p. 62.
4. See Oman, *Wellington's Army*, pp. 189–91.
5. Wellington to Croker, June 1808, quoted in Oman, *Wellington's Army*, p. 90.
6. Quoted in Glover, *Wellington's Army*, p. 51.
7. Quoted ibid., p. 55.
8. Quoted in Oman, *Wellington's Army*, p. 77.
9. Quoted in Glover, *Wellington's Army*, p. 167.
10. Quoted in Duffy, *Borodino*, p. 37.
11. Quoted in Duffy, *Austerlitz*, p. 36.
12. James, *Regimental Companion*, II, p. 200.
13. Oman, *Wellington's Army*, pp. 74–5.
14. Cooper, p. 13.
15. Ibid., pp. 16–17.
16. *Manual for Vol. Corps of Inf.*, pp. 30–35.
17. Hanger, *Reflections on the Menaced Invasion*, pp. 159–60.
18. Wellington to Earl Bathurst, 24 June 1813 (quoted 'Despatches' X, p. 458).
19. *Edinburgh Advertiser*, May 1802.
20. *London Chronicle*, June 1795.
21. Quoted in Rogers, *Weapons of the British Soldier*, p. 94.
22. Hanger, *Reflections on the Menaced Invasion*, pp. 195–6.
23. and 24. Quoted in Hughes, *Firepower*, p. 27.
25. Quoted in Hughes, *Firepower*, pp. 26–7.
26. Henegan, I, pp. 344–6; quoted in Glover, *Peninsular Preparation*, p. 140.
27. Hughes, *Firepower*, p. 133.
28. Circular Order, 25 December 1797, quoted in Glover, *Peninsular Preparation*, p. 141.
29. and 30. Quoted in Lachouque and Brown, p. 513.
31. Simmons, p. 227.
32. Rowlandson, *Loyal Volunteers*, Plate 46.
33. Ibid., Plate 6.
34. Beaufroy, p. 189.
35. Quoted in Glover, *Peninsula Preparation*, p. 226.
36. Bugeaud, quoted in Chandler, p. 348.
37. Guthrie, quoted in Glover, *Peninsular Preparation*, p. 142.
38. Quoted in Chandler, p. 344.
39. 'Gazette des Uniformes', No. 20, p. 15.
40. James, *Regimental Companion*, II, p. 183.
41. Macdonald, p. 67.
42. Quoted in Robson, pp. 154–5.

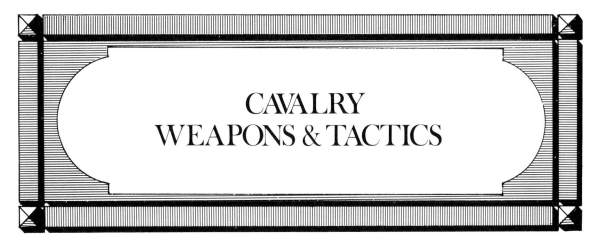

CAVALRY WEAPONS & TACTICS

THE CAVALRY

Despite a bewildering variety of names, all cavalry was divided into three basic categories: heavy, medium and light. The former was specifically designed to execute the charge, a potentially-decisive blow, hence the name: heavy horses and large men to impart maximum impetus. Heavy cavalry included cuirassiers, 'Garde du Corps' (German and Russian), British Household Cavalry, dragoon guards and dragoons; Grenadiers à Cheval, Gendarmerie d'Élite and Carabiniers (French); Prussian dragoons; and during the Revolutionary Wars regiments simply titled 'Horse'.

Dragoons were medium cavalry (one weight lighter than the 'heavies'), despite their original function as mounted infantry who rode into action and dismounted to fight. Though France employed dismounted dragoons, their function during the greater part of the Napoleonic Wars was as *bona fide* cavalry.

Mounted on faster horses and lighter-equipped, light cavalry was used for reconnaissance, protection of an army, and pursuit at the end of a battle, though naturally was equally adept at all other forms of mounted warfare. The consequent prestige of the arm was usually reflected in glamorous uniforms, swaggering bravado and hard-drinking, epitomized in hussar corps, light cavalry copied from Hungarian irregulars, whose costume was perpetuated by the universal fur cap and pelisse. The archetype hussar, the French Comte de Lasalle, epitomized the whole light cavalry spirit by declaring: 'A Hussar who isn't dead at thirty is a blackguard' (he survived to 34). Less prestigious was the ordinary light horse: Chasseurs à Cheval (French), Chevau-Légers and German Chevaulegers, Mounted Jägers (German and Russian) and Light Dragoons (British). Those armed with lances, often wearing uniform styled on traditional Polish lines, were named either Lanciers (French) or Uhlans (German). Other terms included Chevau-Léger-Lanciers and Eclaireurs à Cheval (scout-lancers), both French.

Organization was based upon the cavalry regiment, comprising several squadrons, each sub-divided into troops or companies; one company might be designated 'élite' (authorized in France in 1801, as the 1st Company of the 1st Squadron), differing from the remainder only in matters of dress and sometimes morale. Within the regiment some men might be armed with accurate firearms and designated 'flankers' (skirmishers), or the front rank might be armed with lances (both adopted by the Russian hussars, for example).

In 1791 the establishment of a French regiment included a headquarters consisting of the colonel, two lt-colonels, a quarter-master-paymaster, surgeon-major, chaplain, two 'adjutants' (R.S.M.s), trumpet-major and five 'craftsmen' (saddler, armourer, tailor, cobbler and breeches-maker). Light and carabinier regiments comprised four squadrons (others three), each of two companies, a company consisting of a captain, lieutenant, two sub-lieutenants, a 'maréchal-des-logis-chef' (sergeant-major), two 'maréchaux-des-logis' (sergeants), a 'brigadier-fourrier' (quartermaster-corporal), four 'brigadiers' (corporals), a trumpeter, and fifty mounted and four dismounted troopers. Organization fluctuated, though company strength rarely exceeded a hundred; similarly, changes of terminology occurred in commissioned ranks, 'chef de brigade' and 'chef d'escadron' replacing colonel and lt-colonel in 1793, 'colonel' and a new second-in-command rank, 'major', being restored by Napoleon. Briefly the term 'demi-brigade' replaced 'regiment' during the Revolutionary Wars, each demi-brigade divided into four squadrons of two companies each, each of 116 men; but in practice a whole demi-brigade rarely averaged above 200 or 300 men.

Shortages of horses led to the reduction of the French heavy arm by 1803 to fourteen regiments, and in 1805 twenty-four dragoon regiments were given a mixed establishment of three mounted and two dismounted squadrons each, the latter formed into six-company battalions, two of which formed a dismounted regiment, and three regiments a division. The system was naturally unpopular and saw only limited service.

By 1806, when French cuirassier regiments received a fourth squadron, regimental staff consisted of colonel, major, two 'chefs d'escadron', two 'adjutants-major', paymaster-quartermaster, surgeon-major, 'aide-major', two 'sous-aides-major', two 'adjutants', a corporal-trumpeter and six craftsmen (as above, plus spur-maker); and each company comprised a captain, lieutenant, 2nd-lieutenant, sergeant-major, four sergeants, 'fourrier', eight corporals, eighty-two troopers and a trumpeter.

French hussar regiments remained virtually unchanged in character, but the lancer was an innovation; first adopted by the Polish Chevau-Légers of the Imperial Guard, the lance was used more extensively as two other Guard regiments and ultimately nine line units (the two lancer regiments of the Vistula Legion, six dragoon regiments and the 30th Chasseurs à Cheval) were equipped in this rôle, the line units (converted in 1811) being termed 'Chevau-Léger-Lanciers'.

Other nations had similar cavalry establishments. For example, a British dragoon regiment of 1815 comprised three squadrons, each of two troops, each troop containing a captain, two lieutenants, troop-sergeant-major, three sergeants, four corporals, trumpeter, farrier, and from sixty to sixty-five privates. Regimental strength in action was around 400, but often less. Further tactical sub-divisions included half-squadron (i.e. troop), division (half-troop), and sub-division (quarter-troop).

Austrian regiments each comprised eight squadrons of varying complement, giving in 1805 a nominal total of over 1,400 for cuirassiers and dragoons and over 1,700 for chevaulegers, hussars and lancers. In 1803, like France, Russia 'lightened' her cavalry by reducing the cuirassiers to six regiments and increasing dragoons to twenty-two. Both types had five-squadron regiments, two companies per squadron and over 1,000 men per regiment; hussar regiments comprised ten squadrons each, about 1,900 men per regiment. By 1812, there were five Lifeguard regiments, eight of cuirassiers, thirty-six dragoon and eleven hussar regiments, plus cossacks. After the Treaty of Paris, Prussian cavalry regiments comprised four squadrons, each of two companies of two platoons (Zügen), each squadron numbering 125 men. On campaign it was common to field only two or three squadrons, with two or more regiments combining to form provisional units like the 'Combined Hussars' of the Grande Armée in 1812. Independent ('Normal') squadrons formed from selected personnel ultimately became the Guard Dragoon, Uhlan and Hussar regiments; volunteer units of 'National cavalry' and Landwehr had varied establishments, a regiment usually comprising five squadrons.

For proficient manoeuvre, training was paramount. For a simple movement like 'The Line will retire and form Two Columns' no less than eighteen verbal commands were listed in the British manual of 1808.[43]

Manoeuvre varied with nationality, from three-file column to single- or double-rank line, the charge executed at a gallop whenever practicable, slowly built up from a walk.

Many tacticians considered a third rank of negligible value, restricting the attack to two ranks as Mack instructed the Austrian cavalry. An Austrian manual of 1805 notes:

'The regiment attacks in two waves. The second wave follows the first at the distance of twelve paces. Each wave has two rows, which are separated from one another by the length of a horse's pace. The horses ride one behind the other for cover. The leaders of the squadrons ride half a length in front of the squadron, the leaders of the platoons and subalterns ride in the ranks.'[44]

The front rank comprised experienced troopers; the space between riders was such that their knees were not quite touching. (There are accounts of cavalry being pressed together so closely that the horses could not move, and conversely of the files of opposing units opening to allow the protagonists to pass through one another, the men hacking at the enemy as they rode past.)

Czar Paul's 'Code of Field Cavalry Service' (1796) decreed the two-rank formation, 'for experience shows that the third rank is useless – it impedes nearly all movements, and when anybody falls it proves dangerous to rider and horse.'[45] These regulations were replaced in 1812 by the 'Preliminary Decree Concerning the Order of the Cavalry Service' which included attacks by column of platoons, 'the best formation for any kind of movement,'[46] during which detachments of sixteen men swept out in open order to protect the flanks. Prussian cavalry regulations of 1812 revolved around the basic three-man group, the 'Rotte'. Attacks were made in column or echelon, 'squadron column' being the regiment's four squadrons behind each other, or 'half-squadron column' in which each squadron had two 'Zügen' in line, the regiment having a double-Zügen frontage and eight-Zügen depth. Mounted skirmishers always engaged the enemy with carbines or pistols about 150 to 200 yards in front of the main body.

Whilst swordsmanship was important, the control of larger formations was the decisive factor in cavalry tactics. Napoleon considered that although two mamelukes could outfight three Frenchmen, 300 French could defeat an equal number of mamelukes, and 1,000 French overthrow 1,500 mamelukes;

similarly, Wellington wrote:

'I considered our cavalry so inferior to the French for want of order, that although I considered one of our squadrons a match for two French, yet I did not care to see four British opposed to four French, and still more so as the numbers increased, and order (of course) became more necessary. They could gallop, but could not preserve their order.'[47] In other words, the larger the formation, the more discipline (as opposed to swordsmanship) counted.

The British lack of control often resulted in a charge getting out of hand, careering onward usually to disaster. At Campo Mayor, for example, an audacious charge captured the French siege-train, thundered on for several miles, met fresh French troops, were chased back and lost the captured guns. Few British generals (excepting Paget) had any idea of how a charge should be executed. At Maguilla (11 June 1812) Slade's successful charge dashed on and was routed, about which Wellington wrote:

'It is occasioned entirely by the trick our officers of cavalry have acquired of galloping at every thing, and their galloping back as fast as they gallop on the enemy. They never consider their situation, and never think on manoeuvring before an enemy – so little that one would think they cannot manoeuvre, excepting on Wimbledon Common; and when they use their arm as it ought to be used, viz., offensively, they never keep nor provide for a reserve.

'All cavalry should charge in two lines, of which one should be in reserve; if obliged to charge in one line, part of the line, at least one-third, should be ordered beforehand to pull up, and form in second line, as soon as the charge should be given, and the enemy has been broken and has retired.'[48]

After Waterloo he endeavoured to introduce controlled manoeuvre by his 'Instructions to Officers Commanding Brigades of Cavalry in the Army of Occupation,' which listed the following pointers towards a successful operation:

'1. A strong reserve should be kept to exploit success or cover withdrawal.

2. A cavalry force should be deployed in three lines, the first two deployed and the

37

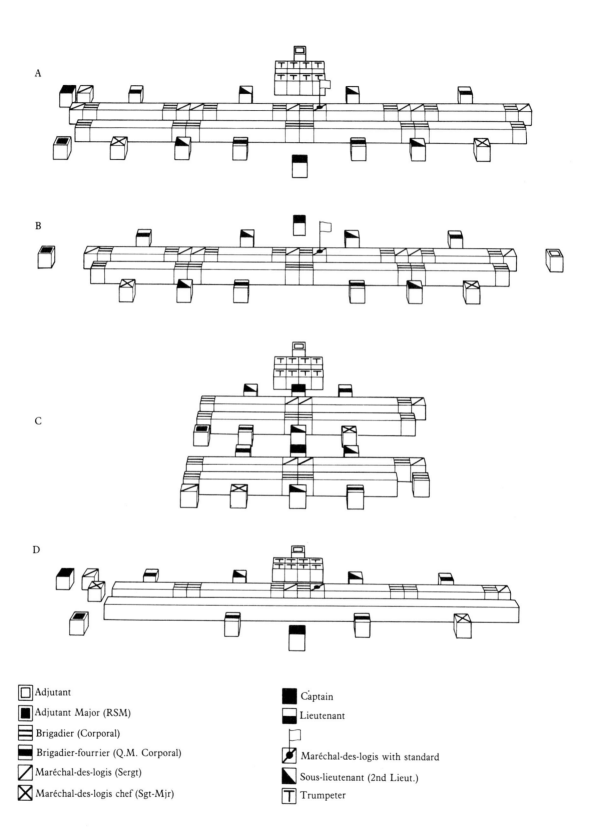

A

B

C

D

Adjutant

Adjutant Major (RSM)

Brigadier (Corporal)

Brigadier-fourrier (Q.M. Corporal)

Maréchal-des-logis (Sergt)

Maréchal-des-logis chef (Sgt-Mjr)

Captain

Lieutenant

Maréchal-des-logis with standard

Sous-lieutenant (2nd Lieut.)

Trumpeter

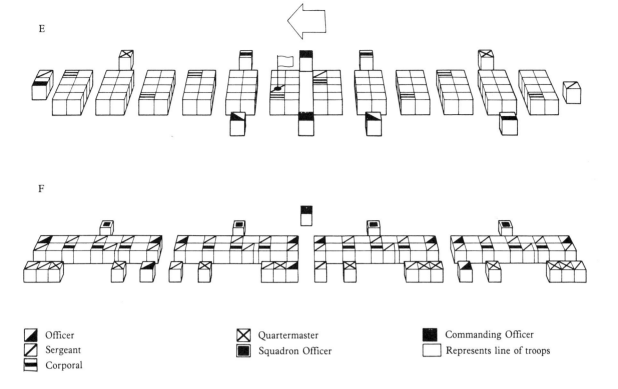

E

F

Officer	Quartermaster	Commanding Officer
Sergeant	Squadron Officer	Represents line of troops
Corporal		

Fig. 21. Cavalry Formations. A. A squadron of French light cavalry in line of battle; B. A squadron of French Light cavalry in 'Colonne serrée'; C. A squadron of French Light cavalry in 'Colonne par divisions' of company frontage; D. A squadron of French heavy cavalry in 'Colonne serrée', preceded by the regimental trumpeters; E. A squadron of French heavy cavalry in column of fours; F. A British cavalry regiment in line in close order.

reserve in column but formed so as to be easily moved into line.

3. When acting against cavalry the space between lines should be between 400 and 500 yards, sufficient for effective support but allowing the front line to retire without disturbing the cohesion of the remainder.

4. Against infantry the second line should be 200 yards behind the first, allowing the second line to charge the infantry before they had time to recover from the charge of the first line.

5. When the first line charged, the supports should follow at a walk to evade involvement in the melée; 'For order in the supports must be rigidly kept – they are useless if they have got into confusion.'[49]

Napoleon's cavalry tactics relied upon the smashing blow of a 'heavy' charge, executed with audacity and discipline. '... it is impossible to fight anything but a defensive war', he wrote, 'unless one has practically achieved parity with the enemy cavalry.'[50] 'Cavalry needs audacity and practice; above all it must not be dominated by the spirit of conservatism or avarice.'[51] To this end, heavy and medium cavalry were used in large bodies for shock-action (his 'reserve' corps of heavy cavalry formed a central striking-force), supported whenever possible by horse artillery and infantry. The actual charge (similar in most armies) was executed as follows: the cavalry would trot for one-third of the distance to the enemy; then canter; then gallop when 150 yards from the target, and only in the last

Fig. 22.   French cuirassiers in action in Russia, 1812. Print after Albrecht Adam.

fifty yards break into the charge 'à l'outrance' when the horses were given their heads; discipline was enforced throughout so that the horses would not become exhausted before the moment of impact and so that an immediate rally could be made to resist counterattack. Massive mounted attacks relied heavily upon adequate support (the failure of the charges at Waterloo was a result of insufficient co-ordination of support), but the successes of Napoleon's cavalry – Eylau the supreme example – proved the validity of his comment: 'Without cavalry, battles are without result.'[52]

Light cavalry were often distributed to make full use of their specialist rôle (in 1812, for example, each of Napoleon's heavy divisions had a light regiment, usually Chevau-Léger-Lanciers, attached), and were often instructed not to seek combat: 'less disgrace attaches to an hussar officer who retreats, than to one who gets embroiled with the enemy in unfavourable circumstances',[53] as a Russian order read. 'Outpost duty' demanded great vigilance, as disaster could overtake the unwary (such as Ney's surprise at Foz d'Arounce, 1811, and Gérard's at Arroyo dos Molinos). Despite lack of official training ('any idea . . . of outpost duty was considered absurd'),[54] many British units became more adept than the French at reconnaissance; for example, the 1st Hussars of the King's German Legion kept a forty-mile line against four times their number of French from March to May 1811, without letting a French patrol through, without losing a vedette, or transmitting a single piece of incorrect information.

Light cavalry was paramount at the end of a battle, covering a retreat or pursuing the

Fig. 23. *Cavalry in combat at Waterloo: Private Samuel Godley of the British 2nd Life Guards –
known as 'the Marquis of Granby' because of his bald head – defends himself successfully against a
French cuirassier. Print published by Thomas Kelly, 1816.*

enemy. Spectacular results could follow the pursuit of a disordered foe; Napoleon wrote: 'After Jena, the light cavalry capitalized the victory all on its own',[55] not only driving the Prussian army to the Baltic but capturing fortresses as well, Lasalle (with typical hussar bravado) with 500 men receiving the surrender of the 6,000 garrison of Stettin!

Long-range raids were rare, though the cossacks were expert at this type of 'hit-and-run' warfare; in fact their loose organization was unsuitable for conventional combat, for as Denis Davidov described an attack of hussars and cossacks on formed troops:

'Colonels, officers, subalterns and many simple cossacks rode at the enemy, but all in vain. The columns rode on, one behind the other, drove us off with shots from their muskets and laughed at our art of cavalry fighting . . . [they] ploughed straight through our cossacks, like a battleship among fishing boats . . .'.[56]

But the cossacks eventually harried the Grande Armée out of existence.

Casualties resulting from a cavalry charge against infantry could fluctuate surprisingly; though Colborne's brigade was all but annihilated at Albuera, the French 4th Line, similarly ridden-over at Austerlitz, escaped with only eighteen dead.

Cavalry sabres were classified in two distinct types, depending upon the manner in which they were employed. Those designed for the cut – the swinging slash with the edge of the blade – were usually curved with a sharpened edge, or straight and wide-bladed with blunt point. Those designed for the thrust – in which the sabre stabbed forwards with the straight arm, like an extended finger – were narrow-bladed with sharpened point and often blunt edge. Some sabres combined the characteristics of both types.

The best employment of a sabre remained a vexed question throughout the period. Marshal Saxe believed the sabre '... should be three square ... and carefully blunted on the edges, that the soldier may be effectually prevented cutting with it in action, which method of using the sword never does execution',[57] but the cut remained the preferred stroke of many, the thrust not being regarded as feasible against a mounted opponent in the British *Rules and Regulations for the Sword Exercise of Cavalry* (1796):

'The *thrust* has only one mode of execution ... a greater degree of caution is required in its application against cavalry ... for if the *point* is parried, the adversary's blade gets within your guard, which is not to be recovered in time ... for which reason the point should seldom or never be given in the attack, but principally confined to the pursuit, when it can be applied with effect and without risk. The case is different in acting against infantry, as the persons against whom you direct the *point* are so much below your own level, that the weight of your sword is not so felt; consequently it is managed with greater facility than with an extended arm carried above the level of the shoulder ... against infantry, the point may be used with as much effect as the edge and with the same degree of security.'[58]

French heavy and medium cavalry used sabres suitable *only* for the thrust (at which they were supremely proficient), even the light cavalry's curved sabres being capable of thrusting. The British chopper-like sabres compared badly, as 'An Officer of Dragoons' wrote about the Peninsular War in the *United Service Journal* (1831):

'The sword of the British heavy dragoon is a lumbering, clumsy, ill-contrived machine. It is too heavy, too short, too broad, too much like the sort of weapon which we have seen Grimaldi cut off the heads of a line of urchins on the stage. The ... light dragoon sabre ... we can answer for its utility in making billets for the fire ... There can be no doubt that thrusting is the proper use to make of the sword; it is a brutal operation...'[59]

Training was essential to produce a good cavalryman. Not only was a good seat vital, but the sword had to become an extension of the arm for the cavalryman had virtually to learn to fence on horseback, to protect his breast, back, bridle-arm and thigh, to execute a blow against cavalry on his right or left, infantry standing, kneeling or even lying down, and often with a cumbersome, ill-balanced sabre. Even the simple cut varied with circumstance, the British 1796 manual emphasizing that against cavalry, all movement should come from the wrist and shoulder, a bent elbow exposing the forearm to the enemy's blade; whereas against infantry a bent elbow was necessary to obtain sufficient sweep for the blow. In the charge it was usual to 'point' the sabre, often with the guard uppermost for maximum protection, this movement with a curved blade resulting in the tip pointing downwards and the cutting-edge uppermost.

The weight of metal and its distribution was important in sabre-design, a cutting weapon needing more weight on the blade to assist the downward slash, and the thrusting sabre requiring a heavy hilt to facilitate the raising of the point. The channels

Fig. 24. Above: *The Cut with the curved cavalry sabre. A British Light Dragoon from* The Sword Exercise of the Cavalry, *1796.* Below: *The Thrust with the straight cavalry sword. A French Dragoon 'Giving Point'.*

Fig. 25. Left: *A French Carabinier, showing the cuirass. Engraving by M. Haider after Gericault.* Right: *French cuirassier officer. Print by Martinet.*

running down a blade (erroneously called 'blood channels') were a method of reducing weight without reducing strength, the deepest channels being found on weapons designed solely for the thrust. Guards varied from the single knuckle-bow or quillon type, providing little protection, to the basket-hilt version, sometimes almost enclosing the entire hand, and counter-balancing too greatly the weight of the blade. But in the hands of a proficient trooper, the sabre, whether blunt or sharp, could inflict horrific injuries, amputations and decapitations being very common. 'It is a brutal operation. . .'.

Britain began the Revolutionary Wars with the 1788 sabre, the light version not curved enough to execute a decent cut and the heavy version an ill-balanced monstrosity, both of very inferior steel. When compared to the sabres and proficiency of their Austrian allies in Flanders in 1793, they were a disgrace. John Gaspard Le Marchant attempted to remedy the situation by copying everything possible from the Austrian cavalry, renowned as swordsmen and for high-quality weapons. His reforms began with the issue of the 1796 *Rules and Regulations* and continued with sabre-design, Le Marchant finding the existing patterns so ill-balanced that many wounds to British soldiers and their horses were inflicted by their own weapons!

Ensuring an improved quality by enforcing stricter controls, Le Marchant copied the

44

Fig. 26.   Cavalry combat between British dragoons and French cuirassiers at Waterloo. Print by R. Havell after I. M. Wright.

Austrian 1775-pattern heavy cavalry sabre for the British 1796 pattern, with a broad, straight blade and pierced 'disc' hilt. Though an improvement, it was still a cumbersome weapon, having a blunt point (some were sharpened regimentally) and prompting Capt. Bragge of the 3rd Dragoons to note in April 1812 the results of an engagement at Bienvenida:

'... scarcely one Frenchman died of his wounds although dreadfully chopped, whereas 12 English Dragoons were killed on the spot and others dangerously wounded by thrusts. If our men had used their swords so, three times the number of French would have been killed.'[60]

The 1796 light cavalry sabre was better, having a wide, curved blade but a single-bar hilt which gave scant protection; but it was so good for slashing that Prussia copied it exactly for their 1811-pattern sabre.

French sabres, despite a number of minor alterations in pattern, retained the same basic design: thrusting-swords with long, narrow blades and multi-barred hilts, and light cavalry sabres designed for the cut but with a sharpened point capable of thrusting, initially with single-bar guard but later adopting the better protection of multi-bar. Some, particularly those of carabiniers, had shell-guards bearing plaques embossed with regimental devices, in this case the bursting grenade. As with French firearms, sabre-patterns were named after the year in the Revolutionary calendar in which they were authorized, *not* the year of actual issue; for example, the '*An* IX' (1800–01) heavy cavalry sabre was not issued until 1803–05, apparently; whilst the '*An* IX' and '*An* XI' light cavalry patterns were not issued until about 1807, old patterns continuing in use even after a newer pattern had been distributed to some units. Two

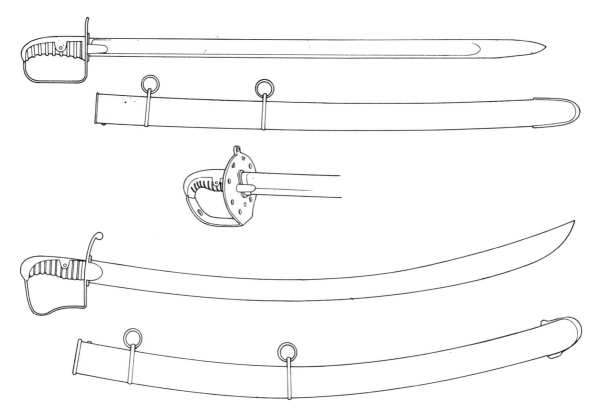

Fig. 27. *British swords.* Top to Bottom: *Heavy cavalry troopers' broadsword and scabbard, 1796 pattern; detail of hilt; light cavalry sabre, 1796 pattern.*

further patterns – the '*An* XIII' for dragoons and light cavalry – were issued even later.

The 'Pallasche' was a German design of sabre with a straight, broad and heavy cutting-blade, the term usually associated also with the huge guard, half-enclosing the hand, often encountered in German and Russian service, sometimes bearing elaborately-embossed designs or cut-out segments. The large guard was rarely seen outside Germanic armies, though British Household Cavalry officers latterly carried such a sabre, and the French '*An* IV' carabinier pattern was not dissimilar. The single-bar guard was common in Germany for all types of light cavalry sabre, though a refinement found on some Austrian weapons was a second bar fitting over the first, hinged to swing out and lock into position to provide extra protection.

Both all-metal and half-metal, half-leather scabbards were used by all nations, the non-metal scabbard (leather, or leather covering a wooden core) in theory keeping the 'edge' on the blade longer than a metal scabbard. In practice it was a negligible point, British 'cutting' sabres all having metal scabbards with apparently little ill-effect on their already dubious efficacy, whilst French thrusting-sabres, also with metal scabbards, had blunted blades to begin with. Leather scabbards, however, were light and more manageable, with no danger of the sword becoming rusted in the scabbard as it could in a metal one. The two common methods of suspension were by a stud on the scabbard fitting into a 'frog' on the waist- or shoulder-belt, or the more common scabbard-rings attached to two slings suspended from the belt.

The campaigns in Egypt prompted the adoption of the oriental or 'mameluke' sabre, a sharply-curved weapon with guardless hilt. Highly-fashionable, particularly amongst light cavalry officers, the pattern was carried

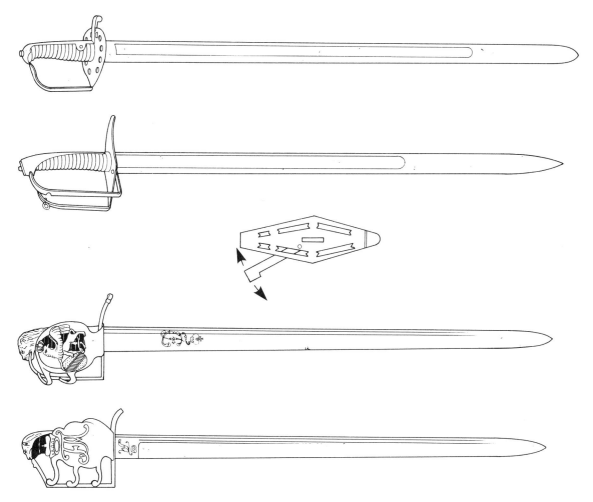

Fig. 28. Top to Bottom: *Austrian heavy cavalry broadsword, 1803; Austrian light cavalry sabre with folding hilt; detail of hilt; Baden dragoon officers' sabre, 1800; Saxon cuirassier officers' sabre, 1800.*

unofficially, becoming so popular that European copies of oriental weapons were produced; they were also favoured by musicians and particularly by drum-majors. Other 'native' weapons included the Caucasian knife/sabre used by Russia's Asiatic irregular cavalry, the 'kindjal' being a double-edged, slightly-curved and guardless short sword; longer-bladed versions were used though the regulation cossack 'shashqa' was not issued until 1834. The mamelukes of the French Imperial Guard carried not only Turkish scimitars but even a Turkish dagger in brass sheath.

Many nations copied the sabre-designs of others, examples being cited above. In some cases this process was aided by the adoption of large numbers of captured weapons, in particular large quantities of French weapons in use by both Prussian and Russian forces in 1812–14. Russia copied the French cuirassier sabre in 1806 (for dragoons) and 1809 (for cuirassiers), replacing the previous German-style weapons; curved sabres introduced in 1809 also followed French lines, except the pommel which curved sharply at the top in an opposite direction to the blade; and so many '*An* XI' light cavalry sabres were captured by Russia in 1812 that the pattern was copied for the 1826 sabre.

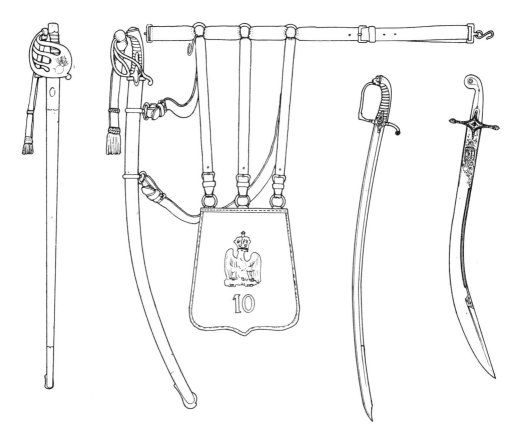

Fig. 29. French cavalry swords. Left to Right: *Carabinier troopers' sabre; cavalry sword-belt, sabretache, slings and sabre of An XI Pattern; Hussar officers' sabre; Mameluke scimitar.*

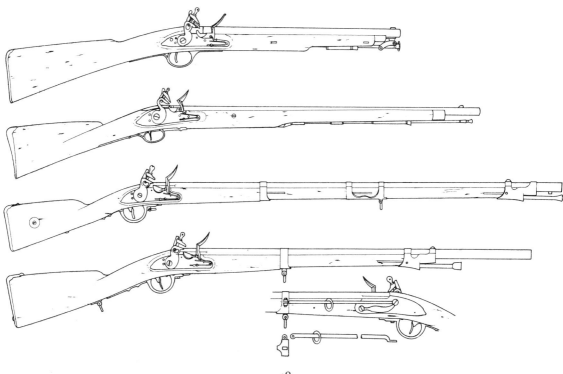

The carbine was a short-barrelled cavalry firearm, not to be confused with the longer-barrelled cavalry musket or the 'musketoon', the latter an imprecise term used by different nations to imply different weapons, usually describing a longer-barrelled carbine with greater range. A characteristic of the carbine was a belt-fitting, allowing the gun to be suspended on a spring-clip from a shoulder-belt.

Despite its short range, the carbine enabled cavalry to fight as skirmishers, both on foot and from horseback, and was thus principally a light cavalry weapon (some heavy units never received carbines). A well-disciplined regiment could even fire a volley from horseback; Parquin records the French 20th Chasseurs à Cheval at Eylau, meeting a Russian charge with a volley of carbine-fire at six paces range, knocking over the Russian first line before charging the remainder with the sabre.

The most common British carbine was the 'Paget', General Henry Paget being credited with its design. It was characterized by its inaccurate, small 16-inch barrel, a lock incorporating a waterproof raised pan and bolt-lock (a 'safety-catch', apparently produced as early as 1806), and a ramrod mounted upon a 'stirrup' or swivel, attaching it permanently to the stock to prevent accidental loss when loading on horseback. A further modification, used by the 16th Light Dragoons at least, was a folding butt, making it even more portable. Other patterns, also named after generals, were the Elliott and Harcourt carbines, the former approved in 1773 but produced throughout the Napoleonic Wars; its 28-inch barrel had a ramrod with bulging end which was secured by fitting into a notch on the stock. The Harcourt apparently was issued only to the 16th Light Dragoons, 500 being supplied by Henry Nock in 1794; its pattern is uncertain but Nock's 'screwless lock' was fitted to some ordinary carbines

from 1797. The Brown-Bess style cavalry musket was reported in March 1796 to be 'very inconvenient, useless and cumbersome', the report recommending its replacement by a 26-inch barrel carbine until which time 'the present Dragoon Firelock should be cut down to … 26 ins so as to be reduced to a Carbine; a Swivel Bar added to it … will give an additional convenience in the carriage and to be carried But [sic] downwards.'[61] A further recommendation, carried into effect for a few years, was a standardization of bores which, as the French realized, greatly simplified ammunition-supply. Though all new weapons were produced in musket-bore for a time, the old system returned, meaning that the cavalryman had to carry two lots of ammunition, for pistol and carbine. The complexity of different bores is exemplified by the following table from James' *Regimental Companion*:[62]

	Drams of powder per cartridge	No. of balls per lb weight
Musket	6	$14\frac{1}{2}$
Carbine, musket bore	$5\frac{1}{2}$	$14\frac{1}{2}$
Carbine pistol, musket bore	$3\frac{1}{2}$	$14\frac{1}{2}$
Carbine	4	20
Carbine pistol	3	20
Common pistol	3	34

Other weapons styled 'carbines' were actually short muskets used by artillery and infantry N.C.O.s.

French light cavalry, train and gendarmes were issued with carbines, but not until 1812 did the heavy cavalry receive them, though some captured Austrian weapons were ordered to be distributed in 1805. The 'issue' pattern was the 1786 musketoon (musket-bore), and after 1801 the 'An IX' pattern, including a bayonet worn from a frog on the

Fig. 30. Left: Top to Bottom: *British Paget cavalry carbine; British Elliott pattern carbine; French Dragoon musket, An IX–XIII Pattern; French cavalry carbine An IX–XIII Pattern, showing reverse side.*

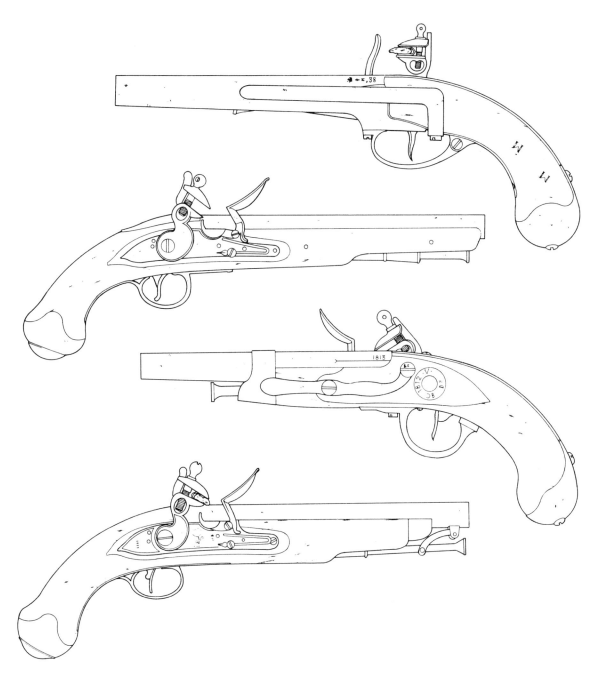

Fig. 31. Top to Bottom: *French 1777 Pattern cavalry pistol; British Light Dragoon pistol; French An XIII Pattern cavalry pistol; British New Land Pattern pistol.*

waist-belt. Other nations issued carbines, but not all as liberally as the French and British; in the Russian hussars, for example, only sixteen men per squadron, the 'flankers', were so equipped after the withdrawal of the general issue in 1812.

Due to the infrequency of its use, contemporary comparisons of carbines are few, though the superiority of the French type (and the manner in which it was handled) was obvious. For example, 'An Officer of Dragoons' writing in 1831 respecting the

Peninsular War reported that '... our light dragoon carbine is so decidedly bad in all respects, that we have only patience to say, the sooner it is got rid of the better.'[63] 'Vanguard', writing in the same publication, describes the duties of light troops in skirmishing in the Peninsula:

'... a man with common observation could not shut his eyes to the glaring fact, that the firearms of the French chasseur, and his capability of acting on foot in cases of emergency, gave him vast advantages over our light dragoons at the out-posts.'[64]

In fact, Stapleton Cotton in 1813 reported that he had ordered the British Household Cavalry to cease to carry carbines (except six per troop), 'as these troops can never be called upon to skirmish, and the horses have already a sufficient load to carry.'[65]

THE PISTOL

Despite the manufacture of vast quantities of pistols (203,137 pairs by French makers until 1814, for example), so that almost every cavalryman had one or two, they were hardly ever used. 'An Officer of Dragoons' recorded the opinion of Marshal Saxe: 'Pistols ... are only a superfluous addition of weight and incumbrance' [sic] and added his own comment: 'We never saw a pistol made use of except to shoot a glandered horse.'[66] The pistol's range was so limited that its discharge was pointless 'till you feel your antagonist's ribs with the muzzle,'[67] at which range it was easier to use the sword.

Nevertheless, Britain issued a bewildering variety of pistols in pistol- and carbine-bore, barrel-lengths varying from the 12-inch 'Heavy Dragoon Pistol' to the 9-inch 'Light Dragoon', as well as a continuous supply from the East India Company. The 1796-pattern cavalry pistol had a ramrod carried in the holster, but this development was not popular and the 'old pattern' was being ordered again in 1801. Variations included the 1796-pattern fitted with Nock's 'screwless lock', bolt-locks like the Paget carbine, and the 'raised pan' which had channels on either side to divert rain-water. The common 'Land Pattern' pistol had a swivel ramrod like the Paget carbine to its 9-inch barrel; another pattern was the 9-inch barrelled carbine-bore 'Dump-ling' pistol with (after 1812) swivel ramrod and raised pan, and in 1814 a 'Squirrel' pistol, perhaps another name for the 'Dumpling'. Unofficial attempts were made to adapt carbine-ammunition to the pistol, so that only one type of ammunition need be carried, by shaking half the powder out of a carbine-cartridge to use it for the pistol; if a soldier in the heat of battle forgot to reduce the charge of powder the recoil would blow the pistol out of his hand.

French pistols had the standard bore (17.1 mm.). The 1777 pistol, characterized by a small amount of woodwork and a steel ramrod set to one side of the barrel, was used until the issue of the 'An IX', which had a stock extending almost to the muzzle; the later 'An XIII' again reverted to the foreshortened stock.

Cavalry pistols were commonly carried in holsters attached to the saddle, but when carried by artillery or engineers (as they were in a number of armies) were suspended in holsters from the waist- or shoulder-belt. They were carried in this manner by most infantry officers. For cavalry regiments not armed with carbines, or with carbines carried in a saddle-boot, the pistol could be hung on the spring-clip of the carbine-belt; a number, usually 'Sea Service' pistols, had a belt-clip attached, a rectangular bar which slipped over the waist-belt, obviating the need for a holster. Small pistols could even be carried in the pockets of a greatcoat.

Huge numbers of privately-purchased pistols were used by officers, ranging from de luxe versions of regulation patterns to ornate duellers; some were produced with detachable shoulder-stocks to turn them into short carbines. Even such finely-made weapons, however, had little effect on the battlefield except at the closest range.

THE LANCE

Traditionally a Polish weapon, the lance was employed by most armies during the Napoleonic Wars, Britain being a notable exception. The lance, however, was issued only sparsely; even France only formed appreciable numbers of lancer units after 1811–12.

The reason for this lay in the characteristics of the weapon, for whatever its advantages the

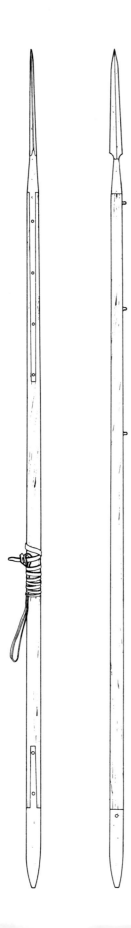

lancer was at a distinct disadvantage in a melée once the initial 'shock' had passed; the fact that a lancer was almost defenceless once the point had been turned was a major factor influencing Britain against its adoption. In addition, specialist training was required to produce a proficient lancer; when the French 3rd Hussars were issued experimentally with lances but without training in 1800–01 they were recorded as not being armed but simply carrying a pole! For skirmishing, scouting and pursuit, however, the lance was lethal, and even in a defensive rôle, with a regiment formed in close order with lances levelled, an impenetrable 'hedge' could be formed at least until the opposition had hacked off sufficient lance-heads to force a way through.

A lance can be 'aimed' at a target with greater accuracy than a sword, so not only could a lancer strike an enemy horseman before coming within sabre-range, against unformed infantry he was an executioner. Colborne's Brigade at Albuera was caught in the flank by Polish lancers; one battalion, the 2/31st, was farthest from the point of impact and was able to form square. The others suffered percentage losses of 85.3 per cent. (1/3rd), 75.9 per cent. (2/48th) and 61.6 per cent. (2/66th). A further use of the lance was demonstrated at Katzbach (1813), when mud prevented the French cavalry from exceeding a walk and heavy rain made the Prussian infantry unable to fire; a square was thus able to hold off the French with a hedge of bayonets until some lancers arrived, their superior 'reach' breaking the square immediately. Prime exponents of the lance were the cossacks, of whom General Wilson wrote that the lance

'. . . is the constant exercise of his youth and boyhood, so that he wields it, although from 14 to 18 feet in length, with the same address and freedom that the best swordsman in Europe would use his weapon.'[68]

Fig. 32. Left: *Front and side views of French cavalry lance, 1812 Pattern (Not to scale.)*

Fig. 33.   Austrian cuirassiers with campaign equipment, c. 1813. Print after J. A. Klein.

43. *An Elucidation ... for the Formations and Movements of Cavalry*, p. 76.
44. Quoted in Wagner, p. 62.
45. Quoted in Duffy, *Austerlitz*, p. 34.
46. Quoted in Duffy, *Borodino*, p. 44.
47. Wellington to Lord John Russell, 21 July 1826, quoted Oman, *Wellington's Army*, p. 104.
48. Wellington to Lt-Gen. Hill, 18 June 1812; 'Despatches' IX, p. 240.
49. Quoted Oman, *Wellington's Army*, pp. 111–12.
50. Chandler, p. 351, quoting Napoleon, *Correspondence* (Paris, 1858–70), Vol. XXXI, p. 426.
51. Ibid., p. 351, quoting Napoleon, *Correspondence*, XXXI, p. 428.
52. Ibid., p. 355, quoting Napoleon, *Correspondence*, XXXI, p. 427.
53. Quoted in Duffy, *Austerlitz*, p. 35.
54. Tomkinson, quoted in Oman, *Wellington's Army*, p. 110.
55. Quoted in Chandler, p. 355.
56. Wagner, p. 62, quoting Tarle, E., *Napoleonovo tazeni na Rus 1812*, p. 313.
57. Quoted in *United Service Journal*, 1831, II, p. 61.
58. Quoted in Rogers, *Mounted Troops of the British Army*, p. 153.
59. 1831, II, p. 61.
60. Bragge, p. 49.
61. Quoted in Blackmore, *British Military Firearms*, pp. 107–08.
62. James, II, p. 183.
63. *United Service Journal*, 1831, II, p. 61.
64. Ibid., p. 206.
65. Quoted in Glover, *Wellington's Army*, p. 50.
66. and 67.   *United Service Journal*, 1831, II, p. 61.
68. Wilson, 'Brief Remarks'; see also *Royal Military Chronicle*, 1812, p. 207.

Fig. 34. *Three illustrations showing British artillery c. 1802, on the march and being manhandled by infantrymen, by bricole. Print after W. H. Pyne.*

ARTILLERY & ENGINEERS

ARTILLERY

All cannon were classified into types or 'natures' by the weight of projectile they fired, an approximate measure at best: thus, a 12-pounder (pdr) gun fired a 12-lb shot, etc., though due to the difference in weight between a British and the heavier French 'pound', a French 8-pdr approximated to a British 9-pdr. Strictly, 'guns' were cannon with a length of twelve calibres or more (i.e. twelve bore-diameters in length); shorter-barrelled cannon, between five and ten calibres long, were termed 'howitzers' and intended for high-angle fire; their 'nature'

was expressed by calibre, (e.g. '10-inch') rather than by weight of shot. Without exception *all* guns were smoothbore and muzzle-loading, cast either in 'brass' (bronze), an alloy giving great strength in relation to weight, or iron; brass and iron guns were used in about equal proportions though the heaviest pieces were invariably iron.

There were considerable variations in calibre between the guns of similar types of different nations; the following table is extracted from Adye's *Bombardier and Pocket Gunner* (1802):[69]

			Calibre (ins)			
'Nature'	*British*	*French*	*Spanish*	*Dutch*	*Russian*	*Portuguese*
36-pdr	—	6.9	6.84	—	6.86	6.8
32-pdr	6.41	—	—	6.4	—	—
24-pdr	5.823	6.03	6.03	5.92	6.0	5.93
18-pdr	5.292	—	5.52	5.45	5.45	5.4
12-pdr	4.623	4.78	4.8	4.76	4.76	4.7
9-pdr	4.2	—	4.2	—	—	4.3
8-pdr	—	4.18	—	4.13	4.17	—
6-pdr	3.668	—	—	3.78	3.78	3.75

(In addition, Britain had 42-, 4-, 3- and 1-pdrs, France 16- and 4-pdrs, Russia 30-pdrs and Portugal 48-pdrs.)

Barrel-weight varied even between guns of the same design and 'nature' (hence the terms 'light 3-pdr', 'long (or heavy) 3-pdr', etc.), and even between guns of identical specification there might be as much as two cwt

variation, necessitating the weight of each gun to be stamped upon the barrel, for example '17-3-1', representing 17 cwt, 3 qtrs, 1 lb. Interminable tables of length and weight are of little interest except to the purist, but the random examples below show the wide variety of cannon in use:[70]

Type	Length (Ft	ins)	(Cwt	Weight Qtrs	Lbs)
British brass heavy 24-pdr	9	6	53	0	9
,, ,, light ,,	5	0	16	3	13
,, iron 24-pdr	10	0	52	0	0
,, ,, ,,	9	0	47	2	0
,, ,, 12-pdr	9	0	32	0	0
,, ,, ,,	7	6	29	1	0
French ,, ,,	8	7	31	2	0
,, ,, ,,	6	10	28	0	0
British brass heavy 6-pdr	8	0	19	1	6
,, ,, new medium 6-pdr	6	0	8	3	27
,, ,, reduced medium 6-pdr	5	6	8	0	22
,, ,, light 6-pdr	4	6	5	0	18
,, iron 6-pdr	8	0	22	0	0
,, ,, ,,	6	0	16	2	0

Although the term 'field artillery' was not generally used during the Napoleonic Wars it is a convenient way of differentiating between artillery used on the battlefield from the heavier pieces used for siege or garrison duty.

Having explained the basic terminology, the actual construction and use of a cannon should be considered.

A cannon was composed of two parts: barrel and carriage. The barrel was a tube of cast iron or 'brass' (alloys of copper and tin with zinc sometimes added, sometimes termed 'Gun Metal') with the centre bored out, few guns after 1750 being cast with the bore already hollow. At the sealed end of the barrel was a knob or 'cascabel', which in later years was attached to various elevating mechanisms. Around the barrel were 'reinforces' or raised metal rings for additional strength, the barrel swelling outwards towards the open end or 'muzzle'. At either side of the barrel was a projecting cylindrical lug or 'trunnion', upon which the barrel rested on the carriage; the trunnions were usually sited on the lower half of the barrel though some nations (including France and the U.S.A.) moved them up level with the bore. At the closed end or 'breech' of the barrel was a small passage connecting the outside with the bore, the 'vent' or 'touch-hole' through which the igniting spark passed. Above and slightly to the rear of the trunnions were lifting-handles or 'dolphins', so called because of their original design in the form of a leaping dolphin.

There were two types of 'carriage', i.e. the wooden, wheeled framework which supported the barrel. Most common was the 'double bracket' carriage, a rectangular wooden framework with the two longer sides of the rectangle constituting the 'trail'. At the front was an axle supporting the two wheels (the term 'wheel' described a spoked wheel of more than twenty inches diameter; smaller wheels were described as 'trucks'). On top of the trail were semi-circular cut-outs to receive the trunnions, secured by shaped metal 'capsquares' which fitted over the top of the trunnions. Some carriages had two pairs of trunnion cut-outs, one to support the barrel in firing position and one further back for the travelling position. The rear end of the carriage included a hole to take the limber-attachment or 'pintle', and bars, rings or holes for the 'handspikes', levers used to traverse the cannon. The whole carriage was banded with iron reinforcing as the discharge was enough to shake a carriage to pieces if not robustly made.

The second type of field carriage was the 'block trail', the trail of which consisted of a single baulk of timber, widening as it approached the capsquares to move forward the gun's centre of gravity and thus make traversing easier. One of the first block trails was designed by Sir William Congreve in 1792 and adopted by the British horse artillery in the following year, but the bracket-trail was predominant throughout Europe.

Though naval carriages were often left in

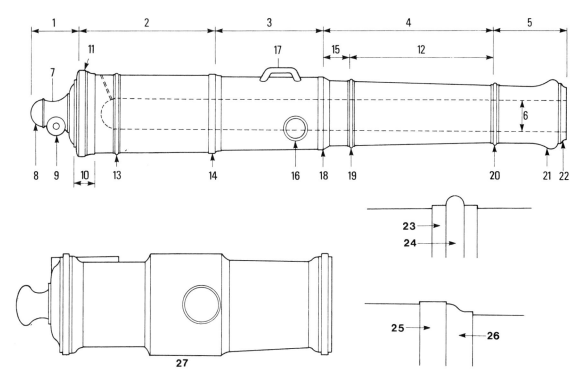

Fig. 35. Parts of the cannon barrel. *1. Cascabel; 2. First Reinforce; 3. Second Reinforce; 4. Chase; 5. Muzzle; 6. Calibre; 7. Cascabel Neck; 8. Button; 9. Elevating Screw Mount; 10. Breech; 11. Base ring and Ogee; 12. Charging Cylinder; 13. First Reinforce Astragal and Fillets; 14. First Reinforce Ring and Ogee; 15. Chase Girdle; 16. Trunnions; 17. Dolphins; 18. Second Reinforce and Ogee; 19. Chase Astragal and Fillets; 20. Muzzle Astragal and Fillets; 21. Swell of Muzzle; 22. Muzzle Moulding; 23. Fillet; 24. Astragal; 25. Ring; 26. Ogee; 27. Howitzer Barrel.*

Fig. 36. Parts of a British Field Carriage. *A. Bracket; B. Trail-plate Eye; C. Trunnion-hole; D. Capsquares and Eye-bolts; E. Lockplate; F. Traversing Stay; G. Limbering-up Handle; H. Traversing Loop; J. Elevating Screw; K. Match or Shot-case.*

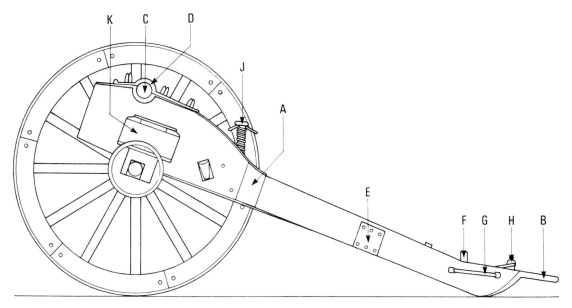

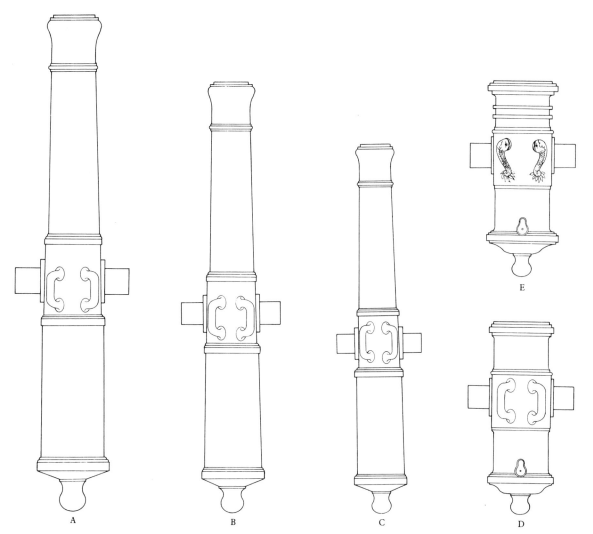

Fig. 37. Barrels of the Gribeauval system, showing the comparative lengths of the different calibres. A. 12-Pounder; B. 8-Pounder; C. 4-Pounder; D. 6-Inch Howitzer; E. 8-Inch Howitzer with 'Dolphin' handles.

'natural' wood, land carriages were usually painted for protection against the weather. Many nations adopted a standard, individual colour-scheme: Britain used the 'common colour', a greenish-grey with metal fittings painted black with a little red paint added; France used an olive-green shade achieved by mixing yellow ochre and black in a ratio of 80:1; Prussia favoured a light greyish-blue whilst the Holy Roman Empire had combinations of yellow and black or black and red. Some Italian states used red carriages with yellow mounts, or even painted the wheels a contrasting colour to the body of the carriage. Spanish carriages may have been blue, though

there is little conclusive evidence; other carriages were apparently just treated with turpentine and left to 'weather' naturally.

Elevation and depression of the barrel was achieved by two methods. The earlier method used a 'quoin', a triangular-shaped wooden block inserted between barrel and the base of the carriage, but later the more efficient screw-elevation was adopted, in which an iron rod projected underneath the cascabel, raising or lowering the barrel according to the movement of the screw of the elevating rod. The two methods were sometimes combined, as in the Russian 1805 System which had a screw passed horizontally through a moveable

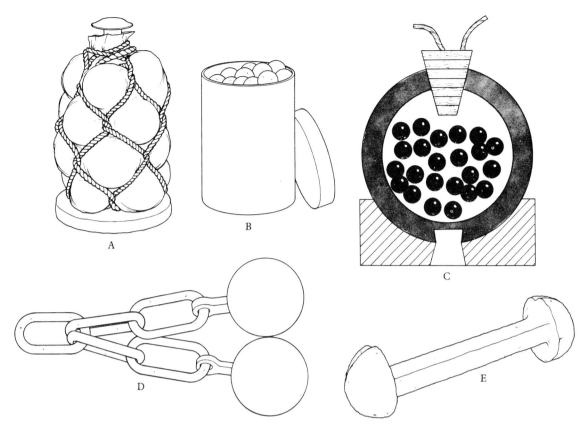

Fig. 38. Artillery projectiles. A. Quilted Grape shot; B. Case, or Canister; C. Spherical Case with 'Sabot' attached to the base, and with a wooden fuze in the top; D. Chain-shot; E. Bar shot.

quoin.

The primary projectile of the cannon was the 'roundshot', a simple iron ball, representing 70–80 per cent. of all ammunition held in the field. It was used to strike down columns of men and demolish obstacles; in the former rôle it was a horrifying weapon, a single ball being capable of killing as many as forty men at 600 or 800 yards, though this was the extreme; Müller estimated that a shot fired at a line of infantry could be expected to kill three men. Though muzzle-velocities of all cannon were similar, the heavier the shot the greater its remaining velocity (i.e. velocity at the target): at 1,000 yards an 18-pdr 840 fps, 9-pdr 690 fps, 6-pdr 450 fps. Therefore, the heavier the shot, the greater its effect, Müller calculating that a 6-lb shot was 50 per cent. more effective than a 3-lb, and a 12-lb twice as effective. Hence the out-gunning of the British in the Peninsula when matching their 6-pdrs against the French 8- and 12-pdrs, leading to the re-introduction of the 9-pdr as the standard British weapon.

A roundshot when fired fell steadily from the height of the muzzle until it struck earth, the 'first graze' (about 400 yards for a 9-pdr at 0 deg. elevation), when it bounced or 'ricocheted' until it hit the ground again (in the above case about 800 yards from the muzzle) at the 'second graze', after which 80 per cent. bounced again (100 yards in the case above). As the entire trajectory was below 'man height' anything in its path would be struck down. As velocity and accuracy decreased with bounces, it was ideal to have the 'first graze' on the target itself, which could be achieved by elevating the barrel: $\frac{1}{4}$ deg. advanced the point of 'first graze' between 100 and 200 yards, a 9-pdr at 1 deg. elevation having a 'first graze' at about 700 yards and the second at 1,000. Even so the trajectory was so low as to preclude any firing over the heads of friendly troops, and in any case the target had to be 'sighted' along the barrel. Ricochet was considerably reduced, of course, in soft ground, and roundshot was much more destructive if it could be fired along a line of men ('at enfilade') rather than through it.

Roundshot could be transformed into 'hot shot' by heating, normally used only for setting fire to ships or buildings, the shot heated in a furnace or portable oven, carried to the cannon in pincers or a spoon, and rolled down the cannon-barrel, igniting the powder-charge. Imbedded in a wooden beam, hot-shot would smoulder for hours; in an experiment in 1771 a 24-lb hot-shot was laid in the open air for four minutes, plunged into cold water three times, then thrown amongst some wood, which burst into flame in seven minutes; doused with water for two minutes, it was alight again in fifty. The expansion of hot-shot (about 1/16th of the diameter) was not sufficient to affect its fit in the barrel.

Despite differences in calibre, 'captured' shot could usually be fired back at its original owner by using a different calibre of cannon from that for which it was originally intended. For example, a French 36-lb shot with a diameter of 6.64 ins could be 'returned' by the nearest British gun capable of firing it, the 42-pdr which normally fired a 6.68 in. diameter shot.

'Common shell' was a hollow iron sphere filled with gunpowder which exploded at a predetermined moment by means of an adjustable fuze lit by the flash of ignition. Shells were fired from howitzers and mortars, fieldpieces not having the high-angle trajectory required. A shell landing before the fuze had burnt down would fizz and splutter on the ground, allowing troops to extinguish it before it burst, highlighting the necessity for considerable skill in trimming the fuze to a precise length. A form of 'air-burst' could be achieved by reducing the propellant charge in order that the shell exploded after the 'first graze'. With the high trajectory, shells could be fired over the heads of friendly troops or even features of terrain.

'Spherical case' was the British secret weapon, invented in 1784 by Henry Shrapnel and eventually bearing his name. First used in 1804, it resembled an ordinary shell but

had a thinner casing, was filled with musket-balls plus a bursting-charge of gunpowder and timed fuze. With careful timing, achieved by adjusting the fuze, it could be calculated to explode above the target, showering musket-balls upon the enemy. Fired from both howitzers and fieldpieces, its wide spread (6-pdr shrapnel had a spread of 250 yards at point-blank range) compensated for the gun's lack of accuracy. It represented between 13 per cent. and 15 per cent. of all British fieldpiece ammunition and up to 50 per cent. of howitzer ammunition. The necessity for *accurate* fuzing was paramount, and Wellington after Busaco commented on this point:

'I have seen our artillery produce great effect on the enemy, and I have been induced to attribute this effect to the use of Shrapnel's shells. But my opinion in favour of these shells has been much shaken lately.

'1st. I have reason to believe that their effect is confined to wounds of a very trifling description ... I saw General Simon, who was wounded by the balls from Shrapnel's shells ... but they were picked out of his face as duck shot ...

'2nd. From the difficulty of judging of direct distances, and in knowing the shell has burst in the air in the proper place, I suspect that an original error in throwing the shells is seldom corrected; and that if the shell is not effective the first shot the continuance of the fire of these shells seldom becomes more effectual ... no doubt, however, that if the shell should be accurately thrown, and burst as it is intended, it must wound a great number of men, but probably none very materially.'[71]

'Case shot' or 'canister' was the universal close-range projectile, consisting of a tin case fitting the bore of the cannon, containing a number of loose bullets. The tin ruptured as it left the muzzle, turning the cannon into a giant shotgun. Limited to a maximum effective range of 600 yards, it was the final weapon for repelling a charge, the 'spread' recorded by Müller as a circle of 32 feet diameter per 100 yards of range. It could even be fired 'double-shotted', i.e. two tins of case or one of case and a roundshot. Most artillery used 'light' and 'heavy' case, the light for a

British 6-pdr containing eighty-five $1\frac{1}{2}$-oz bullets and the heavy forty-one $3\frac{1}{2}$-oz, for example. Heavy case had the longer range (up to 600 yards) and was used offensively by the French, whereas light case had an extreme range of about 250 yards, the British tending to limit the firing of *all* case to about 350 yards.

'Grapeshot' is mentioned by many contemporary writers, usually being confused with canister. Genuine 'grape' consisted of a number of iron balls packed around an iron column attached to a circular base, the whole covered with painted canvas tied with string, giving the appearance of quilting. Extensively used at sea it saw little service on land, as it was not as efficient against personnel as canister, and could damage the bore of brass guns.

Other projectiles were used exclusively for sea service: chain-shot (two roundshot connected by a chain), bar-shot (two roundshot or half-roundshot connected by a bar), knife-blade, expanding and 'dismantling' shot (two-feet-long iron bars attached to a ring), all designed to expand and slice away sails and rigging like a flail.

By this period 'prepared cartridges' of powder inside a fabric or paper bag had totally replaced the ladling of loose powder into the barrel for the propellant charge. 'Fixed ammunition' was that in which the projectile had a wooden shoe or 'sabot' affixed, seated on the powder of the cartridge. Fabric cartridge were preferable to paper in that they left fewer unburnt fragments in the barrel after firing, such fragments having to be removed by a 'worm' or 'wad-hook', a rammer-pole with a 'screw' end.

Having covered the construction and projectiles of fieldpieces, the actual firing-drill should now be described before range, effectiveness and the various national patterns are considered.

Firing-drill varied with nationality, the size of gun and the number of crewmen available, but the following details the basic drill used by all nations. Having unlimbered the cannon, it first had to be aimed, this being the responsibility of the senior gunner. The manoeuvring was achieved by means of 'handspikes', levers usually six to seven feet long, inserted in bars or slots in the trail, this 'traversing' establishing the direction of shot. Secondly, it had to be aligned in the vertical plane to compensate for the target being above or below the gun, and finally an additional 'tangent' elevation to compensate for the drop of shot in flight. The introduction of the elevating-screw greatly speeded the process (eliminating the levering of the barrel with handspikes to inset the quoin), as did the 'tangent sight' fixed to the barrel's base-ring, an adjustable, notched cross-bar used in conjunction with the fore-sight on the muzzle. Both perfected by about 1780, the screw-elevator and tangent-sight made the once-haphazard 'naked eye' gun-laying into a science, though the skill of the gunner was still vital in assessing the 'fall of shot' and consequent adjustments to achieve the correct range.

Before each shot the barrel was swabbed out with a wet 'sponge', a rammer with fleece or similar material nailed on the head. This movement forced a current of air out of the vent which might ignite any smouldering powder, injuring or killing the spongeman; so while the sponging was in progress the third crewman (after the aimer and spongeman), the 'ventsman', placed his thumb in a leather thumbstall over the vent. The fourth crewman, the 'loader', standing in front and left of the muzzle (the spongeman was on the right), then inserted the propellant charge and projectile into the bore. The spongeman then reversed his sponge and forced the charge and shot down the barrel with the wooden rammer-head (the rammer was usually double-headed and about 14 inches longer than the bore). The ventsman then punctured the cartridge by inserting a 'pricker' down the vent, then plugging the vent with a quill or paper tube of mealed powder (after about 1800) or (before 1800) 'quick-match', cotton strands soaked in saltpetre and spirits of wine, the tube or match providing immediate contact between the cartridge and the spark which ignited it. Priming could also be achieved by pouring loose, finely-ground powder into the vent. In British service the ventsman stood to the right of the breech, and in the French to the left. The fifth member of the team was the 'firer', who ignited the

A

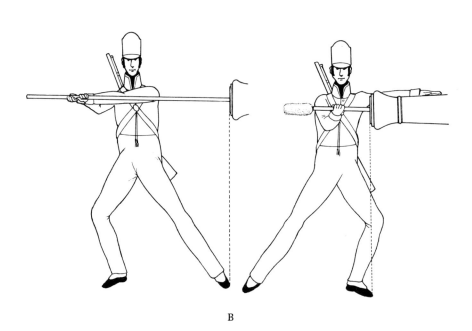

B

Fig. 39. *Gun Drill. A. The position of the crew before loading. The man by the right wheel carries the combined rammer and sponge. the man by the left wheel has a roundshot in his left hand. Behind him can be seen the gun captain with the portfire in his right hand; B. The moment of ramming; C. The movements of the gun captain using the portfire; D. The gun crew at the moment of firing.*

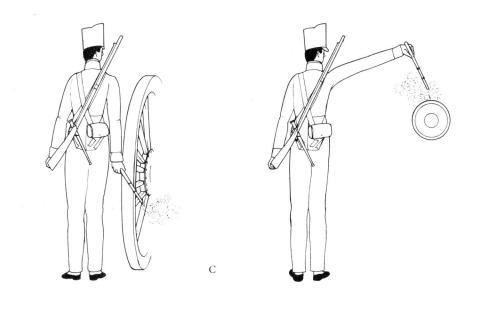

C

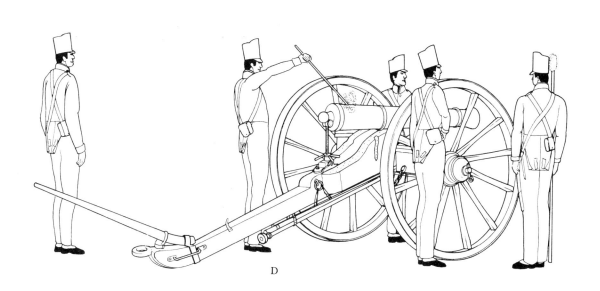

D

charge (when the other men had stood clear) by means of a 'linstock' – a pike holding a piece of burning slow match – or, more commonly, with a 'portfire', a holder for a piece of slow-match which would burn for up to half an hour, lighted from a linstock stuck in the ground at the rear of the battery. Adye details a portfire mixture consisting of 60 parts saltpetre, 40 parts sulphur and 20 parts mealed powder, made into a $16\frac{1}{2}$-inch length which burnt for 12 to 15 minutes.[72] The firer always stood opposite the ventsman. Other methods of ignition, principally by flintlock, were not used on land.

Additional 'packing' for the charge and projectile was provided by the 'wad', made from hay or straw ('junk wads') or turf, the British Ordnance issuing 'punches for sod wads'. A 'grommet wad', used to prevent the ball from rolling out of a depressed barrel, was a rope circle just fitting the bore.

In addition to the five principal crewmen, at least one other was usually included to bring ammunition from the limber or caisson, and one or two more to assist in re-positioning the gun after every shot. No gun-crew could suffer more than one or two casualties without loss of efficiency; crews varied in size according to the type of gun, and extra 'muscle' was often provided by requisitioned infantrymen. For example, standard French guncrews consisted of:

Type	Specialist crew	Non-specialist crew
12-pdr	8	7
8-pdr, 6-in. howitzer	8	5
4-pdr	5	3

Many contemporary records exist of the effectiveness of artillery; not all are compatible and many 'variables' must be considered. The difference between 'maximum' and 'effective' range was often great, the French 12-pdr for example having a 'maximum' range of 1,800 metres but an 'effective' of 900 metres. For roundshot, Müller noted the following test against a six-feet high screen representing a line of men:[73]

Gun	Range (yards)	% of rounds taking effect
3-pdr	450	100
,,	750	34
,,	1,100	20
6-pdr	520	100
,,	950	31
,,	1,200	17
12-pdr	600	100
,,	950	26
,,	1,300	15

The 'Madras Records' trials show similar results, except that the 100 per cent. figure was never attained. Casualties would naturally be heavier in such cases where the target was in more dense formation, such as column. The equivalent French guns were probably slightly more accurate due to the less 'windage', projectiles more nearly fitting the bore, as suggested by the fact that French batteries tended to engage at longer range than British, though at smaller targets the chance of a hit was much reduced, gunners usually refusing to waste ammunition by firing at long range; thus the maximum effective range of *all* fieldpieces can be said to have been between 100 and 1,000 yards, irrespective of the size of the gun. Variations in the quantity of propellant, however, could radically affect the range: Adye quotes a 12-pdr at 2 deg. elevation sending a ball 293 yards to 'first graze' with an 8-oz charge, 350 yards with 12-oz, and 707 yards with 24 ozs of powder.[74]

Müller records the effect on a target 100 feet wide by eight feet high representing cavalry, and 100 by six feet representing infantry, of British 6-pdr canister: 41 per cent. of the bullets were effective at 400 yards and 23 per cent. at 600. From these figures Hughes calculates that from a 6-pdr the following might be expected to take effect:

Range	Hits per round
200 yards	55 bullets, light case
400 yards	36 bullets, light case
600 yards	6 bullets, heavy case

Fig. 40. **Right:** *A Trajectory of a roundshot from a 9-Pounder fieldpiece at 0° elevation; B. At 1° elevation; C. At 2° elevation; D. Problems in firing spherical case shot; E. Different types of artillery fire. (After Hughes.)*

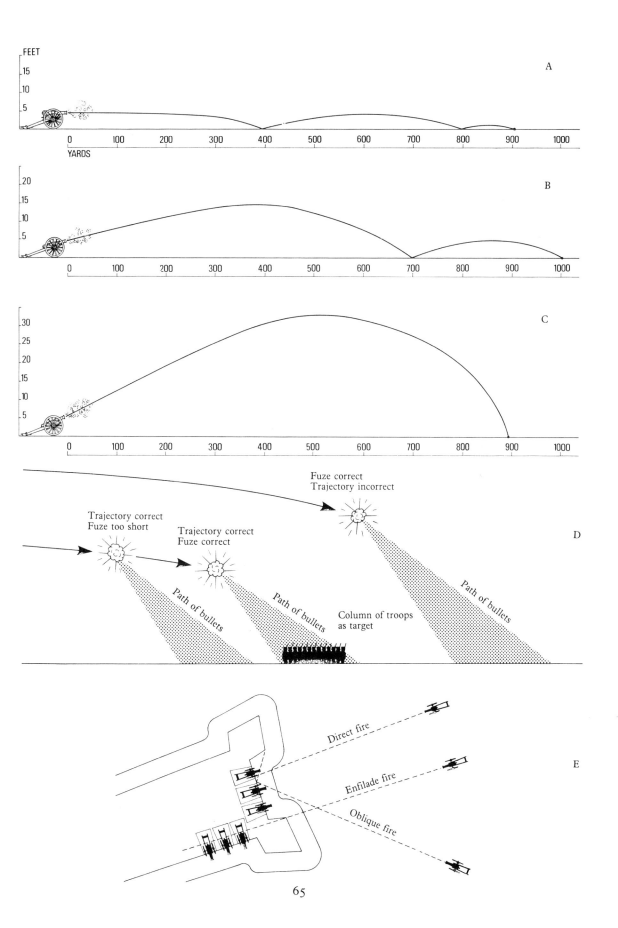

FEET

.15
.10
.5

0   100   200   300   400   500   600   700   800   900   1000

YARDS

A

.20
.15
.10
.5

0   100   200   300   400   500   600   700   800   900   1000

B

.30
.25
.20
.15
.10
.5

0   100   200   300   400   500   600   700   800   900   1000

C

Fuze correct
Trajectory incorrect

Trajectory correct
Fuze too short

Trajectory correct
Fuze correct

Path of bullets

Path of bullets

Column of troops
as target

Path of bullets

D

Direct fire

Enfilade fire

Oblique fire

E

65

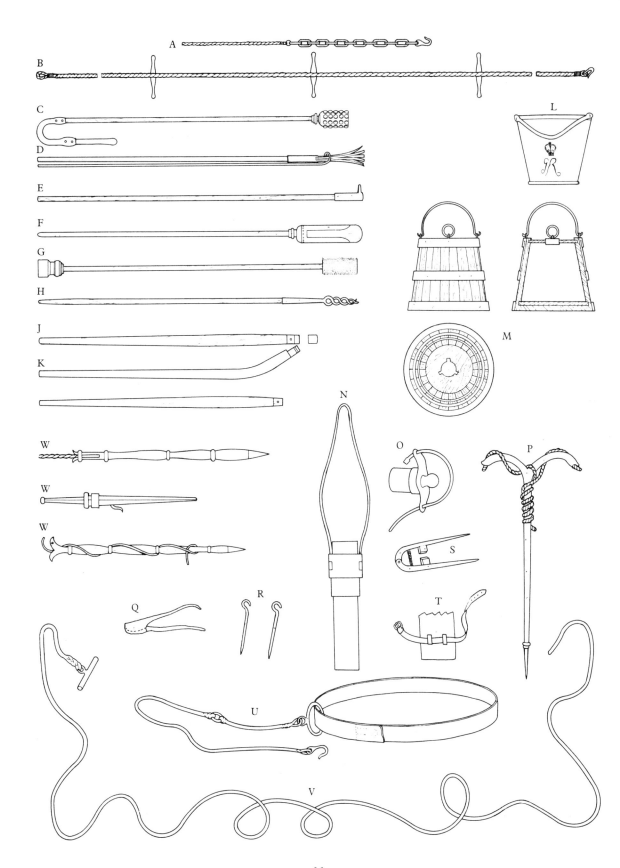

so that a battery of 6-pdrs, firing over 500 bullets at 200 yards range, could expect some 300 hits.[75]

Few trial-records exist for 'spherical case', save a test in 1812 in which between 2 per cent. and 17 per cent. of bullets fired hit the target-screens at 700 and 1,500 yards. The 'Madras Records' suggest that about 10 per cent. of bullets were effective, though the number of bullets contained in each shell was varied: a 6-pdr shell held between 27 and 85, a 9-pdr between 41 and 127, and a 12-pdr between 63 and 170.[76]

There seems to have been an unofficial 'table' of ranges at which various types of shot were used:

British: light case from 0–250 yards; heavy case 250–500; roundshot (guns) or common shell (howitzers) 350–600; roundshot and spherical case over 600.

Other nations: light case 0–250 yards; heavy case 250–500; roundshot (guns) or common shell (howitzers) over 500.

Taking into account 'variables' such as rate of fire, visibility, etc., the 1848 Madras Artillery manual[77] seems to indicate accurately the number of shots each gun could fire upon an advancing enemy:

At advancing cavalry (first half-mile trot, third quarter-mile canter, fourth quarter gallop):

Range from gun (yards)	Rounds fired per gun
1,500–650	7 spherical case
650–350	2 roundshot
350– 0	2 canister

Against infantry:

Range from gun (yards)	Rounds fired per gun
1,500–650	19 spherical case
650–350	7 roundshot
350–100	8 canister
100– 0	2 canister

(It should be noted that Indian artillery carried more spherical case than did British, who would have fired more roundshot; other nations would have fired roundshot instead of spherical case.)

Casualties per shot also varied. Müller (optimistically) calculated that a 6-pdr attacked by infantry would kill thirty men and wound ninety in the time taken to cover the final 400 yards. But on average, well-sited and well-handled artillery could expect to inflict between one and $1\frac{1}{2}$ casualties per shot. In the above case of a battery of six 6-pdrs firing canister, of the 300 hits caused probably no more than 50 per cent. would be effective due to the probability of more than one bullet striking each victim. In practice, there were so many 'variables' that the above 'test' data can hardly be regarded as evidence for what happened in action. So variable were the circumstances that actual casualty figures range from the reported loss of Lannes' troops at Austerlitz – 400 casualties in three minutes from forty guns – to four squares at Smolensk, under fire from twelve guns for three hours, losing only 119 casualties.

Even the noise of a cannon had tactical value, one criticism of the French 4-pdr being that its report was insufficient to demoralize, whereas the loud bang of the 8-pdr and particularly of the 12-pdr did!

Ammunition was stored in the gun-chest ('coffret') or axle-box of the cannon (if such existed), the limber, and in the attached ammunition-waggons ('caissons'). For French ordnance the standard supply was:

Gun	Rounds in 'coffret'	Rounds per caisson Ball	Canister
12-pdr	9	48	20
8-pdr	15	62	20
4-pdr	18	100	50
6-inch howitzer	4	49	11

Fig. 41. Left: *Artillery 'side-arms'. A. Drag Chain; B. English Drag Rope; C. French Crooked Sponge for the light 4-Pounder; D. Searcher with Reliever; E. Searcher; F. Powder Ladle; G. English Sponge and Rammer; H. Worm or Wad Hook; J. English Crooked Handspike; K. English straight hand spike; L. English Water Bucket; M. French Water Bucket; N. Portfire Case; O. Tompion; P. Forked-Linstock; Q. Thumb or Finger Stall; R. Priming Wires; S. Portfire Cutter; T. Vent Cover; U. Bricole; V. Prolonge; W. Portfires. (After Peterson.)*

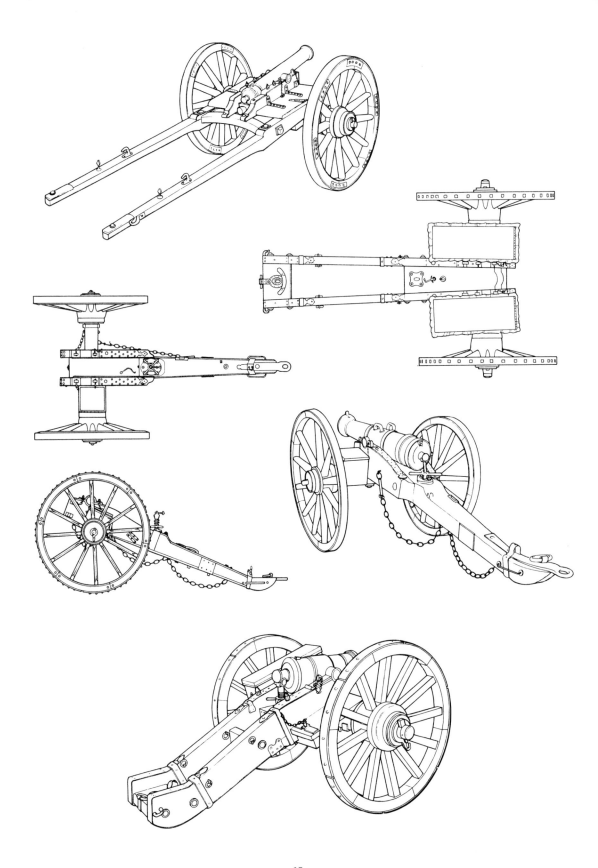

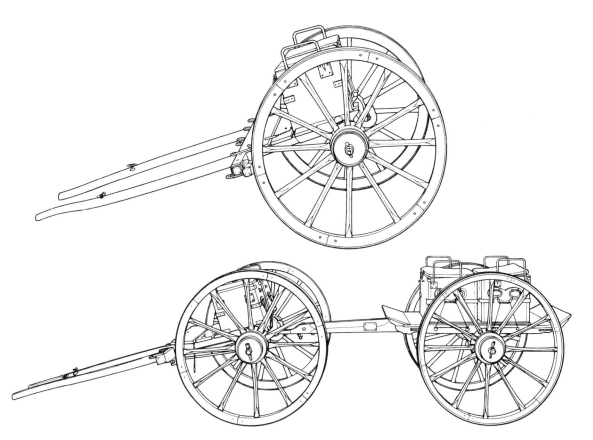

Fig. 42. Left: *British Artillery pieces.* Top to Bottom: *Galloper Gun, 1795; Plan of a Light 6-Pounder on a double bracket field carriage, 1793; Plan and elevation of a block trail field carriage for 6- and 9-Pounders; 9-Pounder gun on a field carriage; heavy 5½-Inch Howitzer, 1786–1819.*

Fig. 43. Above: *British Artillery Limbers.* Top: *9-Pounder Limber.* Below: *Limber with attached ammunition waggon.*

For British Artillery, Adye lists:[78]

Gun	In limber-box	In waggons
12-pdr medium	6 roundshot, 2 canister	120 roundshot, 24 canister
6-pdr heavy	36 roundshot, 14 canister	84 roundshot, 16 canister
5½-inch howitzer	22 shells, 4 canister, 2 carcasses	122 shells, 20 canister, 2 carcasses

Of the two types of waggon, the 'common pattern' contained 72 12-pdr rounds, 120 heavy 6-pdr rounds, 156 light 6-pdr rounds, 288 3-pdr rounds, 72 5½-inch howitzer shells, 24 8-inch howitzer shells, or 20,000 musket-cartridges; the older pattern of waggon carried 66 12-pdr, 120 heavy 6-pdr, 138 light 6-pdr or 60 5½-inch howitzer rounds.[79] British horse artillery carried the following at this time:[80]

Gun	On limber	In one waggon
Light 12-pdr	12 roundshot, 4 canister, 4 shell	52 roundshot, 10 canister, 10 shell
Light 6-pdr	32 roundshot, 8 canister	97 roundshot, 13 canister
5½-inch howitzer	13 shell, 5 canister	41 shell, 10 canister, 4 carcasses

Adye also lists the amount of ammunition normally available in the field with each piece of artillery of the following nationalities at this time (1802) shown in the table.

Gun	Austria		Prussia		Hanover		France	
	Canister	Round	Canister	Round	Canister	Round	Canister	Round
3-pdr	40	184	20	90	50	150	—	—
4-pdr	—	—	—	—	—	—	50	118
6-pdr	36	176	30	150	48	144	—	—
8-pdr	—	—	—	—	—	—	30	71
12-pdr	44	94	20	130	50	150	20	57

'The French horse-artillery waggon, called the *wurst*, carries 58 rounds for 8-pounders; or 30 for 6-inch howitzers.'[81]

Actual quantities of shot fired in action were often smaller than might be expected, due to the need to conserve ammunition because of uncertain re-supply; there are few examples of batteries running out of ammunition in action. At Waterloo, a prolonged artillery action, no more than 10,000 rounds were fired by 78 British guns, averaging about 129 each.

Highest expenditure was by Sandham's company, 183 rounds of 9-pdr ammunition and 5½-inch howitzer shells. During this period Hughes calculates that each gun *could* have fired 250 rounds,[82] indicating that only half the shots which theoretically could have been discharged actually were, proof not only of conservation by the gunners but smoke which obscured the target and therefore slowed the rate of expenditure.

Rate of fire depended upon the time needed to re-lay the gun after every recoil; in practice a rate of two roundshot or three canister per minute was about average, though this could decrease rapidly when the crew became tired (one shot every three or four minutes was not unreasonable in a protracted action), or if the enemy were too close to necessitate re-positioning the gun an almost continuous fire could be maintained for short periods; a competition in 1777 achieved twelve to fourteen unaimed shots per minute, a useless waste of shot under combat conditions. The heavier the piece, of course, the slower the rate of fire: a 12-pdr might average one shot per minute. Recoil was considerable, Adye's table ranging from twelve feet for a medium 12-pdr and light 6-pdr firing roundshot, to 3½ feet for a heavy 3-pdr firing canister. (These tests were carried out on elm planks; in soft ground the recoil would be much less.)[83]

It is difficult to generalize about rates of movement of artillery, the weight of equipment making the condition of the ground a more vital consideration than for infantry or cavalry. Normally, a French gun-team walked at 86 metres per minute, trotted at 189 and galloped at 200, but unless the gunners had transport even a trot was impossible for any distance. Horse artillery, with lighter equipment and the gunners all mounted or riding on the limbers, could achieve considerable speed, as witness Norman Ramsey's celebrated 'charge' at Fuentes de Oñoro. Artillery formations needed frequent halts to rest the horses and close gaps between vehicles, so that on good roads perhaps two and a half or three miles an hour was the average.

For rapid advances or withdrawals without the time-consuming limbering-up, two methods could be used: the 'prolonge', a rope connecting the limber and the gun, in effect enabling the gun to be fired without disconnecting it from the horses, and the 'bricole', by which the gun was manhandled by attaching drag-ropes and leather straps to the carriage and pulling it manually. The rapidity of movement thus achieved is demonstrated by Sénarmont's remarkable artillery 'charge' at Friedland, when his thirty guns opened on the Russians at 1,600 yards, then dragged forward by their crews, fired again at 600 yards, then 300, then 150, and ended by pouring canister at only sixty yards.

Travelling in column, a French battery of six guns and two howitzers would march with all eight guns at the front, followed by the other battery vehicles: eighteen caissons of artillery ammunition, one of musket-ammunition, one of tools and equipment, the forge and a spare gun-carriage. Where roads allowed, a double column was used, the guns always grouped together at the front. Arriving on the battlefield and receiving a post, the battery-commander would reconnoitre to pick the best field of fire: open space in front with no 'dead' (i.e. hidden) ground, preferably with firm ground near the enemy to assist ricochet, and with a gentle slope in front of the gun (more than 1 in 5 made the gun difficult to depress). If the battery could be sited behind marshy ground so much the better, absorbing the enemy's ricochet fire and not throwing up stones when the round-shot landed. Ideally the guns should have been placed on the crest of a hill, with the caissons on the reverse slope, concealed from the enemy; earthworks could be raised for the protection of the battery, or the guns could be concealed from view by infantry who would move away just before fire was opened, thus luring the enemy into an artillery trap. First-line caissons would be about fifty yards behind the guns, the second-line a further fifty, and other vehicles as much as another hundred to the rear; in action, instead of each gun drawing from its own caissons, it was safer to move forward only one or two caissons at a time, all guns drawing from them and thus not exposing more vehicles than necessary to enemy fire, as a single spark could destroy a battery's entire ammunition.

Having selected his position, the battery-commander would bring up his guns, theoretically siting them some six to ten yards apart; but only in massed batteries would guns be so pushed together, twelve to twenty yards between each being usual, to offer a more extended target. To avoid the possibility of enemy enfilade fire the battery would be placed in an uneven line. The length of time taken to open fire varied; horse artillery could be in action almost as soon as the gunners dismounted, but French 8- and 12-pdr batteries needed additional time to transfer the barrels from travelling to firing trunnion-positions. Firing was rarely by salvo, but 'sections' (i.e. each pair of guns) would often fire alternately

When attacked, artillery had little defence if their gunnery failed to repel the enemy; this emphasized the need for co-operation between 'arms', infantry or cavalry protection being vital for a battery. Otherwise they could limber-up and retire, or even engage the enemy in person: twice in 1800 French horse artillerymen protected their battery by mounting and charging the enemy, but such instances were rare. Sharpshooters were a continual menace; there are numerous cases of batteries being silenced or impeded by the accurate fire of a few marksmen.

If over-run, it was vital for artillery personnel to deny the enemy the use of their cannon. Few armies would expose their guns to capture, Russia being an exception; Kutaisov's directive read:

'The artillery must be prepared to sacrifice itself ... Fire your last charge of canister at point-blank range! A battery which is captured after this will have inflicted casualties on the enemy which will more than compensate for the loss of the guns.'[84]

The simplest way of rendering a gun inoperable was to remove a wheel; more permanently, it could be 'spiked', achieved by blocking the vent with a soft iron rod, bent inside with the blow of a rammer. Although 'spikes' were made specifically for this task, with split ends which opened out in the bore, even the hammering of a bayonet into the vent would enlarge it sufficiently to prevent immediate use. More permanent was to wedge a ball at the base of the bore with wooden plugs, necessitating the burning of the wedges to remove it, a time-consuming task; or for permanent destruction a trunnion could be knocked off with a sledge-hammer. Spikings in the field were much simpler, due to the

Fig. 44. Overleaf: *French Artillery pieces, Gribeauval System.* Top to Bottom: *8-Pounder field piece; 12-Pounder field piece and ammunition chest; 6-Inch Howitzer.*

Fig. 45. Overleaf: *French Artillery Waggons.* Top to Bottom: *Gribeauval cannon limbered up; Gribeauval Caisson; Gribeauval Horse Artillery Caisson.*

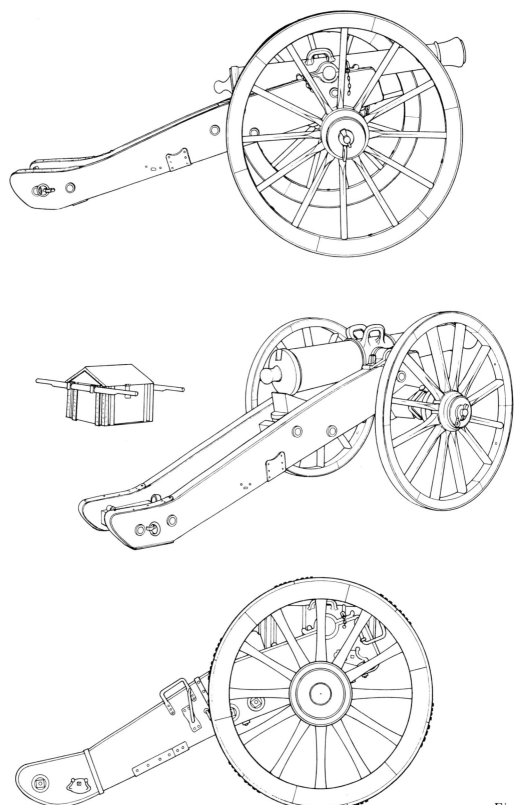

Fig. 44

Fig. 45

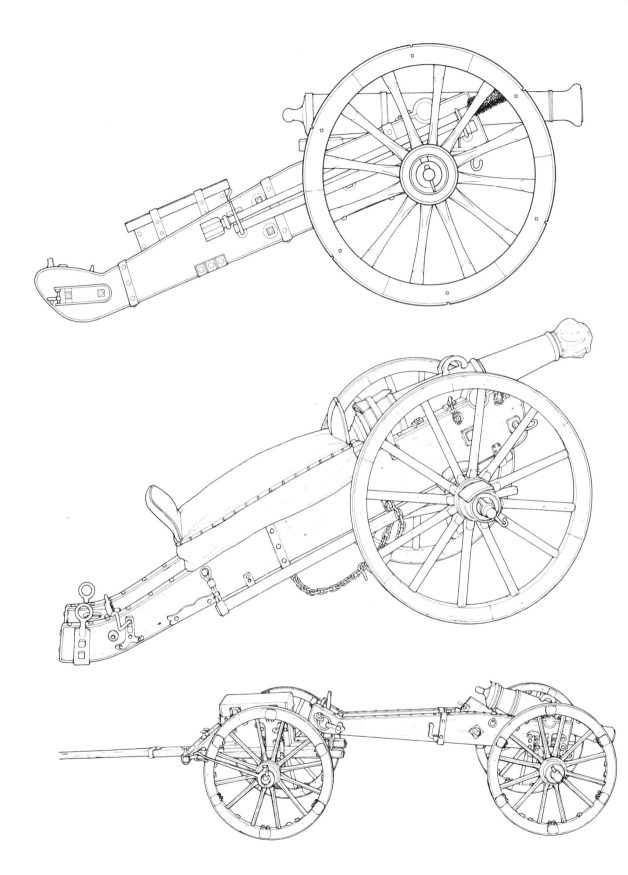

limited amount of time available, thus immobilizing the gun for a shorter period than if a thorough job had been done.

NATIONAL PATTERNS

The excellence of Napoleon's artillery was largely due to Jean Baptiste Gribeauval, who in the years after 1765 re-designed all French artillery with a double purpose: standardization and mobility. Limiting 'field' artillery to 12-, 8- and 4-pdrs and 6- and 8-inch howitzers, he streamlined barrels, introduced reinforced carriages and greatly reduced the weight (a Gribeauval 12-pdr on field carriage weighed 1,600 lbs as against the previous 3,200 lbs). His elevating-screw adjusted the platform upon which the breech rested, instead of being attached to the cascabel in the British fashion (howitzers retained quoin elevation). *All* barrels were brass. The double-bracket trail included two trunnion-positions (for firing and travelling) and a detachable ammunition-chest ('coffret'); 'windage' was reduced by careful calibration of the size of shot, wheels were enlarged and repairs made easier by standardization of design. Other vehicles were also re-designed; the limber had a 'tongue' so that horses could be hitched abreast (six horses for the 12-pdr, four for the others). The four-wheeled ammunition-waggons ('caissons') were divided internally into compartments for easy stowage of powder and shot, and the lid peaked (or rounded with a padded top for the accommodation of gunners sitting astride it).

Napoleon adapted the Gribeauval System, replacing many 8-pdrs with 12-pdrs and many 6-inch howitzers with the heavier version, increasing both range and power; and replaced the 4-pdr with a re-designed 6-pdr for the same reason, to allow many Austrian and Prussian 6-pdrs captured from 1794 to 1800 to be employed and as part of Marmont's plan to replace both the 4- and 8-pdr with an intermediate gun. But the new 6-pdr – part of the 'System of Year IX' – was hastily-produced and found to be an ineffec-tive compromise, lacking the 4-pdr's mobility and the 8-pdr's power; the carriage also tended to be shaken to pieces. Other modifications, such as larger caissons, were successful but although the Grande Armée of 1812 was equipped with new designs, the French in Spain had to use the pure Gribeauval System.

On campaign, the heavier guns were generally held in reserve; the 6- and 8-pdr batteries were attached to advance-guards or divisional parks (though the light horse-artillery was held in reserve), the 12-pdrs largely allocated to Corps and Army reserve parks. Howitzers provided about one-third of divisional artillery though, except for each battery's howitzers, a battery always consisted of one weight of gun. During the Revolutionary Wars all artillery was organized in 'compagnies' (batteries) of four pairs of guns each, this number later retained for field (or 'foot') batteries, horse artillery having six guns per battery, both foot and horse batteries having two howitzers each. Each gun had two caissons attached (three for every 12-pdr and howitzer, and more for Guard pieces – five per 12-pdr and howitzer, three for others). Each battery also possessed a forge, spare carriages and baggage-waggons, raising the total battery establishment to about thirty vehicles and 140 horses. Manpower of each battery consisted of a company of gunners, comprising four sections of two guncrews each (for an eight-gun battery), and a company of drivers from the Artillery Train, a total of about 130 men.

Horse artillery was habitually equipped with lighter guns (4- and 6-pdrs and 6-inch howitzers), and had all their gunners mounted, thus giving them vastly superior mobility. Unlike the 'foot' batteries which had to employ civilian drivers until the foundation of the Artillery Train, horse artillery always had their own drivers. A variation was seen in 1792 when, due to shortages of horses, at least one battery had its gunners riding on the limbers and on 'wurst'-waggons. Horse artillery was grouped into 'squadrons' of two

Fig. 46. Top to Bottom: *Prussian 6-Pounder field piece; Austrian 6-Pounder field piece with padded seat for the crew; Russian 10-Pounder 'Unicorn' equipment.*

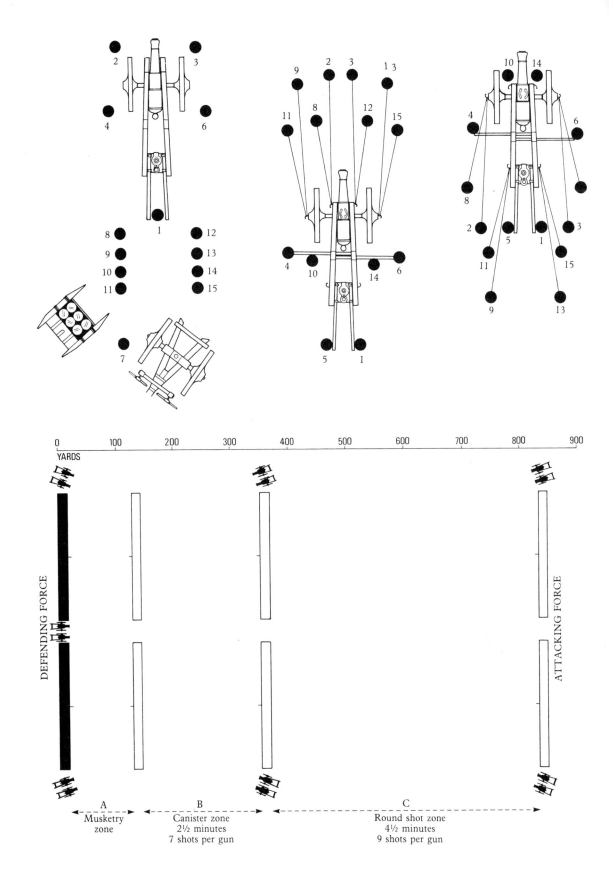

0 100 200 300 400 500 600 700 800 900
YARDS

DEFENDING FORCE

ATTACKING FORCE

A
Musketry
zone

B
Canister zone
2½ minutes
7 shots per gun

C
Round shot zone
4½ minutes
9 shots per gun

76

companies each; the terms 'battery', 'company' and 'division' can be confusing, 'battery' (originally a gun-emplacement) becoming synonymous with 'company', whilst 'division' could indicate a company or an unspecified number of guns.

Though British ordnance had no re-designing comparable to that of Gribeauval, certain innovations were introduced, primarily the 'block trail' adopted for horse artillery 6- and 9-pounders, but not used for other ordnance until after Waterloo; a block trail for the $5\frac{1}{2}$-inch howitzer was designed but never manufactured. Some weights were withdrawn after failure in the Peninsular War: the 6-pdr and 8- and 10-inch brass howitzers were replaced, the 4 2/5th-inch and $5\frac{1}{2}$-inch howitzers remaining in use, and the 8- and 10-inch iron howitzers in use by 1820. Among the wide range of field artillery in use, the brass 12-pdr with barrel from five to nine feet long was obsolete by 1800, leaving the $6\frac{1}{2}$-foot 'medium 12-pdr' and the five-foot 'light 12-pdr'; the six-foot brass 9-pdr was extensively used after 1808; the brass 6-pdr

with barrel-length of between $4\frac{1}{2}$ to eight feet long was obsolete by 1795–1800, leaving the seven-foot 'long 6-pdr' and five-foot 'light 6-pdr' in use; the iron 4-pdr and brass 1-pdr were obsolete by 1800 and 1815 respectively; the brass 3-pdr from three to seven feet long was also obsolete by 1795–1800, leaving the six-foot 'long 3-pdr' and $3\frac{1}{2}$-foot 'light 3-pdr'. Iron guns (excepting the 4-pdr) were restricted to garrison and siege service.

An artillery battery (termed 'brigade'), both foot and horse, had six guns each. In the Waterloo campaign the foot batteries were equipped with five 9-pdrs and a $5\frac{1}{2}$-inch howitzer each. Of the horse artillery 'troops' (batteries) at Waterloo, two were equipped as in the Peninsular War: five 6-pdrs and a $5\frac{1}{2}$-inch howitzer. Four other troops had 9-pdrs and a $5\frac{1}{2}$-inch howitzer each, and one troop six $5\frac{1}{2}$-inch howitzers. In 1815 a foot battery comprised five officers and ninety-seven other ranks plus an officer and eighty-seven men from the Corps of Drivers. Mercer detailed his 'G' Troop, Royal Horse Artillery in 1815:

Five 9-pdrs and a $5\frac{1}{2}$-inch howitzer, 8 horses each:	48 horses
Nine ammunition-waggons (one per gun plus one spare per 'division'), 6 horses each:	54
One spare-wheel cart:	6
Forge, curricle-cart, baggage-waggon, 4 horses each:	12
Six mounted detachments, 8 horses each:	48
Two staff-sergeants, two farriers, collar-maker:	5
Officers' horses lent by Board of Ordnance:	6
Officers' baggage-mules:	6
Spare horses:	30
Two horses per officer, one for surgeon, personally-owned:	11
Total complement of animals:	226

Personnel: captain, second-captain, surgeon, three lieutenants, three sergeants, three corporals, three bombardiers, farrier, three shoeing-smiths, two collar-makers, wheeler, two trumpeters, eighty gunners, 84 drivers.

The troop comprised three 'divisions' of two 'subdivisions' each, a subdivision being one gun, crew, and ammunition-waggon; each division was commanded by a lieutenant, each right subdivision by a sergeant and the left by a corporal. The troop could also be split into two 'half-brigades' of three sub-

divisions each, one half-brigade commanded by the captain and one by the second-captain.

Other artillery included 'gallopers', light guns with the trail in the form of 'shafts' to harness directly to the horse (often attached to cavalry regiments), and the bizarre 'War

Fig. 47. Left Above: *Diagrammatic view of a French gun crew in action. Crew members numbered one to fifteen.* Left: *When firing.* Centre: *Advancing by 'Bricole'.* Right: *Retreating by 'Bricole'.* Below: *Diagram of a theoretical advance against artillery and infantry.*

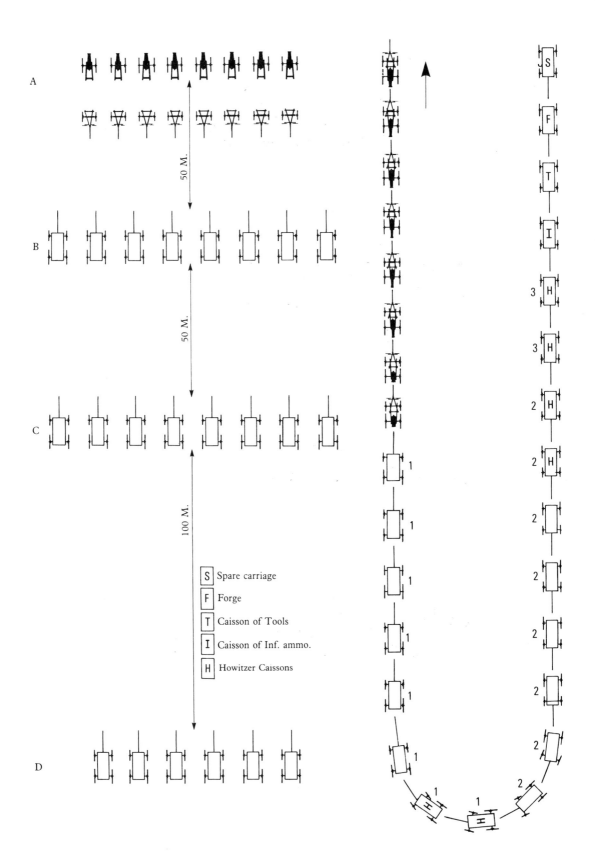

A

50 M.

B

50 M.

C

100 M.

D

S | Spare carriage
F | Forge
T | Caisson of Tools
I | Caisson of Inf. ammo.
H | Howitzer Caissons

S
F
T
I
3 H
3 H
2 H
2 H
2
2
2
2
2
2
2
1
1
1
1
1
1
1
1
1

Chariot' designed by one Mr Sadler of Pimlico for the use of his volunteer Sharp-shooters, a light four-wheel, two-horse carriage with two 3-pdrs on a swivel-mounting, crewed by two gunners and a driver, the guns handled with 'alacrity and safety'[85] with a range of two furlongs.

Like France, Russia re-designed the artillery by Alexi Arakcheev's 'System of 1805', introducing lighter carriages and limiting fieldpieces to light and medium 6- and 12-pdrs. Russia also used the 'Unicorn', a long-barrelled howitzer designed in 1757, which had greater range and accuracy than the French 6-inch howitzer, and which existed in 3-, 10- and 20-pdr versions, the lightest being withdrawn after Friedland. Carriages were of the double-bracket variety with horizontal screw-elevation, all barrels were brass and in 1811 improved 'Karbanov' gun-sights were fitted. Lighter pieces had four-horse teams and 12-pdrs eight or ten. The net result was lighter and faster artillery which '... is so well horsed, so nimbly and so handily worked, that it bowls over almost all irregularities of surface with an ease, lightness, and velocity that give it great superiority.'[86] Battery-composition reflected the excessive quantity of Russian artillery, 'heavy field batteries' comprising eight 12-pdrs, two light and four heavy unicorns, 'light field batteries', eight 6-pdrs, four medium and two light unicorns, and 'horse batteries', twelve 6-pdrs. Wilson remarked unfavourably on the Russian practice of providing excessive numbers of guns:

'... out of all proportion to the infantry ... particularly inconvenient and embarrassing in countries and seasons where forage was not to be procured. Occasionally, indeed, by the delays it compelled, it endangered the safety of the army.'[87]

Prior to the reforms of Archduke Charles from 1806 to 1809, Austrian artillery was inefficient when compared to the French, with insufficient trained crewmen and no permanent train. Concentrations of fire were rare as the lighter artillery was distributed piecemeal among the infantry and only the heavier organized in reserve batteries. The basic types were 3-, 6- and 12-pdr guns and 7-pdr howitzers, with the double-bracket trail, though one unusual feature was the 'wurst'-type padded seat on the trail of horse artillery guns, allowing four gunners to ride upon the carriage. By 1809, when infantry guns had been discontinued and organization established to provide concentration, the artillery commanders were too inexperienced to use its full potential.

The Prussian artillery arm had to be re-constructed after the débâcle of 1806, the number of pieces in that year (4,614) falling to only 149 in 1808. The basic fieldpieces were the 6- and 12-pdr gun and 7- and 10-pdr howitzer, with crews of nine, thirteen, twelve and fifteen respectively; the double-bracket trail had a Gribeauval-style ammunition-chest which was removed for action. Organization in August 1813 consisted of six 12-pdr foot batteries, thirty 6-pdr foot batteries, twelve 6-pdr horse batteries and one battery each of 3-pdr cannon and 7-pdr howitzers. All batteries comprised six guns and two howitzers, the 7-pdr in the 6-pdr batteries and the 10-pdr in the 12-pdr; each battery was subdivided into four sections. The expansion of 1813 resulted in some batteries containing only guns, with no howitzers.

Spanish artillery generally followed the Gribeauval system whilst retaining traditional Spanish barrel-design, and British-style iron

Fig. 48. Left: *French eight-gun battery in firing line. A. Gun and limbers in the firing line; B. Line of 1st Caissons; C. Line of 2nd Caissons; D. Line of 3rd Caissons of the 4th Section, and Battery vehicles.*
Right: *French eight-gun battery in column. 1. 1st Line Caissons; 2. 2nd Line Caissons; 3. 3rd Line Caissons; H. Howitzer caissons; I. Infantry ammunition carts; T. Tool Carts; F. Forge; S. Spare carriage.*

Fig. 49.   Artillery transported on improvised sledges during Napoleon's crossing of the Alps. Print after J. Girardet.

guns. At the beginning of the Peninsular War governmental parsimony and theft resulted in four-gun instead of six-gun batteries, totally devoid of draught-animals (deducting the four complete batteries sent to Denmark with La Romana, the remaining 216 guns and caissons had only 400 animals). Spanish gunners rarely joined the routine 'sauve qui peut' which followed every Spanish defeat but fought until the end, resulting in huge losses of equipment and trained personnel. Eventually the artillery had to be dragged by mules yoked tandem-fashion and goaded by men on foot, the slowest imaginable locomotion. Constant losses of guns also resulted in the use of ancient and archaic guns, particularly in the siege-train.

TACTICS AND OTHER ARTILLERY PIECES

Only when large quantities of artillery were massed together did the arm assume an offensive rôle in its own right, the allocation of batteries to small tactical formations being able only to support the actions of those formations. But the allocation of artillery to 'divisional reserves' enabled two or three batteries to be massed together at decisive points, a combined bombardment exerting greater influence than the individual fire of the component parts. Following the decisive actions of Marmont's massed batteries of

nineteen and eighteen pieces at Castiglione and Marengo, artillery concentrations continued to exist at 'divisional park' level, though the massing of artillery at Corps level was rare in the French forces, due to the reticence of divisional commanders to surrender their guns to a 'Corps park'. The Imperial Guard was devoid of such jealousy and the large Guard park was used *en masse* as an army reserve, becoming one of the deciding features of Napoleonic warfare. Sénarmont's thirty-eight-gun artillery 'charge' at Friedland, already mentioned, turned the course of the battle and thereafter Napoleon attempted to hold even larger masses of artillery in reserve to strike the decisive blow; at Wagram a 102-gun battery was employed, its only partial success due to a better-prepared enemy and lack of French co-ordination. At Lützen sixty Guard pieces appeared from behind a ridge, repelling the enemy; at Bautzen a seventy-six-gun battery had limited effect due to inappropriate terrain and Russian fieldworks; at Dresden the artillery was inexplicably ordered to withdraw and the 80-gun battery at Leipsig blew a hole in the enemy line but the supports failed to take advantage. Breakthroughs achieved by artillery fire demanded careful co-ordination of other arms, a task in which Napoleon often failed, never exploiting the massed-battery tactic to its full potential.

Similar bombardments were used by

Fig. 50.   A British artillery battery in position at the siege of Badajoz, 1812. Contemporary print.

armies other than those commanded by Napoleon: Sénarmont broke the Spanish at Oçana and Medellin (the tactic could not be used against Wellington, who would fight only on ground unsuitable for artillery), by Wellington (accidentally) at Vittoria and Bülow at Gross Beeren, but only Russia was as expert as the French. Thanks to their enormous quantity of artillery, they formed *two* massed batteries at Eylau (sixty and seventy guns). Kutaisov, unlike many others, believed that artillery-fire should be directed against the enemy guns except in a defensive battle, and advocated massed batteries to effect a breakthrough, introducing more guns as the battle continued. At Borodino he forgot his own importance as artillery commander and was killed leading a bayonet-charge, so that much of his artillery reserve was *never* ordered into action.

'Battalion guns' were common at the end of the eighteenth century, being light field-pieces belonging to infantry battalions and crewed by members of the battalion. The system was not as effective as might be imagined, and largely died out around the early 1800s (Britain, for example, trained an officer and thirty-four men per battalion to handle the unit's two 6-pdrs, and an officer and eighteen men per cavalry regiment to crew the 'gallopers', but by 1799 'battalion guns' were virtually extinct). The principal objection was the reduction of the unit's

mobility: 'If you want to prevent your troops manoeuvring, embarrass them with guns' as General Lespinasse wrote in 1800.[88] Napoleon believed them to be morale-boosters ('The more inferior the quality a body of troops, the more artillery it requires';[89] a comment appropriate also to the number of guns allocated to larger formations); he withdrew battalion artillery after the Peace of Amiens but, due to the declining standard of infantry, re-issued the guns in 1809, originally two 3- or 5-pdrs per battalion captured from Austria, later 4-pdrs. They were again abolished in 1813. Adye notes the allotment of battalion guns in other armies (1802): Denmark, two 3-pdrs; Austria, three 6-pdrs; Hanover, two 3-pdrs; Prussia, two 6-pdrs 'to a battalion in the first line' and two 3-pdrs 'to a battalion in the second line.'[90]

Heavier cannon were required to batter holes in fortresses. Too large and cumbersome for use in the field, they formed the army's 'siege train' which travelled slowly to a besieged fortress. Whilst 24- and 18-pdrs were the usual siege artillery, much larger pieces – 42- and 32-pdrs – were also utilized, manufactured in both iron and brass. Gribeauval retained the earlier Vallière siege-patterns, 16- and 24-pdrs. Due to their ponderous movement, however, siege-trains had sometimes to be improvised by the use of naval guns and gunners; prior to Cuidad Rodrigo Wellington had to resort to a

Fig. 51. French artillerymen defending their guns when overrun by British cavalry at Waterloo. (Engraving after W. B. Wollen).

veritable museum of Spanish and Portuguese ordnance dating back to the 1620s, these guns having no standard calibre, no calibrated ammunition and consequently weak effect, prone to 'drooping' or vents becoming unworkable. Eventually Wellington received proper 24-pdrs but for the second siege of Badajos he was sent Russian 18-pdrs which his ammunition did not fit! Even this siege-train had to rely upon eight pairs of bullocks per gun for transportation, with ammunition hauled on ox-carts. The 24-pdr was invariably preferred, the difference between its shot compared to that of an 18-pdr '... is far greater than would be conceived ... no engineer should ever be satisfied with 18-pounder guns for breaching when he can by any possibility procure 24-pounders.'[91] Ammunition-expenditure during a siege could be considerable: the breaching-batteries at Badajos used 2,523 90-lb barrels of powder, 18,832 24-pdr roundshot and 13,029 18-pdr roundshot, almost 5,000 mule-loads of ammunition, not including canister and shell.[92] Siege-guns had a much slower rate of fire than fieldpieces, the twenty-three rounds

per hour for $15\frac{1}{2}$ hours a day maintained against San Sebastian being reckoned an incredible feat.

Similar large cannon were used for garrison duty, with a wider assortment of carriages. Carriages often resembled naval patterns, occasionally iron but usually wood, with small iron 'truck'-wheels (wooden trucks were restricted to sea service). Heavier ordnance used quoin-elevation, the barrels being too heavy to use a screw-elevator. For both garrison and siege-work guns were ideally sited on wooden platforms to prevent the guns sinking into the ground. In garrison 'traversing platforms' could be used, upon which the gun was securely fixed, the entire platform being traversed on a pivot which made aiming both faster and easier. To reduce recoil the rear trucks could be replaced by a wooden block, forming a 'rear chock carriage', or the trucks could be removed completely, producing a low-recoil 'sliding carriage'. Garrison-guns with full-size wheels could also be mounted on platforms, the direction of recoil being controlled by wooden rails on the platform. Carronades were used occasion-

Fig. 52A. Napoleon personally aims a cannon at Montereau. Print after E. Lamy.

Fig. 52B. A French artillery battery-position at Toulon, 1793. Print after Jung.

ally for garrison-duty; originally manufactured at the Carron foundry near Falkirk they were short, large-bore cannon secured not by trunnions but usually by a loop cast on to the underside of the barrel, mounted on wooden carriages with two or four trucks. Used almost exclusively at sea, the carronade existed in 68- to 6-pdr versions, with a range between 230 yards for a 12-pdr at point-blank elevation to 1,280 yards for a 68-pdr at 5 deg. elevation.[93]

Mortars were shell-guns designed for high-angle fire, almost exclusively used for siege and garrison work due to their great weight

Fig. 53. Left Above: *French mobile artillery accompanying a cavalry advance, at Dierhoff, 18 April 1797. Print after Coginet & Girardet.*

Fig. 54. Left Below: *French artillery battery at Frankfurt-am-Main, 1792, showing the use of brushwood 'blinds' to shield the position. (Print after H. Lecomte).*

Fig. 55. Above: *British artillerymen and a piece of ordnance upon a garrison carriage. Print by I. C. Stadler after C. Hamilton Smith.*

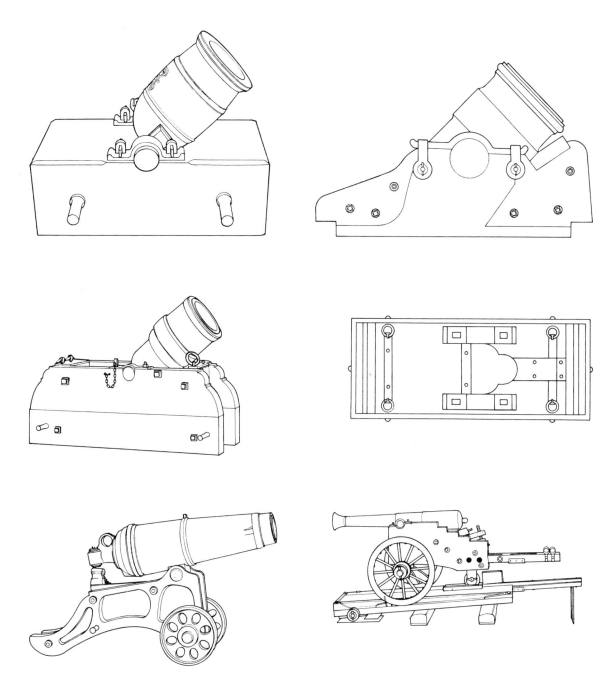

Fig. 56. Top to Bottom, Left to Right: *British Coehoorn Mortar on a wooden bed, 1814; French 10-Inch Gribeauval Mortar; British 10-Inch Mortar on a wooden bed; Plan of a wooden bed; Garrison artillery British carronade on an iron Land Service carriage; Prussian 12-Pounder cannon on a garrison carriage.*

and immobility. Their very short barrels were fixed on to wooden 'beds' bereft of wheels, supported on trunnions positioned at the rear of the breach; all recoil was absorbed by the bed, necessitating most sturdy construction, the simplest beds (for small mortars) consisting of a single block of wood with a hollowed-out depression to accommodate the barrel. Elevation was by quoin inserted at the front of the bed, but a quicker method was to position the barrel permanently at 45 deg. and vary the range by reducing or increasing the amount of powder used as propellant; for example a British 13-inch mortar at 45 deg. had a range of 245 yards with a 14 oz charge and 2,706 yards with an 8 lb charge.[94] British mortars ranged from the 36-cwt 13-inch iron mortar, 3 ft 7½ ins long, through the 8-, 10- and 5½-inch ('Royal') versions to the 4 2/5th in. brass 'Coehorn' mortar, only 1 ft 1½ in. long and weighing ¾ cwt, so light as to be carried by two men and used in the field, despite its alarming jump into the air when fired. Napoleon retained Gribeauval's 12- and 8-inch mortars but replaced the 10- and 6-inch. Like howitzers, mortars were 'chambered'; that is, the part of the barrel containing the charge was smaller in diameter than the bore.

Mortar-bombs resembled howitzer-shells – iron spheres filled with powder and sealed by a tapered wooden fuze – but were often thicker at the base to ensure landing fuze-uppermost. The effect of mortar-bombs falling almost vertically from their high trajectory could produce startling results, such as the exploding of the Almeida magazine in 1809. Bags of stones could be fired as anti-personnel devices, large mortars or 'perriers' being designed for the purpose; Britain had 'stone mortars' of up to 13-inch bore.

Incendiary shells or 'carcasses' originally consisted of tarred canvas bags, later cast-iron cases with three or five holes in, filled with combustible mixture and the fuze-holes filled with powder. Once ignited they were almost impossible to extinguish, burning-time ranging (according to Adye) from three minutes for an 11-lb carcass to eleven minutes for a 213-lb carcass fired from a 13-inch mortar. The filling was a compound of 50 parts saltpetre, 25 sulphur, 5 antimony, 8 rosin and 5 pitch, or 'Valenciennes composition' comprising 50 parts saltpetre, 28 sulphur, 18 antimony and 6 'rosin or Sweedish [sic] pitch', the latter cast in cylindrical blocks and inserted into an ordinary 'common shell'.[95] For illumination-flares, 'light balls' were used, fired from a cannon and comprising an oval iron framework covered with painted cloth, containing mixtures of saltpetre, mealed powder, sulphur, resin and linseed oil. Each had three fuzes protruding from the cloth cover, ignited by the flash of the cannon. 'Smoke balls' were used mostly at sea, intended for concealment or for the suffocation of men working in confined spaces, being mixtures of saltpetre, corned gunpowder, sea coal and antimony, in a tarred papier-mâche case. The most primitive illumination consisted of a barrel of combustible material, rolled to the bottom of a ditch to illuminate a breach.

A normal, wheeled gun-carriage was known as a 'travelling carriage', but for mortars and guns on garrison carriages other modes of transportation had to be used. A garrison-carriage and gun-barrel could be loaded on to a four-wheel 'devil carriage', the carriage upside-down on top of the devil, the barrel slung below the rear axle. A flat-bed, four-wheel 'platform carriage' could also be utilized, with both barrel and carriage laid on top of the platform; and for short distances a barrel could be slung below a two-wheel, shafted 'sling cart'. Mortars were usually transported by devil or sling-cart, the beds following on a separate vehicle. To move a gun-barrel from such a vehicle on to its own carriage, a three-legged 'gin' (or 'gyn') was used, a sixteen-foot high structure from which a block-and-tackle was suspended. In an emergency, when gins were unavailable, drills existed for improvising a crane out of a limber, also useful for hauling guns uphill. A further improvisation was that used by Napoleon when crossing the Alps: the manufacture of sleds from hollowed-out logs in which gun-barrels were placed, allowing the gun and its carriage to be dragged over terrain impassable for wheeled vehicles.

Rockets were an innovation in European warfare, only Britain and Austria seriously

Fig. 57.   British artillery in action at Waterloo. Print after George Jones.

employing them, both of the type designed by Sir William Congreve and first used in action in 1805. In construction, a rocket consisted of a head containing a charge of various types, attached to a stick, the longer varieties made in sections and joined with iron ferrules. Launching required some nerve but little equipment: the rocket could be laid along the ground, on a tripod, on an inclined bank or on a 'rocket car' (a vehicle not used in action during the Napoleonic Wars), angle of fire depending upon the gradient against which the rocket was leaned.

As envisaged by Congreve's 'Details of the Rocket System' (1814) the weapon had much to recommend it: cheap, easily-portable (a mounted 'Rocket Troop' of 172 men without any vehicles could carry 840 missiles), and deceiving to the enemy, a 'Rocket Cavalry-man' carrying the heads under his shabraque and the poles on his shoulder resembling a lance (pennons and lance-heads were provided). But in practice they were unreliable, prone to fly off course and even double back

Fig. 58.   Austrian Mortar battery bombarding the city of Lille, September 1792. After Bertaux.

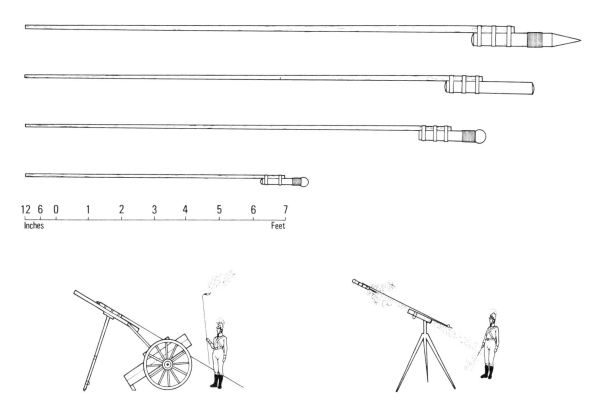

Fig. 59. Rockets and sticks. Above, Top to Bottom: *32-Pounder Carcass; 24-Pounder Case-shot; 18-Pounder Shell; 6-Pounder Shell.* Below Left: *Rocket fired from a rocket cart.* Right: *Rocket fired from a tripod, in the case of smaller rockets.*

upon the firers. This unreliability led to few occasions of use in action, though 40,000 were fired at Copenhagen in 1807 and British rocket troops served in Spain, America, Leipsig and Waterloo, despite Wellington's disapproval: 'I do not wish to set fire to any town, and I do not know any other use for rockets.'[96]

Rockets fell into three classes: 'heavy' (8-, 7- and 6-inch diameter of head with 24, 22 and 21-feet sticks respectively) used as incendiaries or for explosives for long range (2,100 to 2,500 yards); 'medium' (42-, 32- and 24-pdrs); and 'light' (18-, 12-, 9- and 6-pdrs), the 32-pdr being the lightest 'bombardment' rocket and the heaviest 'field' rocket. Heads were originally bound in paper but from 1806 in thin sheet iron cases, the largest (8-inch) weighing 3 cwt. Incendiary-heads were made like carcasses, containing 25 to 50 lbs of explosive; the 'medium' pattern could carry roundshot or shell and the 24-pdr could carry canister which burst in the air over the target.

Signal-rockets and parachute-flares to 'illuminate the atmosphere for nearly ten minutes'[97] were also used. Congreve proposed that the heavy rockets be restricted to sea service, the 24- and 18-pdrs for rocket cars, the 12-pdrs for 'rocket cavalry' and the lighter ones for rocket infantry; in the event, only the cavalry saw active service. Austrian rocket-batteries comprised twenty-four 'launchers' each, using 24-, 16-, 12- and 6-pdrs.

The principal use of rockets was to shatter enemy morale, as G. R. Gleig reported:

'... the confusion created in the ranks of the enemy beggars all description ... you see it coming yet know not how to avoid it. It skips and starts from place to place in so strange a manner, that the chances are, when you are running to the right or left to get out of the way, that you run directly against it; and hence the absolute rout which a fire of ten or twelve rockets can create....'[98]

Hand-grenades – in effect miniature shells

– were long redundant by the Napoleonic period, though still occasionally used at sea, fired from cannon or from a musket bearing a cup-attachment. One intriguing late mention of hand-grenades is contained in a report of February 1798, when the garrison of Templemore, Tipperary, turned out for a false alarm of insurrection with 'grenades ready, matches lighted'.[99] A primitive 'grenade' could be improvised by rolling a lighted howitzer-shell down an incline into the enemy ranks.

VISIBILITY

The Artillerist's Manual and British Soldier's Companion (1839–59) included the following account of visibility under ideal conditions with the naked eye:[100]

'Good eyesight recognises masses of troops at 1,700 yards: beyond this distance the glitter of arms may be observed. At 1,300 yards infantry may be distinguished from cavalry, and the movement of troops may be seen; the horses of cavalry are not, however, quite distinct but that the men are on horseback is clear. A single individual detached from the rest of the corps may be seen at 1,000 yards but his head does not appear as a round ball until he has approached up to 700 yards at which distance white crossbelts and white trousers may be seen. At 500 yards the face may be observed as a light coloured spot; the head, body, arms and their movements, as well as the uniform and the firelock (when bright barrels) can be made out. At between 200 and 250 yards all parts of the body are clearly visible, the details of the uniform are tolerably clear, and the officers may be distinguished from the men.'

In combat, however, dense clouds of smoke were produced by the ignition of gunpowder, frequently forming the 'fog of war', greatly reducing the theoretical rate of fire as targets were obscured, and demanding considerable skill to determine at what moment a volley should be fired through the swirling smoke-screen.

GUN-EQUIPMENT

Each piece of artillery was equipped not only with the 'sidearms' – rammer, handspikes, etc. – needed for actual firing, but also with a wide range of additional equipment carried on the limber or attendant waggon. An example is the list of stores given by Adye[101] for a British heavy 12-pdr in addition to carriage and ammunition:

Eighteen portfires, one 'apron of lead' (a foot-long, 10-inch wide sheet weighing 8 lbs 4 oz),[102] two 'sponges, with staves and heads', one wad hook with stave, two traversing handspikes, one 'tampion' (a plug used to close the muzzle), three straps for lashing side-arms, one gun-tarpaulin, one limber-tarpaulin, one linstock, two pairs drag-ropes, three padlocks with keys, 28 lbs slow-match, one 'spring spike', two 'common spikes' (both for 'spiking' the gun), two 'punches for vents', one 'budge barrel' (for powder), six 'couples for chain traces', one spare sponge-head, one spare rammer-head, one claw-hammer, one set of priming-irons, one pair draught-chains, one powder-horn, one French water-bucket, one felling-axe, one pick-axe, one bill, two spades, one 'skain' of 'tarred marline' (skein of tarred rope), one skein of tarred twine, one skein of 'Hambro' line', one lb packthread, one firkin of grease (one firkin = nine gallons), two grease-boxes, one lb tallow, one dark lantern, one lifting-jack, one 'waggon with hoops and painted covers, Flanders pattern', one 'wad miltilt', one tanned hide, one set 'Men's harness (twelve to a set)', one set chain horse-harness, one set harness-traces, one 'wanty' (leather waggon-rope), ten hemp horse-halters, five short whips, ten nose-bags, two corn-sacks, two sets forage-cords, one waggon linch-pin, two 'body-clouts' (for waggon), two 'linch-clouts' (for waggon), thirty-two sixpenny clout-nails, one spare ladle-stave, two tube-boxes, two portfire-sticks, one cutting-knife, one pair scissors, $\frac{1}{2}$-oz worsted, two needles, two leather cartouches, three copper powder-measures and two thumb-stalls.

Howitzers possessed even more equipment, including mallets, pincers and other tools for fuzing shells. Though powder-ladles were made obsolete by the use of the prepared cartridge, they were usually held in store in case of emergency.

RATIO OF ARTILLERY TO TROOPS

Considerable significance was put upon the 'correct' ratio of the number of guns to the total strength of an army, this usually being expressed as a figure of 'guns per thousand men'. A random sample of Napoleonic battles for which reasonably accurate figures are available is given below:

Contrary to what might be expected, in each battle the side with the highest proportion of artillery was defeated. Whilst it is dangerous to presume too much from this fact, it should be noted that too much artillery could be as bad as too little, excess guns slowing down the rate of manoeuvre. This was particularly true, for example, at Eylau, when the Russians' 460 guns represented a ratio of almost six per thousand men. The most vital factor, nevertheless, was the quality of the gunners and the skill with which the artillery was handled.

		Troops (approx.)	*Guns*	*Guns per 1000 men*
AUSTERLITZ	French	73,200	139	1.89
	Allies	85,400	278	3.25
BORODINO	French	133,000	587	4.41
	Russians	120,000	640	5.33
LIGNY	French	80,000	210	2.62
	Prussians	84,000	224	2.66
MARENGO	French	28,000	23–29	Approx. 1
	Austrians	31,000	100	3.22
SALAMANCA	Allies	59,000	60	1.01
	French	48,500	78	1.6
VITTORIA	Allies	75,300	90	1.19
	French	66,900	138	2.06
WAGRAM	French	170,500	500	2.93
(6 July 1805)	Austrians	146,600	450	3.06

ENGINEERS

Engineers' duties ranged from the construction of roads, fieldworks and bridges to the fortification and besieging of cities, mining, entrenching and map-making. The French engineers were the best in Europe, as they had been in the eighteenth century; as Foy wrote, 'All Europe has been covered by our redoubts and entrenchments...'.[103]

French engineer organization fluctuated greatly, particularly during the Revolutionary Wars, comprising companies of sappers, miners and the corps of officer engineers, initially part of the artillery but a separate entity from April 1795. Ultimately eight sapper battalions existed (reduced to five after 1812), from 1806 each battalion possessing its own vehicles, part of the engineer train battalion. Companies usually operated independently, and engineer officers were attached to every headquarters to supervise

constructions carried out by untrained labourers and infantry. Pontoon-trains were under artillery control, but permanent bridges were the responsibility of engineer personnel, who eventually possessed their own pontoon-equipment. Naval personnel were also attached to assist the engineers; in 1809, for example, Napoleon's engineer park consisted of an 800-strong naval battalion, 1,200 marines, nine sapper, three miner, three pontoon, four pioneer and two artillery companies, in addition to the two sapper and one pontoon company possessed by each corps.

The quantity of equipment carried is surprising; Napoleon's 48-waggon engineer train in 1809 transported some 30,000 tools, the variety illustrated by those used in the capture of Badajos in 1811: 100 miners and 483 sappers had 1,700 pickaxes, 170 miners' picks,

1,700 shovels, 1,700 long-handled shovels, 680 felling axes, 1,020 billhooks, 1,802 artificers' tools, 253 miners' tools, 8,318 kg. of machinery and stores, 35 waggons, 10 waggons of bridging-equipment and 230 draught horses.[104] So fine were the tools that captured ones were prized by the British above all; as Wellington wrote, 'Is it not shameful that they should have better cutlery than we have?'[105]

The British engineer corps comprised the Royal Engineers (officers only); the Corps of Royal Military Artificers (N.C.O.s and privates only), which became the Royal Sappers and Miners in 1812–13; the Royal Staff Corps, formed as part of the Quartermaster-General's Dept in 1800, who, though skilled, rarely served abroad; and the Barrack Artificer Corps, formed in 1805 when the removal of the Barrack Office from Ordnance control prevented repairs to barracks being made by the Artificers. In 1809 there were only 179 members of the Royal Engineers, only seventeen of whom were sent to Portugal. Though they performed sterling service and lost heavily (eleven out of twenty-four killed at Badajos [1812] and eleven out of eighteen at San Sebastian), Wellington commented: '... equipped as we are, the British army are [sic] not capable of carrying on a regular siege.'[106] Both personnel and equipment were lacking. Of the twelve Artificer companies in semi-permanent garrison in 1809, eight were in Britain, two in Gibraltar and one each in Nova Scotia and the West Indies, in a 'state of vegetation';[107] skilled in 'domestic' arts like carpentry, they were inexperienced in field duties. In 1809 only two sergeants and twenty-seven men were with the Peninsula army, augmented two years later by two sergeants and fifty-seven men 'who had never seen a sap, battery or trench constructed.'[108] Before Ciudad Rodrigo 180 infantry had to receive elementary training in sapping, and at Burgos miners were acquired by requesting ex-coal diggers to volunteer from the line! Such inexperience resulted in mis-conducted sieges and consequent heavy casualties, ill-positioned trenches 'leaving poor officers and troops to get into and across the ditch as they can.'[109] When Wellington blamed the casualties of Badajos on inefficient engineer organi-

zation, the Royal Sappers and Miners were increased to 2,800 and the equivalent of four companies served at San Sebastian. Transport was usually lacking; in 1813 Wellington's engineers had a total of only 120 mules and even in 1815 Flemish waggons and civilian drivers had to be hired, 'many ... of bad character, so that frequent desertions took place.'[110] Even personal arms were wretched; some had muskets but others are recorded as carrying blunderbusses or pikes.

Austria had *five* engineer corps, often competing with each other for personnel. Engineers and Sappers and Miners had their own establishments and trained officers, but before 1800 the rank and file had been misfits transferred from line regiments. Civilian recruits – young, healthy, unmarried, at least five feet four and literate – were accepted, greatly improving the standard. The Miners were employed not only in their specialist rôle but as ordinary engineers as well; the fourth unit was the Pioneer Corps, until 1809 not even controlled by the Director-General of Engineers, and doing the same job as the Sappers; their separate identity resulted from their national composition, 50 per cent. Bohemians and 35 per cent. Moravians, almost all specialist tradesmen. The fifth corps was the Pontoniers, six companies strong, and so elementarily trained that they needed Pioneer assistance for bridge-building!

Prussia reorganized her engineers in 1809 into fifty-six officers of the Engineer Corps and three Fortress Pioneer Companies, each of 123 of all ranks. The arm was expanded until by 1815 there were nine Field Pioneer Companies, eight Fortress Companies and one Landwehr unit, the Mansfeld Pioneer Battalion. Russia's small engineer corps was particularly adept at the construction of fieldworks, contributing far more than their limited numbers might suggest.

Infantry regiments in most armies included pioneer sections, distinguished by often-colourful uniforms, leather aprons, beards and axes, the latter three being jealously-guarded 'trademarks'. They were responsible for the construction of shelters and minor fortifications and often preceded the unit in attacks on prepared positions, to demolish

Fig. 60.   Crossing a river by pontoon: Prussians at the Rhine, August 1792. Print after J. Volz.

obstacles in the attackers' path. Regimental pioneer-sections were small; a British battalion in 1815, for example, had a pioneer-corporal and ten men, carrying between them eleven billhooks, three saws, three 'broad axes', two felling axes, eight spades, three pickaxes and three mattocks.

PONTOONS

Portable bridges were necessary equipment for any field army, pontoon-trains coming under the authority of engineers or (as in the French army) artillery. Pontoons were shallow, box-like boats with sloping prow and stern, made of wood or tin on a wooden framework, transported on four-wheel vehicles. According to Adye[111] the standard pontoon was 21 ft 6 ins long at the top and 17 ft 2 ins at the bottom, 4 ft 9 ins wide and 2 ft 3 ins deep, each pontoon equipped with: four baulks 22 ft 8 ins by one foot wide, one 22-foot gang-board one foot wide, six 11 ft 6 in. 'chesses' 2 ft 4 ins wide, two oars, an anchor, 'graplin', 'setter', four iron bolts, two mounting bars, four binding sticks, four spring-lines, four 'faukes', a cable, sheer-line,

boat-hook, maul, pump, windlass and four pickets. (A further variety, 'Colonel Congreve's Wooden Pontoons', were 26 ft long at the top, 23 ft at the bottom, 2 ft 8 ins deep and 2 ft 3 ins wide.)

Adye describes how a pontoon-bridge was constructed.[112] First, both river-banks were made solid by the laying of fascines. A cable was then carried across the river and fixed to a 'picket' (stake), and drawn taught by a windlass. Each pontoon was launched with two men in, and rowed downstream until one end could be lashed at right-angles to the cable (with a second cable at the other end if the river flowed strongly). Each boat was connected to its neighbour, about its own breadth apart, by diagonal lashing, with anchors fixed upstream. The 'baulks' were then laid at right-angles across the pontoons, and on top of them the 'chesses', forming the surface of the bridge, held by gang-boards along the outer edge of the bridge. Such a bridge would support between 4,000 and 5,000 lbs but care had to be taken, vehicles keeping a good distance from each other and cavalry leading their horses across to avoid undue movement. Usually two pontoon-bridges were built in conjunction, one for traffic each way and if sufficient were available the pontoons could be lashed directly together, with no space between, allowing a greater weight to pass over.

Pontoons could be improvised from local river-craft; the British engineer Squires, for example, bridged the Guadiana in April 1811 with two trestle-tiers connected by five moored boats, until swept away by the river, whereupon the boats were used as 'flying bridges' (ferries) and a 'slight narrow bridge'[113] improvised from spare pontoons and wine-casks. Similarly, Major Sturgeon improvised a repair to the broken bridge at Alcantara in 1812 by construction of a suspension-bridge of a network of rope overlaid with planks.

Pontoon-building could be hazardous, particularly under fire, though it could be vital. General Eblé, for example, commander of the French 'Pontoniers' in 1812, though ordered to burn his pontoons at Orsha, kept enough equipment to construct two bridges over the Beresina, over which the remnant of the Grande Armée was able to make its escape.

FORTIFICATIONS

To describe all the types of defence utilized during the Napoleonic Wars would entail a history of fortification beginning with the medieval castle, as all ages of fortification were used.

The basic theory of fortification was that no army could operate or leave its lines of communication unguarded with any sizeable enemy presence in the rear. Thus a fortified city could not be bypassed without risk, particularly if its garrison were capable of sallying out; thus, enemy fortresses had to be 'reduced' (captured) before any lengthy advance could continue. Furthermore, fortresses provided a refuge for a field army, supply-depôts, and could protect an army's flank. Most effective were defensive-chains of fortresses, like the 'Quadrilateral' in Italy (Mantua, Verona, Peschiera and Legnano), or Vauban's border-defences which twice saved France in 1792–93; as Carnot remarked, they were 'the defensive arms of states, and the counterparts of the shield of the individual soldier.'[114]

Fortresses were usually constructed in a standard, geometric design, with fabric of stone, usually covered with earth, or of earthworks alone, the latter cheaper to build but difficult to maintain. An earth covering absorbed roundshot which would ricochet off unprotected stonework and send stone-splinters flying like shrapnel. The language of fortress-construction is incomprehensible to the uninitiated, so is explained below.

The standard shape was the 'bastion', a four-sided construction with an open end, and a 'point' towards the enemy. Four or five such bastions grouped in a circle formed a 'citadel', the central point of a fortified place, around which the main defence-works were placed, often in two or three concentric rings, each defensible alone but connected to the others by passages. The main fortress-wall or 'enceinte' consisted of a high, almost-vertical stone wall or 'revetment' backed by earth, with a wide rampart-top or 'terreplein', from which artillery and muskets could be fired through gaps or 'embrasures' in the 'parapet'. At the bottom of the wall on the outward side was a wide ditch with a lower wall parallel to the revetment, giving the ditch an unscaleable face on both sides; at the top of this lower wall was a walking-space or 'covered way', protected by a wooden palisade and firing-step from which defenders could shoot across the 'glacis', a gently-sloping earth bank up which any attacker would have to charge. The ditch, ideally impassable by assault, was the most vital part of any fortification.

Along the enceinte bastions protruded, allowing the space between them to be swept by cross-fire. To protect the enceinte between bastions, 'detached works' could be built, either triangular bastions termed 'ravelines' or 'demi-lunes', or independent, detached forts some distance away. Other fortifications included 'retrenchments' (interior works covering the site of a likely breach), 'redoubts' (powerful works inside a bastion), 'redans' (V-shaped works open at the rear) and 'cavaliers' (raised gun-platforms). Some fortresses boasted 'casements' – vaulted chambers in the wall in which guns could be sited.

The capture of a fortress demanded great

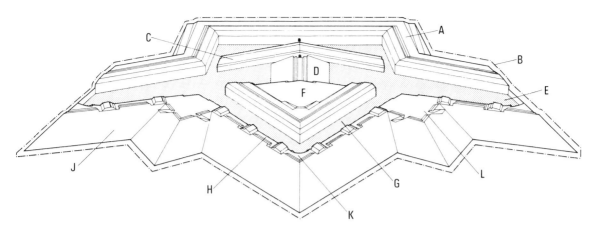

Fig. 61.   Vauban's First System of Fortification. A. Curtain; B. Part of Bastion; C. Tenaille;
D. Caponier; E. Main Ditch; F. Ravelin; G. Ditch of Ravelin; H. Covered Way; J. Glacis;
K. Salient Place of Arms; L. Re-entrant Place of Arms.

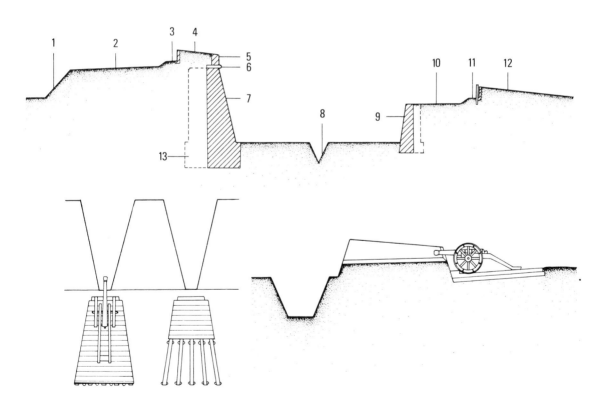

Fig. 62.   Above: The cross section of a fortification. 1. Talus; 2. Terreplein; 3. Banquette;
4. Parapet; 5. Tablette; 6. Cordon; 7. Scarp Revetment; 8. Cuvette; 9. Counterscarp Revetment;
10. Covered Way; 11. Palisade; 12. Glacis; 13. Counterfort. Below: Plan and elevation of part
of a battery constructed on a wooden foundation.

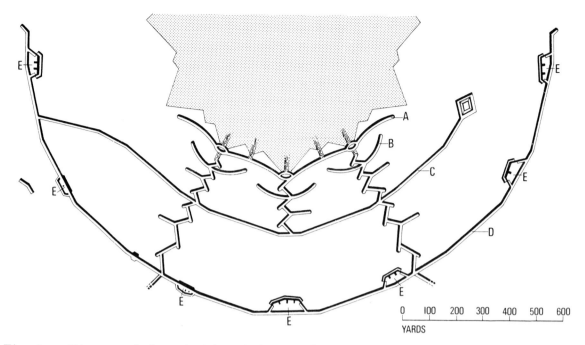

Fig. 63. Diagram of the principles of siege work. A. Third Parallel; B. Demi-Parallel; C. Second Parallel; D. First Parallel; E. Batteries.

expenditures of energy and equipment. First came the 'investment' – cutting communications of the fortress with its nearest support, achieved by judicious troop-placement. The opening of a 'practicable' breach – one which could be stormed – began by the digging of a 'parallel', a trench in front of the wall to be assaulted. This trench, usually begun at night, was pushed forward by zigzag trenches until a second, third, and fourth parallel took the besiegers close to the enceinte, breaching-batteries firing upon the selected point of storm. Particularly deadly was working in the final parallel, 'when every bullet takes effect – when to be seen is to be killed – when mine after mine blows up at the head of the road ... when the space becomes so restricted that little or no front of defense [sic] can be obtained, and the enemy's grenadiers sally forth every moment to attack the workmen ...'[115]

Once the breach was open and the defenders forced to retire to the enceinte, it was usual for the attackers to 'offer terms', to call upon the garrison to surrender. If the offer were declined and the besiegers unable to wait

until the garrison starved, an assault would be launched, inevitably a bloody affair. The breach would be barricaded with debris and 'chevaux-de-frise', wooden planks with imbedded stakes or sword-blades, and planted with 'mines', charges of powder and shells ignited below the attackers. A garrison's refusal to surrender was regarded as legitimate cause for the sack of a city once the besiegers got inside, horrific affairs like Badajos, Ciudad Rodrigo and Saragossa.

Mining could be used to tunnel beneath the enceinte, the burning or exploding of the tunnel bringing down the wall above; counter-mining by the garrison resulted in hand-to-hand fights in the blackness of the mine-shafts.

There were few innovations in fortifications during the Napoleonic Wars other than those associated with weapon-improvement. Among new defence-works were the 'Lines of Torres Vedras', a series of mutually-supporting forts protecting Lisbon; and the French constructed a series of block-houses behind their own lines in Spain, protecting lines of communication from guerrillas.

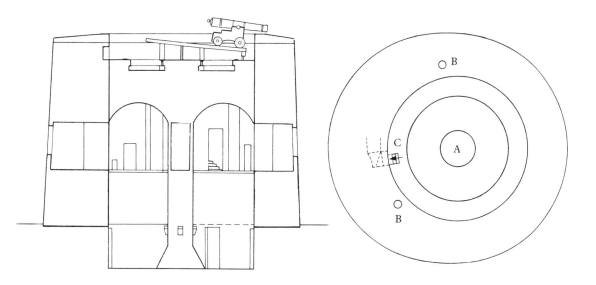

Fig. 64. Plan and section of a Martello Tower. A. Pivot; B. Chimney; C. Access stairs.

The Martello tower was another innovation, copied from an immensely-strong circular tower at Mortella [sic] Point in Corsica, whose tiny garrison offered a protracted resistance to the British in 1794. It so impressed them that a series of similar towers was built along the south and east coasts of England in preparation for the anticipated French invasion. Circular or elliptical in plan, the original proposal for 'Bomb Proof' towers suggested a height of 33 feet and interior diameter of 26 feet. They usually had two or three floors and a door set half-way up the wall, accessible only by ladder. On the upper storey – a flat, lead-covered roof – cannon were situated, often one heavy (18- or 24-pdr) and two light, fixed on traversible mountings which gave a complete field of fire over the six-foot parapet. A typical garrison comprised an officer and twenty-four men. The walls (widening towards the base) were at least six feet thick, stone with often a stucco finish. Their strength was indicated by the demoli-

tion of Martello 68 at Eastbourne in 1860, which required 100 rounds *each* from a 100-pdr, 80- and 40-pdr rifled Armstrong guns, immeasurably more powerful than any Napoleonic cannon.

Earthwork fortifications could be raised before a battle, the Russians being particularly proficient as the Raevsky Redoubt and Bagration 'flèches' (arrow-shaped constructions) at Borodino testify. Simpler to construct was an 'abatis', a barricade or parapet of felled trees. 'Fascines' were used for crowning defences or filling parapets, being bundles of brushwood or branches, often about eighteen feet long by nine inches diameter; 'gabions' were earth-filled wicker-work baskets, between two and a half and three feet high by two feet diameter, used for bolstering a trench or providing a parapet. An easier alternative was the sandbag, about two feet long by eight inches wide, Adye noting that 250 sandbags were needed for each fathom of battery.

69. Adye, p. 153.
70. Ibid., pp. 154–6.
71. 'Supplementary Despatches', VII, p. 304; see also Chambers p. 104.
72. Adye, pp. 218–19.
73. Quoted in Hughes, *Firepower*, p. 37.
74. Adye, p. 161.
75. Hughes, *Firepower*, p. 40.
76. Ibid., p. 38.
77. Quoted in ibid., p. 43.
78. Adye, pp. 15–16.
79. Ibid., pp. 16–17.
80. Ibid., p. 17.
81. Ibid., p. 21.
82. Hughes, *Firepower*, p. 65.
83. Adye, p. 229.
84. Quoted in Duffy, *Borodino*, p. 87.
85. Rowlandson, *Loyal Volunteers*, Plate 46.
86. Wilson, *Journal*, p. 30.
87. Wilson, 'Brief Remarks'; see also *Royal Military Chronicle*, 1812, p. 205.
88. Quoted in Chandler, p. 340.
89. Napoleon, *Correspondence*, XIX, p. 361, quoted in Chandler, p. 340.
90. Adye, p. 9.
91. Jones, *Journal of Sieges*, I, p. 145.
92. Ibid., I, pp. 209–10.
93. Adye, p. 72.
94. Ibid., p. 203.
95. Ibid., pp. 70–71.
96. Quoted in Glover, *Wellington's Army*, p. 101.
97. Congreve.
98. Gleig, *The Subaltern*, pp. 290–91.
99. Sir J. Carden, 15 February 1798; quoted in Packenham, p. 36.
100. See Hughes, *Firepower*, p. 26.
101. Adye, pp. 11–14.
102. Ibid., p. 8.
103. Quoted in Chandler, p. 365.
104. Jones, *Journal of Sieges*, II, p. 386; see Glover, *Peninsular Preparation*, p. 107.
105. Wellington to the Earl of Liverpool, 11 February 1812; see Brett-James, *Wellington at War*, p. 233.
106. Wellington to Lt-Col. Torrens, 7 April 1812; 'Despatches', IX, p. 49.
107. Pasley, *Elementary Fortifications*, quoted in Glover, *Wellington as Military Commander*, p. 173.
108. Quoted in ibid., p. 173.
109. Wellington to Maj. Gen. Murray, 28 May 1812; 'Despatches', IX, p. 183.
110. Pasley, *Course of Military Instruction*, II, p. xii, quoted in Glover, *Peninsular Preparation*, p. 108.
111. Adye, pp. 217–18.
112. Ibid., pp. 62–4.
113. Napier, *Peninsular War*, III, p. 499.
114. Carnot, *De la Défense des Places Fortes*, Paris, 1812, quoted in Duffy, *Fire and Stone*, p. 20.
115. Jones, *Journal of Sieges*, I, pp. xiv–xv.

Fig. 65. Napoleon undertakes his own reconnaissance. Print after Raffet.

STAFF & SUPPLIES

TACTICAL FORMATIONS

The Brigade was an administrative grouping of two or more battalions or cavalry regiments, to which orders were issued and which acted as a tactical entity; it was commanded by a field officer of one of the component battalions or by a junior general officer. Two or more brigades formed a Division, commanded by a general officer, with a divisional artillery park and sometimes a light cavalry brigade attached. Two or more infantry divisions comprised a Corps, with light cavalry and a reserve artillery park either instead of, or in addition to, divisional parks. Commanded by a marshal or senior general the Corps was a self-contained army, complete with commissariat, capable of independent action.

Methods of organization varied. For example, France favoured the establishment of 'Reserve' Cavalry Corps, comprising heavy cavalry divisions with light brigades attached as skirmishers, enabling enormous masses of heavy cavalry to be concentrated. In the Austerlitz campaign, both Russian and Austrian armies were run at regimental level, with no permanent brigade, divisional or Corps organization; the Russians realized the folly of such a system, Barclay de Tolly instituting a semi-permanent organization by which two three-battalion regiments (one of which was in the reserve or 'Supply' Army) formed a brigade, two line and one light brigades a division, and two divisions a Corps, with artillery and cavalry attached at Corps level.

Wellington instituted the first British divisional system in 1809, only brigades existing prior to that year. During the Peninsular War it was customary for each Anglo-Portuguese infantry brigade to include rifles or light infantry as skirmishers, and each division artillery and administrative units, but only the Light Division had a permanent attachment of cavalry. Cavalry brigades were grouped in a single division (two in 1811–12) for administrative reasons only, it usually being impossible to manoeuvre any cavalry formation larger than a brigade. There was no official 'Corps' organization though two, later three groups of divisions were made semi-independent, with divisional staff expanded to form a 'Corps headquarters'.

There was no fixed size for brigade, division, or Corps; thus in Napoleon's army in 1805 Corps-strength ranged from Soult's IV Corps (41,000) to Augereau's VIII Corps (15,000).

STRATEGY

Although strategy does not fall properly within the scope of this book, a brief mention is necessary to illustrate the inter-relation and co-ordination of 'arms' within a Napoleonic army.

By eighteenth-century concepts, strategy (the manoeuvre of an army towards an objective) and tactics (the conduct of a battle) were seen as separate entities, but Napoleon considered both part of the same subject, thus employing strategical ploys on the battlefield, and vice-versa. Due to the French system of foraging, Napoleon was unhampered by the enormous supply-trains of other armies and was thus able to pursue a '*blitzkrieg*' policy. He broke every campaign into three parts: move to contact the enemy, battle, and pursuit, all merging into a single concept. Whilst *every* campaign was different, there existed underlying features, applied according to circumstance.

First, the plan: Napoleon believed that a single target should be selected, preferably the enemy's main field army; that the army should move by a single line of operations, keeping lines of communication open; that he should always move against the enemy's flank and rear, turning the enemy's most exposed flank to isolate him from reinforcements. Great flexibility and good co-ordination were required to concentrate large bodies of troops quickly and effectively, requiring discipline, good staff-work and the ability to move rapidly over comparatively short distances.

Napoleon's favourite manoeuvre was the envelopment ('la manoeuvre sur les derrières'). To avoid a 'frontal' battle – both sides lined up and battering away until one withdrew, costly even to the victor (e.g. Borodino), Napoleon would hold the enemy's attention by a feint frontal attack, whilst slipping a large force, hidden by terrain or cavalry screen, to threaten the enemy's flank or rear. Successfully achieved, this manoeuvre isolated the enemy army from its supports, whereupon Napoleon would begin a general advance, leaving his adversary two alternatives – surrender or fight on ground not of his own choosing. To remedy the situation, the enemy commander could continue his action with the initial holding force, which Napoleon would provide with an adequate reserve or retire and draw the enemy deeper into the trap; or the enemy could risk dividing his force in an attempt to cut Napoleon's communications, a temporary break in which was unimportant due to the French ability to live off the land; or the enemy could move against the main French force, i.e. that which had turned his flank, and fight on Napoleon's terms with an army disorganized by the withdrawal from their original position. Enemy reinforcements would be temporarily blocked by Napoleon's 'corps of observation', interposed between the theatre of operations and the route of reinforcements. Napoleon employed 'la manoeuvre sur les derrières' some thirty times, most successfully in 1805 when he achieved a crushing and bloodless victory over the isolated Austrian general Mack at Ulm. Its success lay in taking the initiative immediately, cutting communications and shattering the enemy's strategic position and morale by encirclement. The only effective answer was to disregard the flanking movement and push on regardless, as the Allies did in October 1813 and March 1814, only feasible when the enemy enjoyed a superiority in numbers over Napoleon and had enough supplies to invalidate a temporary break in communications.

Another favourite strategic manoeuvre employed by Napoleon was 'the strategy of the central position', adopted when the French were faced by two or more numerically-superior enemy armies supporting each other. Napoleon realized that numerical superiority on the battlefield, not in the campaign, was the deciding factor, so would launch a '*blitzkrieg*' at the enemy's weakest point, the juncture of the two armies; thus, by interposing himself between two enemy forces, Napoleon commanded the 'central position', from where he would detach one wing as 'corps of observation' to hold off one enemy army, whilst the remaining French annihilated the other, having more troops available for the battle than the enemy. Part of the victorious French would be assigned to pursue the defeated enemy, whilst the remainder would move to support the 'corps of observation' and destroy the second enemy force; in other words, divide and conquer. But this ploy had its failings; though Napoleon could switch the emphasis from one flank to the other thanks to a centrally-placed reserve, it was difficult to control both wings with absolute precision as even Napoleon could only be in one place at once! Equally, due to the necessity of switching from one enemy to another, no decisive pursuit could be made; consequently Napoleon, advocate of the single, decisive victory, used the 'central

Fig. 66.   Napoleon and his staff at Leipzig. Print by Molte, after Grenier.

position' move only when necessary.

The third of Napoleon's general manoeuvres was the 'strategical penetration'; when faced by a cordon of enemy forces, Napoleon would smash through at a weak point and march rapidly deep into enemy territory, creating a situation favourable for the employment of one of the previous systems. All three manoeuvres could be merged in the same operation, adapted according to changing circumstances, to baffle and demoralize an enemy operating according to 'conventional' tactics.

'It is often in the system of campaign that one conceives the system of battle,'[116] wrote

Napoleon; thus in tactics, as in strategy, he aimed for a single, decisive victory, concentrating on all-out attack. Only three times did he fight a purely defensive battle (Leipsig, La Rothière, Arcis), and then only after an initial attack had failed. Enemies who attempted to counter-attack suffered more than those who remained on the defensive, so part of Napoleon's plan was to tempt the enemy to attack, as at Austerlitz where he deceived the enemy into under-estimating French strength.

As in strategy, envelopment was the key to success. There were two types of flank-movement: one executed by a large force acting independently of the main body, and an outflanking movement by part of the French line of battle, the former threatening the enemy's rear and the latter forcing him to re-deploy or change his front, which rarely led to a complete dislocation of the enemy position as did the former. Even the appearance of a flank-manoeuvre, not an attack, could be sufficient to demoralize an enemy, as at Mount Tabor when two judicious cannon-shots caused the flight of the enemy.

There were three basic types of battle, capable of combination into a single operation. Firstly, the straight frontal combat, with no attempt at manoeuvre, costly to the victors and usually allowing the vanquished to withdraw in some order. Secondly, a battle on two fronts, with a distinct break between the actions (corresponding to the strategic 'central position' for allocation and transfer of troops), for example Jena-Auerstadt and Quatre Bras-Ligny. Thirdly was the Napoleonic battle par excellence: the strategic battle depending upon manoeuvre, envelopment and breakthrough. The flexible French Corps system allowed the first Corps in contact to fight a holding action, with the remaining Corps close enough to lend rapid support, each Corps being capable of holding a superior enemy for at least a day. As French reinforcements arrived the enemy would be compelled to commit his reserves, whilst Napoleon's enveloping force would reveal itself at the moment in which the enemy had committed all his reserves, this revelation often timed by Napoleon's watch, measured literally to the minute, the exact moment for revelation being signalled to the commander of the enveloping force by cannon-shot or, if closer at hand, by message borne by A.D.C.

With this threat to his rear and lines of communications, the enemy general had two choices: order a general withdrawal, usually impossible as Napoleon increased pressure on the front to coincide with the flank attack, or transfer troops from the front (his reserves already committed) to meet the flank attack. Napoleon launched his hitherto-concealed 'masse de rupture' against the sector of the line thus weakened, this strong striking-force plunging into a gap blown open by the Guard artillery and dividing the enemy force in two.

At this point, only the scale of the victory was left undetermined. By pressing the retiring enemy with light cavalry and horse artillery, allowing no time to reform, Napoleon could end a war by a single battle. Even when the plan did not go smoothly, French organization and Napoleon's planning were so flexible that improvisations could be made without damaging the general scheme. But ironically Napoleon's last battle was the very reverse of classical Napoleonic warfare: *Napoleon* commanded the 'static' army whilst Blücher performed the rôle of the Napoleonic enveloping attack, forcing Napoleon to commit his reserve and thus being hoisted by his own tactical petard.

THE STAFF

The organization of general staff and headquarters varied greatly between armies but maintained a basically similar framework.

Following the Revolution, a new staff hierarchy was created by France in 1790 with ranks including Generals-in-Chief, Lieutenant-Generals, 'Maréchaux-de-Camp' (Major-Generals), and Adjutant-Generals as chiefs of staff for the Lieutenant-Generals; the latter rank and 'Maréchal-de-Camp' was later replaced by 'Général de Division' and 'Général de Brigade' respectively. Lower ranks included Aides-de-Camp, 'Adjoints' (Assistant-Adjutant-Generals) and for a short time the sinister political commissars, 'Représentants en Mission' or 'Représentants du Peuple aux Armées'. A typical divisional staff might be organized with a General of Division in command, assisted by two Adjutant-Generals; each brigade commanded by a General of Brigade; with divisional artillery and engineer commanders attached to headquarters. All general officers had aides-de-camp to act as couriers, and usually other 'personal' staff – secretaries, grooms, surgeons, etc.

Napoleon's 'Imperial Headquarters' (numbering about 800 persons in the Jena campaign, for example) included not only military staff but his 'household' – Master of Horse, Grand Master of the Palace, etc.; all Napoleon's A.D.C.s were general officers themselves, each with a staff of ordinary aides

Fig. 67.   A French staff officer reconnoitres the enemy, while a chasseur *holds his horse. Print after Meissonier.*

for routine (though dangerous) courier service. Inside Imperial Headquarters were two departments, the Imperial Cabinet and Army Headquarters, the latter the office of the Chief of Staff. The former included secretarial staff, the Statistical Office, and Bacler d'Albe's Topographical Office which not only provided the cartographical services but acted as Napoleon's 'Operations Room'. The Chief of Staff's Office transferred the strategical plan into reality by the issue of movement-orders, supply-instructions, etc., to accomplish which there existed a complex organization of departments and General Staff Cabinets, supervising the entire running of the army from quartermaster duties to the accommodation of prisoners of war.

This enormous bureaucracy which accompanied Napoleon's army on campaign contrasted with the simpler system employed by Wellington in the Peninsular War, with far fewer number of troops to be supervised and in a limited sphere of operations. With this, and fewer capable subordinates, Wellington dispensed with a Chief of Staff, this being shared by the Military Secretary (simply a junior officer responsible for the transmission of orders) and the Quartermaster- and Adjutant-Generals. The Quartermaster-General's Department was responsible for all commissariat organization, topographical surveys and ultimately intelligence; the staff consisted of Assistant QMGs and Deputy Assistant QMGs, usually officers seconded from line regiments and attached not to headquarters but to individual units. The Adjutant-General's Department was responsible for all discipline and statistical matters, and similarly consisted of Assistant AGs and Deputy Assistant AGs. Attached to General Headquarters were other departments and staffs: officers commanding Royal Artillery and Engineers; the Provost-Marshal and his Staff Corps Cavalry responsible for enforcing discipline, deserters and prisoners; and the Corps of Guides, used as couriers and interpreters. The attached Civil Departments comprised the Inspector of Hospitals' Medical Department, the Purveyor's Department (responsible for hospitals), the Paymaster-General and staff, and the Commissariat, the latter headed by the Commissary-General, assisted by Deputy CGs, Assistant- and Deputy Assistant-Commissaries and others, an Assistant-Commissary being attached to each infantry brigade and cavalry regiment. Heavy baggage was the responsibility of the Storekeeper-General.

Junior staff appointments included Brigade-Majors and A.D.C.s, the latter fewer in number than those of the French, regulations limiting Major-Generals to one, Lieutenant-Generals to two and even Wellington to only three (though numerous supernumerary A.D.C.s were used, their subsistence coming from the general's own pocket). Contrasting with France, Britain had virtually no trained staff officers, the entire army having only ten (the Quartermaster-General's Permanent Assistants), of whom in 1813 only four were with the field army. All other staff positions, excluding general officers, were filled by officers 'on detachment' from line regiments. Staffs were very small; in autumn 1813 the Peninsula army's QMG had only four British officers and an A.D.C., and the Adjutant-General four assistants and one trainee, this paucity partly due to the almost self-sufficient brigade system, the brigade-major (liaison officer between headquarters and brigade staff) being the only permanent appointment. Ironically, the general staff list was overloaded; in November 1812 there were 518 general officers, of whom only 200 were employed in staff duties, only forty-two with the Peninsula army; of the three senior Major-Generals in 1811 none had seen service since 1783!

Staffs of other armies varied between two extremes: the Spanish staff of Cuesta's heyday, for example, though multitudinous, were totally useless; others, like the Austrians, were so proficient at staff-work that in the Austerlitz campaign they even took over the running of the Russian army, which was scarcely able to move without Austrian administrative personnel and guides. A characteristic of inferior staff organization was the excessive number of useless people gathered around a general (Napoleon's staff, though vast, was proficient), for example the Russian General Buxhöwden who in 1805 not only dragged behind him eleven carriages and as many carts but no less than ninety-six animals and 139 servants and staff.

INTELLIGENCE

The gathering of intelligence rested largely with spies of one variety or another. 'Observing officers' rode deep into enemy territory, sometimes clandestinely, gathering information about enemy troop-movements. They were aided by 'correspondents', residents reporting troop-movements in their own area, like Dr Patrick Curtis of the Irish College at Salamanca, whose network of agents supplied Wellington with much valuable information. Others were spies in the conventional mould, like Napoleon's agent Charles Schulmeister, a master of disguise who infiltrated Austrian headquarters in the 1805 campaign (he was discovered but set free by the Austrians after a beating)!

Reports from such observing officers and agents were collated with information gathered by the army's outposts and from the interrogation of prisoners. Napoleon's intelligence-system included a file of enemy regiments, covering strength, morale and efficiency, each compartment of the file representing a location; regimental details were noted on a playing-card and moved to the correct compartment according to the latest reports.

Cyphers were used when there was a danger of couriers being intercepted. They were vital to the French in the Peninsula, though Wellington's code-breaker, Capt. Scovell, even mastered the Great Paris Cypher. As Scovell was attached to the Quartermaster-General's Department most intelligence work was passed there rather than to the Adjutant-General's Department which should have been responsible.

Accurate maps were a vital part of intelligence-work, often made by cartographers attached to the army, such as the 'sketching officers' who mapped on a scale of three

Fig. 68.   Different concepts of staff officer. Left: *A French general and his escort. Print after Meissonier.* Right: *'A Major Part of the Town of Portsmouth' – Major Nathan Ashurst, 1807. Print after Robert Dighton Sr.*

inches to a mile under the direction of Quartermaster-General Murray in the Peninsular War. Otherwise, inaccurate civilian maps had to be used, such as Lopez's map of Spain which caused Masséna such trouble. In British service this item was replaced by the more accurate Faden's map, which was itself so bad as to deserve 'to be burned by the public hangman.'[117] The fine French Topographical Department does not seem to have operated in Spain at all, though it was a vital contributing factor to Napoleon's successes elsewhere. The supply of *accurate* maps could affect a general's strategy; for example on the day of Vimiero Wellington had ordered an advance on Mafra, as 'I should have brought the army into a country of which I had an excellent map and topographical accounts ... and the battle ... would have had for its field a country of which we had a knowledge.'[118]

SIGNALLING AND COMMUNICATIONS

Communications between military formations was largely a matter of courier, bearing either written or verbal messages, accomplished on the battlefield by the Aides-de-Camp attached to every general officer, whose high mortality-rate frequently resulted in the non-delivery of orders. For the bearing of messages over greater distances, relays of riders or even post-chaises were employed, some units being raised for the purpose, like the Allied Corps of Guides (composed of Portuguese and renegade Italians) in the Peninsula.

For short messages various mechanical devices could be used. The semaphore was first introduced by Claude Chappé, who installed twenty-two stations between Lille and Paris in 1792, capable of transmitting

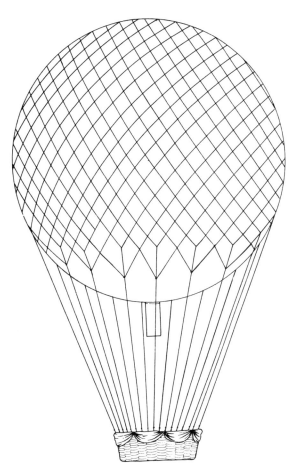

Fig. 69. A French Observation Balloon, 1794.

letters and words by means of three moveable arms on a vertical pole. This 'Tachygraphe' as Chappé named it, later 'Telegraph', was adopted by the French army at the instigation of Lazare Carnot, whose chain of stations linking Paris with the Rhine frontier transmitted news of the capture of Condé in 1793 in twenty minutes. Despite maltreatment by the authorities which led to Chappé's suicide, the telegraph prospered during the Empire, the small but efficient Military Telegraph Service manning chains of signal-stations connecting Paris with other major cities and the seat of war, flag-relay posts connecting campaign headquarters with the nearest permanent semaphore station. In good weather messages could travel at an astonishing 120 miles per hour.

With the telegraph virtually inoperable in snow or fog, messages were still transmitted by horseback, sometimes with disastrous consequences. In April 1809 Napoleon dispatched a message to Berthier by telegraph, following it with a qualifying message half an hour later by courier. The telegraph message, delayed by bad weather, took six days to arrive; Berthier received the horse-borne second message two and a half days before the first, presumed that the second message was in fact the first, and acted upon it, with consequences which could have been tactically catastrophic.

Other nations also used various systems of message-machine. By 1796 Lord George Murray, Director of Telegraphs at the British Admiralty, had erected a chain of twenty-four stations between London and Portsmouth, each with a wooden framework on which letters were displayed. In 1797 one Richard Edgeworth, having devised a semaphore-system to transmit race-results from Newmarket to London, proposed a 'Tellograph' visible by telescope at 15 miles, with a portable version for use in the field, but no system was adopted until Admiral Popham's two-arm semaphore devised in 1803. In 1806 this device transmitted a message and reply between London and Portsmouth in two minutes. Such devices, though static, were used on campaign (the semaphore-station at Elvas relayed news of the fall of Badajos on 11 March 1814 to Wellington by the 14th), but no attempt was made to introduce signal-systems on the battlefield, probably because powder-smoke would have made all attempts futile. In 1808 Joseph Connolly proposed a mobile system consisting of seven-feet square sheets hung between two pikes, costing £2 to produce and visible at three miles 'by the use of six-guinea telescopes', but despite successful tests nothing came of the idea. Improvisations actually used in the field included the removal of two windmill-arms by Sir William Congreve at Menin in 1793, signalling with the two remaining arms.

Other devices included the hoisting of coded combinations of balls or flares on church-towers or flagpoles and the employment of carrier-pigeons. Most rudimentary was the beacon-chain on the coast of Britain, to be lit in case of invasion. The effectiveness – and drawback – of the system was demonstrated in 1804 when the beacon-watch at Home Castle mistook a domestic fire in Northumberland for the signal of invasion, the local defence forces turning out with incredible alacrity as the whole chain of beacons was ignited.

AERIAL OBSERVATION

Guyton de Morveau of the French Committee of Public Safety instigated the first employment of captive balloons in a military capacity, the 'lre Compagnie d'Aërostiers' being created under J. M. J. Coutelle and N. J. Conté on 23 March 1794. The world's first military 'aircraft' was constructed at the Château de Chalais-Meudon, the hydrogen-balloon 'L'Entreprenant', powered by the passing of steam over red-hot iron, the use of sulphuric acid being forbidden in the interests of the production of gunpowder. Secured by two cables, 'L'Entreprenant' had a crew of two – pilot and observer.

Coutelle, commander of the Aërostier company, joined the French army at Mauberge, using his balloon to report the positions of the Austro-Netherlands army outside the city, signals being transmitted by flags, luminous balls hung over the side of the basket, or written messages in sandbags slid down the cables by small rings. On his fifth ascent Coutelle encountered history's first anti-aircraft fire; when a roundshot glanced off the bottom of the basket he ascended a further 1,300 feet until out of range! From Mauberge the company moved to Charleroi, the appearance of the balloon in the sky apparently demoralizing the Austrians into immediate surrender. Next day Coutelle took up General Morlot as observer for the full ten hours of the Battle of Fleurus, the information relayed to the ground contributing to French victory. A second balloon section was formed, serving at Donauwörth and Würzburg (where a balloon was captured). On one occasion Coutelle was airborne in so strong a wind that sixty-four men hanging on to the cable could barely control it; fearful for his safety, the Austrians sent a message to the effect that if Coutelle would

descend they would allow him to visit their headquarters. Coutelle declined!

In 1796 France possessed 'L'Entreprenant' and three other balloons, 'Céleste', 'Hercule' and 'Intrépide'; in 1797 Napoleon took one section to Egypt but it was never employed successfully, and the whole corps – excepting a detachment in Egypt – was disbanded in 1799, not to re-appear (except for an abortive experiment in Algeria) until the Franco-Prussian War. The principle of aerial observation was sound, but too revolutionary for the somewhat hidebound military theorists of the day.

RATES OF MOVEMENT

The movement of an army depended upon the speed of march physically possible, the amount of artillery and baggage, the state of the roads and the hours of daylight, all variable quantities.

In British service in 1801 there existed three 'steps' for infantry: 'Ordinary Time', 75 paces to the minute; 'Quick Time', 108; and 'Wheeling Step', 120, used only for manoeuvre; each pace was thirty inches. Similar 'steps' were used by most armies, Russia for example having a slow pace of 75 to the minute and a quickstep of 120 (added in 1803), in their case executed in a 'goose-step' with unbended knee. France used a 25.6 in. step, 76 paces to the minute in ordinary time and 100 in quick time, so that in theory the British should have marched faster; on campaign, the reverse was true.

Though cavalry travelled quickly over short distances, Adye estimated the 'usual rate of marching' to be seventeen miles in six hours, 'but this may be extended to 21, or even 28 miles in that time'[119] ... 'military horses *walk* about 400 yards in $4\frac{1}{2}$ minutes. *Trot* the same distance in 2 minutes 3 seconds, and *gallop* it in about 1 minute.'[120]

An average speed for an army was about fifteen miles per day, though even this would exhaust the horses if maintained. Some nations were renowned for ponderous movement: Russia, usually encumbered by an excess of artillery; Spain, armies lethargic, ill-disciplined and short of horses; and Austria, whose armies moved quickly only under certain circumstances. For example, in

Fig. 70. British regimental baggage- waggon, c. 1802. (Print after W. H. Pyne).

Fig. 71. Right Above: British infantrymen loading baggage and their families on to a regimental waggon. Print after W. H. Pyne.

Fig. 72. Right Below: A halt on the march: French troops at rest in the Russian campaign of 1812. Print after Albrecht Adam.

1809 an Austrian army took eighteen days to advance from the River Inn to the Isar; the left wing covered the same distance, in rout, in two days!

Sustained effort could wreck an army. At the beginning of the Peninsular War Junot's French marched from the French border to Lisbon, taking 43 days to cover 640 miles, the first 300 at twelve miles a day on main roads and the remainder, over minor roads, averaging eighteen miles a day. This left the cavalry and artillery behind, having to be re-horsed en route and arriving in Lisbon ten days behind the infantry! Later in the war Wellington marched 80,000 men from the Portuguese frontier to Vittoria over the same poor roads at over fifteen miles per day, without affecting the efficiency, due both to superior organization and experience and to the season (midsummer, as against October–November for Junot).

Extraordinary feats could be achieved by trained units or horsemen. Wellington's A.D.C.s could cover four miles in eighteen minutes, twelve miles in an hour, and with a relay of horses about sixty miles a day.

Wellington himself rode the 174 miles from Ciudad Rodrigo to Badajos in 76 hours, and even more spectacular was the 595-mile ride of Sir Charles Vaughan, from the Tudela to Corunna via Madrid and Salamanca, in nine days (Vaughan himself mis-calculated the 188 leagues to be 790 miles, a figure accepted by Fortescue and Oman). A similar mis-calculation has distorted the most rapid infantry march of the Napoleonic Wars, that of the British Light Brigade to Talavera, '62 miles in 26 hours', due to the different 'leagues' in use in Spain ('Legales castellana' = 2.63 English miles, maritime leagues = 3.49 miles, 'Géograficas' leagues = 4 miles, and 'Legales España' = 4.21 miles). The *actual* distance covered by the Light Brigade would seem to be 42 miles in 26 hours, plus four or five miles beyond Talavera, a prodigious feat nonetheless.[121]

Napoleon's speed of march constantly astonished his opponents; on 13 November 1805 Lannes' and Soult's Corps arrived at Vienna after marching 152 miles (plus detours) in thirteen days on poor roads; and Davoût entered Berlin on 25 October 1806 after marching 166 miles and fighting the Battle of Auerstädt in only fourteen days.

Climatic conditions could drastically reduce the rate of movement, both dust-clouds in summer or snow-drifts in winter, heavy rain turning roads into a quagmire which sucked off boots and even drowned men, or burning sun causing heatstroke. Even a blocked road – such as that closed by fire at Wavre – could have a decisive bearing upon the outcome of a battle.

RATIONS, SUPPLIES AND TRANSPORT

Nauseating though contemporary recipes now seem, the British army was comparatively well-provendered. Adye records the daily 'Complete Ration of the small Species.'[122]

'Flour, or bread	1½ lbs	
Beef	1	
or Pork	½	
Peas	¼ pint	
Butter, or cheese	1 oz	
Rice	1 oz	

'When the small species are not issued, 1½ lbs of flour or bread, with 1½ lbs of beef, or 10 oz of pork, forms a complete ration: or 3 lbs of beef; or 2 lbs of cheese; or half a pound of rice.'

When, of course, it *was* issued. John Shipp describes a typical meal provided by an unscrupulous landlord: '... fat pea soup ... suet dumplings heavy as lead ... greasy puddings, and fat stews made of the offal of the house for the past month, with fat an inch thick on the top....'[123] Alcohol was provided, often in startling quantity: aboard ship, says Adye, each group of six men should receive four gallons of beer, two pints of spirit or four pints of wine per day.[124] In the Peninsular War the standard daily ration was 1 lb of meat (travelling on the hoof), 1 lb of 'biscuit' or 1½ lbs of bread or rice, and one pint of wine or ⅓ pint of spirit. Other nations' rations, however, were much worse: for example, prior to British re-organization, the Portuguese soldier was given ¼ lb of fish and 1½ lbs of bread on Sundays and Fridays, and on other days ½ lb of beef, 1½ lbs of bread and a quart of wine. The fish and meat were usually rotten, the wine sour and the bread baked with sand to save flour! Army 'biscuit' was either rock-hard (at least one British officer saved his life by stuffing his jacket with biscuit and thus turning a musket-ball), or alive, as Charles Napier wrote: 'We are on biscuits full of maggots, and though not a bad soldier, hang me if I can relish maggots.'[125] In British service, the ration was made daily whenever possible, for a larger issue usually resulted in the troops eating as much as possible and selling the remainder to buy alcohol.

Wellington wrote: 'No troops can serve to any good purpose unless they are regularly fed.'[126] This was the duty of the commissariat, transporting rations from depôts to the army; in mid-1813 this amounted to 100,000 lbs of biscuit, 300 head of cattle and 200,000 lbs of forage-corn *per day* for Wellington's army. As each mule carried 200 lbs of supplies plus its own feed for the round trip (in other words, six days' biscuit for thirty-three men, rum for one hundred or rice for twenty men), enormous mule-trains were required. The depôts or 'magazines' were ideally situated within three or four days' mule-march of the army, supplies being taken to the depôts by bullock-carts and river-boats, coming not only from Portugal but by ship from Britain and the U.S.A.

France used the other classic method of food-supply: living off the land by foraging. This process increased an army's mobility and manoeuvrability, and was closely-tied to the Napoleonic *'blitzkrieg'* theory of warfare, and worked reasonably well until barren country was encountered, though even in fertile terrain required a wide dispersal of forces to avoid the total exhaustion of any one area. Throughout the Peninsular War and particularly in Russia, however, starvation was an ever-present companion of the French armies. The system of foraging also had strategic drawbacks; though it allowed a commander to ignore temporarily his lines of communication, it presented strict limits: as Marmont wrote to Napoleon in February 1812: 'If the army marches against Rodrigo now we should not be able to stay there for three days for lack of food. We should achieve nothing as the enemy knows we cannot stay there....'[127]

Russia adopted the same policy. As Wilson wrote of the Russian commissariat: 'This may be dismissed in three words – There is none at all...[128]... their regular food of the coarsest and plainest quality, and so precarious ... that the usual and best mode of supply, even in their own country, is by rapine....[129] ... where the magazines are lost, or the army is compelled to leave them at a distance, every one must nearly take care of himself....'[130]

Thus, the Napoleonic soldier was often on the brink of starvation, which a few random examples illustrate. In the Eylau campaign neither French nor Russians had anything but potatoes and water; in fact on 25 December 1806 General Lasalle's gift to Marshal Murat, a princely gift indeed, consisted of a loaf of bread and a bottle of wine, sent by special courier! One Russian soldier complained to the Czar that for seven days he and some comrades had only a piece of hide, softened in water, on which to chew. The ultimate pangs of hunger invariably led to the consumption of the army's horses and, occasionally, to cannibalism. The latter practice occurred frequently on the retreat from Mos-

cow and even in the Peninsula, where rascally muleteers were recorded as selling 'pork slices' from a French corpse!

Even more than food, forage for horses was vital to keep an army mobile. On service a horse could carry three days' food, corn in a sack behind the saddle and hay slung in nets wherever possible. Frequently the forage was provided by regimental parties detached for the purpose, though it was often despatched from depôts by the British in the Peninsula, a mule carrying six days' corn for three horses, plus 20 lbs over.

Supply-trains were enormous, even excluding the droves of 'camp followers'. For example, each British brigade and cavalry regiment in the Peninsula required about 150 mules, whilst a horse artillery troop is recorded with seventy-one mules for bread, twenty-four for rum, twelve for rice, sixty-nine for forage and twenty-nine spares: total 205 mules. In addition to commissariat-animals, each unit had animals to carry camp-kettles, medical stores, ammunition, etc., plus officers' baggage, the latter on a sliding scale according to rank: lieutenant-colonel ten, major seven, captain five, subaltern one, etc. (General Order, 1 September 1809). Even so British trains never approached the enormity of those which trailed behind other armies, the Spanish for example.

Waggon-trains originally depended upon civilian drivers, and even civilian contractors to supply and maintain the waggons, usually a hopeless system as both contractors and frequently the officials in charge were riddled with corruption. Until 1807 this system was used by France, the waggoners (nicknamed 'Royal Cart Grease') despised and the contractor, the Breidt Company, termed 'a band of rascals'[131] by Napoleon. In 1805, for example, instead of providing the thirty transport-brigades they had promised, the company fielded only six brigades, of which only sixty waggons remained available by December. Napoleon was served so badly in

Fig. 73. Overleaf Left: *Various French wag-gons.*

Fig. 74. Overleaf Right: *Various Russian waggons.*

the Eylau campaign that he scrapped the previous arrangements and instituted the Carriage Train Corps, which grew in size to twenty-three battalions, each possessing 140 waggons, a total often either exceeded or not reached in the field. In addition, each battalion or cavalry regiment after 1805 had two waggons, plus one for officers' baggage, a total invariably exceeded on campaign. So many waggons were lost in 1812 that thereafter all manner of civilian carriages were pressed into service.

Britain supplanted its civilian waggoners with the infamous Royal Corps of Waggoners in 1794: 'Of this Corps little need be said, as its miserable state became proverbial in the Army; it failed completely in every part, and the only trace remaining of it is a heavy charge on the half-pay list of reduced Officers.'[132] In 1799 the Royal Waggon Train was formed, and by the time of the Peninsular War was apparently chiefly used for the transportation of wounded (its waggons were unsuitable for Portuguese by-roads), though it was not until 1810 that the commissary officers were given military rank, being members of the Civil Service until that date; they ranged from brilliant organizers to downright thieves. Paltry though the commissariat was, the government tried to reduce it further during the Peninsular War, Huskisson noting: 'The Waggon Train is an annoyance on foreign service and useless at home;'[133] but Wellington refused to send home the two troops scheduled for reduction.

The old system of relying on depôts could severely limit the manoeuvrability of an army; before Valmy, for example, the Prussians had to halt every sixth day to bake a week's bread before moving on (they later possessed a more sophisticated 'Train' which supplied services such as remount-depôts and postal services in addition to usual duties; detachments of 'Truppentrain' were seconded to individual units to drive regimental vehicles as well). Napoleon persisted with his foraging system ('We must separate to live but unite to fight')[134] until barren terrain compelled him to write in February 1807: 'Circumstances have forced me to return to the system of depôts.'[135] These depôts concentrated upon armaments though bread was produced for current consumption and as a reserve; supply-trains were normally allowed to carry only between four and seven days' rations of flour and biscuit, to feed the army when battle was imminent, when the usual foraging was impossible. Ration-food was also carried by the individual; at the beginning of the 1812 campaign, for example, some French soldiers were given four 16-oz biscuits and a cloth 'sausage' to hold 10 lbs of flour.

Living off the land had advantages, but could be disaster to an army unaccustomed to the art of forage. Austria (of whom one veteran claimed that their 'tail' of waggons was so immense and the officers so unwilling to be parted from their comforts that they lost half a march on the French every day) attempted to emulate the French mobility by living off the land; the system was a disaster to the inexperienced Austrians who not only starved but were unable to concentrate rapidly when necessary.

Such a system occasioned not only dispersal of forces but loose organization on the march. A French émigré in Bavarian service recorded the march of the French from Ulm to Vienna in 1805:

'... the victorious army ... appeared ... no longer anything but an army in rout, but rout in advance ... this torrent took the direction of Vienna, and henceforth there was nothing but an "arrive qui peut".....'[136]

Yet at the first alarm this milling mass was instantly transformed into orderly units. As the quality of the French army declined, so the straggling increased: an estimated 60,000 men were 'absent' after Eylau and in 1809 five travelling courts-martial were established: 'Every straggler who, under pretext of fatigue, leaves his corps for the purpose of marauding, will be arrested, tried by court martial, and executed on the spot' (14 May 1809).[137]

Despite a number of regulation patterns of vehicle, many baggage-waggons were impressed from the local population or privately-purchased civilian vehicles. The British in the Peninsula were equipped with waggons sent from Britain (unsuitable for local conditions), and a few 'spring waggons' for the transportation of wounded, but depended almost entirely on great numbers of Portuguese ox-carts. These primitive vehicles with wicker-work sides, solid wheels and turning axles which made an excruciating noise, were painfully slow – two miles an hour was a fair speed – and too small, but were used because they were suitable for local terrain and could be driven and repaired by any peasant. Regimental baggage-trains marched in the following order: oxen for the day's meat; then vehicles drawn by horses or mules; carts drawn by oxen; mules bearing ammunition; baggage of the staff; mules carrying camp-kettles or tents; and finally baggage of regimental officers.

Excessive transport impeded an army's progress, particularly over poor roads in bad weather. Wellington eventually forbade the use of bullock-carts for transporting reserve ammunition because of blockages caused by these slow-moving convoys. In Poland in 1806–07 the roads so deteriorated in winter that nothing would move without a double- or treble-team.

There was comparatively little use of vehicles for the transportation of troops. Where roads allowed, France used this system in limited quantities; in 1805, for example, a column of Imperial Guard went from Paris to Strasbourg by 'post' – troops packed four or five to a two-wheeled cart and twelve per four-wheel waggon, covering sixty miles a day by changing horses at 'posting-stages' about ten miles apart. It was both exhausting for the men and wearing on equipment. Similarly, Kutuzov employed some 2,233 Austrian two-horse carts in 1805, the first part of each column riding ahead of those on foot to give the men a brief (if uncomfortable) rest. Other improvisations included such episodes as the commandeering of Irish jaunting-cars and carriages by the Dumbarton Fencibles, racing to the battle of Arklow (1798).

Ingenious vehicles were occasionally designed specifically for the transportation of troops, one such 'military fly' reported by the *London Chronicle* (1796):

'... a carriage for the rapid conveyance of troops from place to place. It is a light waggon, which carries fifty men, with their arms, baggage, &c. drawn by six horses a-breast, harnessed as in a coach, and ridden by two postillions. This machine is calculated to travel upon an average nearly as fast as a stage coach: it went quite round the park, carrying its full complement of men, in ten minutes. They are accommodated with seats, one higher than the other, so constructed that the men's legs are out of each other's way. The arms, accoutrements, &c., are deposited in a kind of narrow chest in the centre of the waggon....'[138]

Under active service conditions, however, it would probably have proved too cumbersome.

Sledges were used over snow when available; small, two-man vehicles pulled by a single horse were much used by the Grande Armée in 1812, and even adopted a defensive function. Marbot dismounted the 23rd and 24th Chasseurs à Cheval and formed a sledge-transported brigade, drawn into square at night to resemble a 'Wild West' waggon-laager: with each man armed with two muskets it provided a mobile fort secure from marauding cossacks.

Water-borne transport was only of use when an army had unchallenged domination of the sea (as had the British in the Peninsula), or when rivers and canals coincided with the position of the army. In 1812, for example, Napoleon organized convoys of river-boats and barges to supplement the waggon-trains moving from Dantzig and Königsburg to the army.

MEDICAL SERVICES

During the Napoleonic Wars medical knowledge was limited, methods of treatment primitive and hygiene non-existent. *Any* wound, no matter how slight, could result in death from neglect or gangrene, with amputation a universal palliative. As one British surgeon wrote about those with severe wounds:

'... a simple inspection of their wounds, with a few words of consolation, or perhaps a little opium, was all that could be recommended ... prudence equally forbids the rash interposition of unavailing art, and the useless indulgence of delusive hope.'[139]

Disease was a greater threat even than battle-wounds. From 1793 to 1797 in the West Indies 80,000 British troops died or were permanently disabled by fever. In 1811, a hard-fought year in the Peninsula, Britain lost 22,953 men; of these, some 2,000 were killed in the Peninsula and 100 in Java, with over 4,000 in the Peninsula and 15,000 elsewhere dying or being disabled through sickness. In 1807, out of every 196 Frenchmen admitted to hospital, only forty-seven were wounded. Unable to determine the cause of diseases, the medical establishment had no idea of how to combat them; when in 1809 the British Physician-General was asked to investigate the epidemic at Walcheren, he declined as '... he was not acquainted with the diseases of soldiers in camp and quarters.'[140] 'Remedies' included bleeding, pouring twenty-five buckets of cold water from a third-storey window on a man suffering from 'Guadiana fever' (probably malaria), and the 'cure' prescribed by one doctor: '... the best of living and at least two bottles of Madeira per diem.'[141]

France possessed the most enlightened medical service thanks to a number of enlightened surgeons like Pierre François Percy and, in particular, Dominique Jean Larrey, surgeon-in-chief of the Imperial Guard and perhaps the greatest humanitarian of the age. 'Revolutionary fervour' had led in 1792 to the abolition of all medical schools (privileged institutions being anathema), the training establishments which replaced them being largely useless. Only in 1803 were the old faculties resurrected, the medical services in the meantime depending upon a few gifted surgeons like Larrey, Percy and the Physician-in-Chief, René Desgenettes (the ci-devant Baron Des Genettes).

Effective treatment of wounds depended upon early casualty-evacuation, originally dependent upon slow-moving carts or 'fourgons' which might take 24 or 36 hours to transport wounded to the nearest dressing-station. In 1793 Percy began despatching surgeons on horseback to the battle-front, and in 1799 designed a four-wheel 'wurst wagen', a caisson with a padded top to seat up to eight medical orderlies, to treat men as soon as they were wounded. Actual evacuation was completed by Larrey, who invented the 'flying ambulances', two- and four-wheel sprung carriages with covered roofs and provision for two and four stretcher-cases respectively, but though they were used as early as 1793 the parsimony of the administration prevented any widespread introduction. In 1797 Larrey organized ambulance-trains, each 'ambulance' of 340 men comprising three divisions of 113 men each plus one surgeon-in-chief, each division comprising a surgeon-major, fourteen assistant-surgeons, four quartermaster personnel, a military police lieutenant, six N.C.O.s, two musicians, twelve mounted and twenty-five dismounted orderlies, eight two-wheel and four four-wheel ambulances and drivers, and four 'fourgons' crewed by four N.C.O.s, a trumpeter and twenty men. Only in the Imperial Guard, however, was Larrey's system truly effective, the benefits of early treatment and proper care being evident in the Guard's casualty-figures for Aspern-Essling and Wagram: out of 1,200 wounded, 600 by August had returned to their units, 250 been evacuated to France and only forty-five had died. Outside the Guard, however, the problem was almost as bad as ever; despite Larrey's overall command of medical services for the 1812 campaign personnel and equipment were so inadequate due to governmental parsimony that in the 24 hours after Borodino Larrey had to perform 200 amputations himself; and in 1813 the situation was so chaotic that Larrey had to resort to transporting the wounded from Bautzen in straw-filled wheelbarrows. Other unusual innovations included the use of camel-panniers for the transportation of casualties in Egypt, and latterly the equipping of orderlies with pikes which doubled as stretcher-poles.

The British army possessed a small number of medical 'staff' who supervised hospitals, and regimental medical officers (one surgeon and two assistants per battalion). Evacuation relied upon carts or commissariat-waggons which rode so badly as to finish off many wounded before they even reached hospital; Wellington would allow no systematic transportation of casualties as such vehicles would have impeded movements of the offensive part of the army. Hospitals usually resembled charnel-houses, even those with beds putting two patients in each. Small wonder that when Harry Smith went to Lisbon in 1810 to have

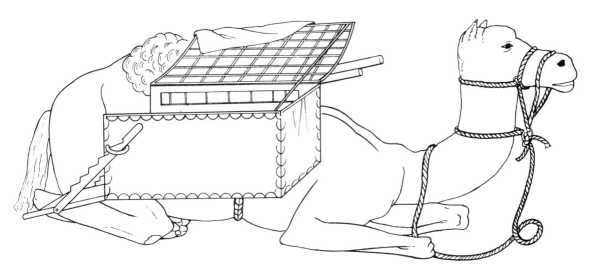

Fig. 75. A French camel litter as used in Egypt. Light wooden framework with silk or cotton panels and roof. The ramp at the back was held by a notched bar.

Fig. 76. Larrey's ambulances. Above: *Two-wheeled and* Below: *Four-wheeled examples.*

Fig. 77. *The appalling sight of a battlefield: Borodino. Print after C. G. Faber du Faur.*

Fig. 78. *The common neglect of the wounded: injured French soldiers left to their own devices. Print after Raffet.*

a bullet removed from his leg the surgeons advised him to keep his stiff leg rather than risk having the ball extracted!

Lack of knowledge, care and interest all contributed to make the 'butcher's bill' of the Napoleonic Wars far greater than it should have been. Even today humanitarians like Larrey remain largely unknown, whilst the instigators of the carnage have been almost immortalized. As Percy remarked in 1799, 'One would believe that the sick and wounded cease to be men when they can no longer be soldiers.'[142]

IRREGULARS

The term 'irregular' is used to describe any unit not classed as part of a 'regular' army.

The statutory British home-defence force, the Militia, existed as a number of county infantry battalions, recruited by ballot, a form of conscription which enabled balloted men to buy exemption by providing a 'substitute' to serve in their place. Though never required to serve abroad *en masse*, militiamen were latterly allowed to volunteer into line regiments, providing the regular army with a constant supply of trained recruits. After the Militia came the Volunteers, local-defence companies who drilled for a few hours a week and were not required to serve outside a specified area – town, county or military district – and then only in cases of civil disorder or invasion. Including cavalry ('yeomanry') and artillery, the volunteers originally comprised only those who could afford to purchase their arms and equipment; the formation was given a wider social basis after 1803, the 'establishment' of that December numbering some 463,134 British volunteers. Volunteer artillery was restricted to manning shore-batteries, the Government considering the allocation of fieldpieces to be unwise. Training and equipment varied from very good to occasionally wretched, though morale (in as much as it was possible to estimate that of troops not on active service) was high. The volunteers were largely replaced in 1808 by 'Local Militia', an attempt to organize the hundreds of independent units into cohesive battalions. The militia and volunteers' main contribution was to relieve regular troops for active service, security and

law-enforcement being largely the duty of these auxiliary troops. 'Fencibles' – both infantry and cavalry – were similar to the regular army, save that they could not be ordered out of the country in which they were raised without their consent; a few did serve abroad, in the ''98' in Ireland and one unit in Egypt.

France implemented a limited *'levée en masse'* (mass-conscription) at the start of the Revolutionary Wars, but the main second-line troops were the National Guard (formed 1789) who, when called upon, could perform with distinction (as at La Fère-Champenoise), though not all were so steadfast. Other auxiliaries included the 'Gardes d'Honneur' of individual towns, and the National Guard system was adopted by many nations in the French sphere of influence.

A form of *'levée en masse'* was activated in Prussia in 1813, the mass-conscription of men aged seventeen to twenty-four to form 'Landwehr' units, who fought alongside the regulars; in fact it is a moot point whether the 'Landwehr' should be classed as 'irregulars'. The Austrian Landwehr was much inferior, though numerous: in 1809 there were 200,000 Landwehr and 40,000 members of Hungarian and Croatian 'insurrections' (home-defence corps). Out of 175 battalions at or near Wagram, thirty-one were Landwehr or similar, though even the Minister of War termed them 'a body without a soul';[143] when mobilized in 1809 two battalions refused to march at all and another attacked its commander with bayonets! 'Freikorps' were another German innovation, being small units or companies of middle-class volunteers attached to regular corps, adept at scouting and skirmishing, and acting as a training-ground for officers and N.C.O.s. 'Burgwehr' were town-guard units, also German; and the 'Landsturm' was a popular insurrectionist movement established in Prussia in 1813, intended to encompass *all* males between eighteen and sixty years, wearing no uniform and acting as guerrillas; it was a total failure as it was bound by government restrictions and lacked the necessary spontaneous support.

'Guerrilla' warfare originated in Spain during the Peninsular War, in a massive

Fig. 79. Popular enthusiasm: the departure of the Paris National Guard for the battlefront, September 1792. Print after Coginet.

popular movement to expel the French. Despite an attempt to regularize the size of guerrilla bands in 'partidas' in December 1808 they ranged from a handful to the 8,000 men controlled by Espoz y Mina, one of many guerrilla chieftains who became folk-heroes. The guerrilla contribution to the Peninsular War has been under-estimated, for not only did they wreak havoc by cutting French communications, they also accounted for, by one estimate, one hundred Frenchmen *per day* throughout the entire war. Inevitably much simple banditry was disguised as patriotism and on both sides the most horrific atrocities were perpetrated. The Portuguese militia was of value only in relieving regular troops from garrison duty whilst their *'levée en masse'* or 'ordenança', often armed only with sharpened vine-poles, was of negligible value.

The cossacks were the most effective 'ir-regulars' of the period: nomadic tribesmen, superb horsemen, trained from childhood and unswervingly loyal to the Czar, yet un-disciplined, prone to looting and barbarity. They were organized in tribal groups or 'voiskos', with chieftains or 'atamans' as officers, and the 'hetman' (general) over all. Superb light horse, avoiding contact except upon their own terms, they favoured the 'hit-and-run' tactics which speeded the destruc-tion of the Grande Armée in 1812. Similar auxiliaries – tartars, bashkirs and kalmuks – were of less value, many armed in medieval fashion. The Russian version of the *levée en masse* was the *opolchenie*, crudely-armed

Fig. 80. Cossacks with a local guide, c. 1813. Print after J.A. Klein.

peasants who lacked equipment but not spirit; at Maloyaroslavets they '... not only stood as steady under the cannonade as their veteran comrades, but charged the sallying enemy with as ardent ferocity'[144] according to General Wilson. Eventually they received grey kaftans, cloth or fur caps and firearms. Partisan-bands were formed in Russia in 1812, often from local opolchenie around a nucleus of cossacks and regular hussars, producing folk-heroes like Denis Davidov; haphazard bands of peasants armed with agricultural implements also existed, and were responsible for most of the atrocities inflicted upon French stragglers in 1812. The Russian authorities, ever afraid of insurrection, refused to allow these irregular forces the freedom of action demanded by guerrilla warfare; for example,

an enterprising private Chetvertakov raised a partisan band of up to 4,000 men in the Gzhatsk region in 1812, but was branded a trouble-maker and compelled to return to his regiment. In all over 90,000 Russian irregulars served in the 1812 campaign.

'FOREIGN CORPS'

A number of armies included contingents of foreigners, serving as mercenaries, 'émigrés' (fugitives from their own country) or, like the fine Swiss troops in French service, supplied by client states under contracts of employment. In addition, some ordinary units contained large numbers of foreign-born personnel; in 1812, for example, the French 11th Hussars and 14th Cuirassiers were

Fig. 81. 'Foreign' troops made up a large proportion of Napoleon's army in 1812; here a French cuirassier observes Bavarians tending a casualty. Print after Albrecht Adam.

Dutch, the 7th and 8th Chevau-Léger-Lanciers Polish and the 9th German, the 111th and 113th Line Italian, the 123rd to 126th Dutch and the 129th German, the latter also including some of the 1,000 conscripted Lithuanian peasants also distributed to the Illyrian Regiment.

French émigré units served with other nations during the Revolutionary Wars and some, augmented by ex-prisoners, mercenaries and other riffraff served throughout the period. Germany provided troops to several nations, some smaller states having made a regular industry of supplying troops for cash: as late as 1793 Hanover, Hesse-Cassel, Hesse-Darmstadt, Baden and Brunswick supplied 33,750 men to Britain, and 7,300 more in the following year. The Duke of Brunswick's 'Black Legion' had a chequered career, raised for Austrian service, transferred to British and fighting under their own colours at

Waterloo. The quality of 'foreign corps' varied from the excellence of the Franco-Swiss and the British King's German Legion, to trash like the mutinous rabble of Greeks, Croats, Serbs and Albanians in Froberg's Regiment in British service, 1804–07. The practice of enlisting deserters and ex-prisoners drastically reduced the quality.

Many individuals served in foreign armies: French émigrés, many Germans in Russian service, and many second- or third-generation Irish in the Spanish army (whose 'foreign' regiments – Irish, Swiss, Neapolitan, etc. – contained a large percentage of Spanish-born foreigners). Britain employed many Germans (George III being Elector of Hanover), French émigrés, plus a few Canadians, Americans and Portuguese. The career of one officer illustrates the inter-change of personnel between armies, the anonymous writer 'Capt. Fritz'; from an aristocratic Mecklen-

Fig. 82. Infantry from the Duchy of Warsaw march to the attack, observed by Napoleon. Print after Raffet.

burg family, he served as a Prussian hussar officer until 1806 when he attached himself to the Russians, then joined the Brunswick Legion in Austrian, later British service, transferred to the King's German Legion and served in the Peninsular War, fought with the Russian army at Borodino and rejoined the Prussians in 1813! Officers even fought on different sides: von Kruse the Nassauer served with the French in 1813 and against them at Waterloo. More unusual was the career of the British 97th; raised from Tyroleans (called Swiss) for Austrian service, they were captured in Italy by the French who sold them to Spain at a dollar a head; captured by the British in Minorca they were formed into the Queen's German Regiment and were ultimately taken into the British line!

AMPHIBIOUS OPERATIONS

Though control of the sea was a vital factor affecting trade and the supply of overseas contingents, amphibious operations were few and any landings usually unopposed.

Transporting troops by sea was unpleasant, the troopships hopelessly insanitary and disembarkation by longboat fraught with difficulty, even worse for horses than for men, there often being no other way of landing them other than throwing them over the side and letting them swim to shore. There were no special boats used for disembarkation, though Napoleon gathered fleets of barges for his proposed descent upon England, in addition to the fanciful 'rafts' of enormous size planned by eccentric designers.

Naval actions could radically affect the course of warfare on land, for example the destruction of the French fleet in Aboukir Bay, and the very presence of a naval force capable of landing troops – for example the diversionary attacks by the British on the coast of eastern Spain during the Peninsular War – could occupy large numbers of troops which could have been employed to greater effect elsewhere.

Marines, originally infantry units raised

Fig. 83. British troops landing upon an enemy-held coast. Print by M. Dubourg after J. A. Atkinson.

for service aboard ship, were either from specialist corps or from detachments of line troops seconded for the purpose, even dismounted cavalrymen being used occasionally in this rôle. At sea, marines were used as sharpshooters, firing from the deck and fighting-tops, and occasionally to repel boarders. Equally, they could serve on land, as the French Guard Marines did; Russian marines fought in the 1812 campaign and the French Marine Artillery – actually 'coast artillery' employed to garrison seaports – served in the 1813 campaign.

116. Napoleon, *Correspondence*, XII, No. 10032, quoted in Chandler, p. 178.
117. General Graham, quoted in Glover, *Wellington's Army*, p. 133.
118. Quoted in ibid., p. 133.
119. Adye, p. 179.
120. Ibid., p. 167.
121. See Verner, pp. 487–9.
122. Adye, p. 225.
123. Shipp, p. 16.
124. Adye, p. 226.
125. Napier, *Life of C. Napier*, I, p. 166; quoted in Brett-James, *Life in Wellington's Army*, p. 110.
126. Wellington to Lord Wellesley, 8 August 1809; 'Despatches', V, p. 11.
127. Marmont, 26 February 1812; quoted in Glover, *Peninsular War*, p. 31.
128. Wilson, 'Brief Remarks'; see *Royal Military Chronicle*, 1812, p. 205.
129. Ibid., p. 205.
130. Ibid., p. 203.
131. Napoleon, *Correspondence*, XIV, No. 12178.
132. Le Mesurier; see Glover, *Peninsular Preparation*, p. 273.
133. Quoted in Glover, *Wellington's Army*, p. 18.
134. Quoted in Rogers, *Napoleon's Army*, p. 98.
135. Napoleon to Darut, 2 February 1807, quoted in Rogers, *Napoleon's Army*, p. 99.
136. Comeau, *Mémoires des Guerres d'Allemagne*, p. 219; see Petrie, *Napoleon and Archduke Charles*, p. 25.
137. Saski, *Campagne de 1809*, III, p. 366; see Petrie, *Napoleon and Archduke Charles*, p. 25.
138. *London Chronicle*, 29 October 1796.
139. Dr Adam Neale, quoted in Glover, *Wellington's Army*, p. 128.
140. Quoted in ibid., p. 126.
141. Quoted in ibid., p. 129.
142. Percy, *Journal des Campagnes de Baron Percy*, Paris, 1904, p. 16; quoted in Richardson, p. 2.
143. Quoted in Petrie, *Napoleon and Archduke Charles*, p. 27.
144. Wilson, 'Narrative'; quoted Brett-James, *1812*, p. 215.

UNIFORMS & EQUIPMENT

UNIFORMS

The Napoleonic Wars produced the most colourful array of uniforms ever, but although patterns are much-recorded the tactical implications are often overlooked. Originally, uniforms had a triple purpose: to identify friend from foe; to raise morale; and, by the adoption of epaulettes and tall head-dress, to over-awe the enemy. All these considerations could have been achieved without the over-elaborate and impractical costumes designed by military clothiers, but few contemporary writers urged for uniforms to be made more functional. On campaign, however, individuals made their uniforms as comfortable as possible until 'uniformity' was sometimes non-existent, partly due to uniforms becoming worn-out with no replacement available. Thus can be found hundreds of quotations like that of Ross-Lewin of the British 32nd in 1814:

'No one ... could possibly have discovered ... the original colour of our clothing, for it was so patched with a diversity of colours, and so bespoke a variety of wretchedness that ... we must have borne an undesirable resemblance to Falstaff's ragged regiment.'[145]

The tactical implications were more important, particularly when similarity of uniforms could cause confusion. Wellington, attempting to prevent the adoption of French-style uniform by the British in 1811, made this point:

'There is no subject of which I understand so little ... I think it indifferent how a soldier is clothed, provided it is in an [sic] uniform manner; and that he is forced to keep himself clean and smart, as a soldier ought to be ...'

He then quoted the capture of an 11th Light Dragoons officer to illustrate

'... one thing I deprecate ... any imitation of the French, in any manner. It is impossible to form an idea of the inconvenience and injury which result from having any thing like them ... Lutyens and his piquet were taken ... because the 3rd Hussars had the same caps as the French *Chasseurs à Cheval* and some of their hussars; and I was near being taken on the 25th September from the same cause. At a distance, or in an action, colors [sic] are nothing: the profile, and shape of a man's cap, and his general appearance, are what guide us; and why should we make our people look like the French? ... there is no such mark as the English helmet, and, as far as I can judge, it is the best cover a dragoon can have for his head ... I only beg that we may be as different as possible from the French in every thing. The narrow top caps of our infantry, as opposed to their broad top caps, are a great advantage to those who look at long lines of posts opposed to each other.'[146]

Confusion in battle also occurred because of common items of 'service dress' worn by most armies, oilskin or fabric shako-covers, greatcoats and loose trousers, making bodies of troops virtually indistinguishable at a distance. For example, Nassau and Prussian troops fought each other at Waterloo, both believing the others to be French, whilst during the Peninsular War French and

Spanish infantry wearing blue uniforms and 'broad top caps' with white covers were often confused. When the distinctive 'Tarleton' helmet was replaced in 1812–13 by the British light dragoon shako, and the bicorn by the maned helmet, men so dressed looked exactly like the French in silhouette. The French Hanoverian Legion, wearing red uniforms, lost several men killed at Busaco by their own side mistaking them for British. Fearing a repetition their commander requested that they might wear their greatcoats at Fuentes de Oñoro; the request was rejected and the Hanoverian Legion were again mistaken for British redcoats. Attacked by their own side, they lost 100 men before retiring from the firing-line, whereupon the sight of red uniforms appearing through the smoke threw the French rear into confusion! Similar mistakes occurred due to the similarity between French gendarme and Spanish cavalry uniform, Napoleon himself suggesting that gendarmes 'should be distinguished from the Spaniards by some peculiarity of uniform, such as a white stripe on the arm.'[147]

In the 1814 campaign the wide variety of allied uniforms made the adoption of a similar mark imperative, following the wounding of a British staff officer at La Rothière by a cossack, and considering that the Prussian army had units dressed in British and Portuguese uniforms. From 2 February, therefore, all allied personnel wore a white brassard on the left upper arm, a return to the 'field sign' of the seventeenth century.

Confusion was sometimes deliberate. The British 71st, for example, tricked the French in October 1811 into believing them to be Portuguese militia by wearing their greatcoats and concealing the diced band on their shakos with black crepe. The French made an injudicious attack on the 'militia' and were bloodily repulsed.

Most staff officers favoured magnificently-laced uniforms (the British, often preferring plain uniforms or civilian dress, were an exception); but laced uniforms drew the fire of sharpshooters and several commanders were killed because of being identified by their costume. Some staff officers realized the danger; for example, when William Warre, an English A.D.C. to Marshal Beresford in the Portuguese army, wrote home for a new hat, he instructed that it

'... must not be gold laced, as the new regulation is ... I suppose our good chiefs do not think our Generals or Staff get killed off fast enough that they order them cocked hats with gold binding. It must only be meant for Wimbledon. There are no Voltigeurs there, and a gold laced cocked hat, though very ugly, is a very harmless thing – not here.'[148]

Yet another function of uniforms was pointed out by Wellington:

'... the state of the Spanish troops ... an exertion ought to be made immediately to clothe them in the national uniform. By the adoption of this measure, the practice which prevails ... of throwing away their arms and accoutrements and running away, and pretending to be peasants, would be discontinued. Large bodies could not change their clothing ... and it is probable that as they would not only find no security, but rather increase their danger by throwing away their arms and accoutrements in their flight, the State would not so frequently sustain the loss of these valuable articles. Another advantage ... from the more general use of the national uniform is, that it would be in the power of the general to punish the troops who misbehave before the enemy ... when a number of peasants are collected together with arms in their hands, and in the garb of peasants, it is difficult to fix a mark upon those corps or individuals who have behaved ill, which shall point them out as objects of excretion to the whole community ... if the whole army wore the national uniform, it would be possible to disgrace those who should misbehave, either by depriving them of it, or by affixing some mark to it, which would tend more effectually than any thing else to prevent a repetition....'[149]

But although fine uniforms attracted recruits, the theory that they also improved morale did not always apply; the King of Naples, for example, discussing a project for re-uniforming his army, is reported to have remarked: 'Dress them in blue, in red, or yellow; they will run just the same!'[150]

Fig. 84. Infantry equipment. Left: *'Line' infantry style worn by a grenadier of the British 3rd Foot Guards, showing the knapsack with mess-tin affixed. Print by Martinet, 1815.* Right: *Rifle corps style worn by the North York Militia, 1814, including powder-horn. Print by R. & D. Havell after George Walker.*

PERSONAL EQUIPMENT

The infantryman's burden was remarkably similar in most armies: usually a knapsack worn on straps passing over the shoulder and under the armpit, a leather cartridge-box on a belt over the left shoulder, often a second belt over the right shoulder supporting a bayonet and/or sabre, a water-canteen, rolled greatcoat or blanket atop the knapsack or slung across the body, and often a mess-tin and haversack. Thus equipped, a man might have 60 lbs about his person, with little consideration given to the way in which it was carried. Cross-belts compressed the chest and, if the knapsack-straps were connected by a breast-strap, could seriously impair breathing. Unless the cross-belts were connected at the back the cartridge-box and bayonet could become entangled and the soldier thrown off-balance; particularly guilty must have been the untidy Bavarian equipment

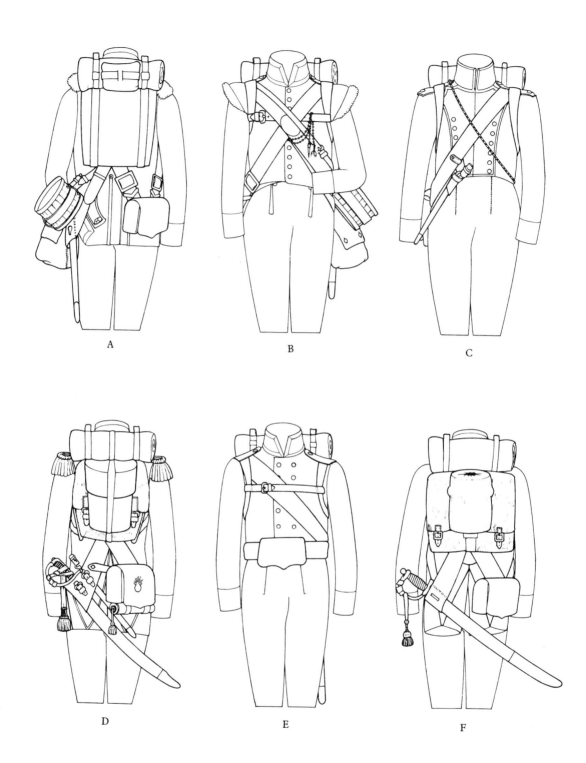

A

B

C

D

E

F

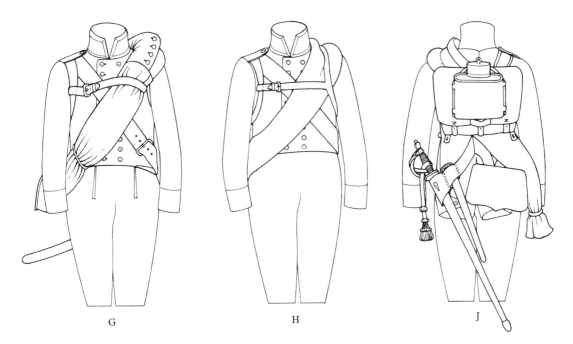

G   H   J

Fig. 85. Infantry Equipment. A, B. British, 1812–15; C. French Fusilier; D. French Grenadier; E. Prussian Fusilier; F, G. Prussian Musketeer; H, J. Russian.

worn before the adoption of French-style patterns. The '... load of arms and accoutrements considered by the peasantry under their ordinary habits to be impracticable'[151] was sufficient to cause collapse and even death, Costello of the British 95th claiming that their 70–80 lbs weight killed some 400 of the regiment before the remainder learnt to throw away all but the most essential items.

A typical set of equipment, with weight, is listed by Sergt Cooper of the British 7th Fusiliers on the march to Vittoria:[152] musket and bayonet (14 lbs), pouch and sixty rounds of ball (6 lbs), canteen (1), mess-tin (1), knapsack (3), undress jacket ($\frac{1}{2}$), two shirts ($2\frac{1}{2}$), two pairs shoes (3), trousers (2), gaiters ($\frac{1}{4}$), two pairs stockings (1), four brushes, comb and button-stick (3), cross-belts (1), pen, ink and paper ($\frac{1}{4}$), pipe-clay (1), two tent-pegs ($\frac{1}{2}$), three days' bread (3), two days' beef (2), and water in canteen (3). In addition could be a greatcoat (4 to $5\frac{3}{4}$ lbs), extra ammunition, four bill-hooks per squad and an iron camp-kettle between ten soldiers (replaced by a light tin kettle in March 1813, carried by the men in turn instead of mule-

back as before). In addition each man had a 'little semi-circular tin saucepan, with its soup-plate in it,'[153] and often extra food: fourteen or fifteen days' bread carried by the French, six days' by the Portuguese, etc., though the British could only be trusted with two or three days' supply at most; Wellington in fact ordered a twice-daily inspection in 1812–13 to ensure that the food was still in the individual's possession! For a man designated a 'handicraft' (cobbler, etc.) he would have the tools of his trade to carry, but fortunately a greatcoat and blanket were rarely carried together: 'The Duke of Wellington tried it in the year that his army entered France, but it distressed the troops greatly....'[154]

The common knapsack was of simple construction, frequently made of goat- or calf-skin with the hair left on, fastening satchel-fashion by buckled straps. The French knapsack, of this pattern, did not have the extra breast-strap as did those of Prussia and Austria. British knapsacks were made of painted canvas, originally of the same pattern or 'envelope' form, the latter opening flat for

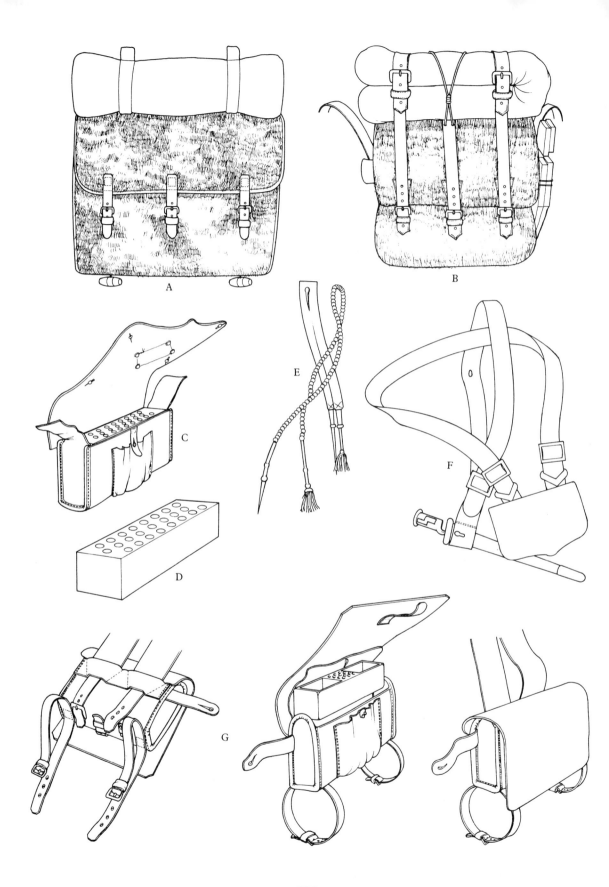

Fig. 86. Left: *Knapsacks and cartouche boxes. A. French cowhide infantry knapsack; B. Austrian knapsack with folded blanket and tent pegs; C. Cartouche box; D. Wooden block to hold cartridges; E. Wire pickers and brushes for cleaning the touch-hole and pan of the musket; F. British Foot Guards pattern equipment; G. French cartouche box showing* (Left) *rear view,* (Centre) *view when open, and* (Right) *front view.*

Fig. 87. Above: *A typical knapsack of painted canvas, marked to the 10th North British Militia (Edinburgh), c. 1800.*

the sides and flap to be folded over the contents, which pattern continued in use despite the introduction in 1805 of 'Mr Trotter's' knapsack, a rectangular, wooden-framed construction covered with canvas. Originally painted in regimental colouring, with regimental devices, all British knapsacks were ordered to be painted black in 1808 and to bear the regimental number. More unusual was the cylindrical knapsack used by the Russian army and replaced by a rectangular leather pattern.

Cartridge-boxes contained a variety of fittings, either wood or tin compartments or a wooden block drilled with holes, both to hold cartridges. The underside of the flap often included a small pocket to hold spare flints and tools, though the 'picker' and wire brush were usually attached to the shoulder-belt where they were more accessible for their use in cleaning the touch-hole and priming-pan of a musket-lock. Another pattern of pouch was worn on the front of the waistbelt; more accessible, it was favoured by light infantry. Smaller pouches worn at the side of the waistbelt-clasp were used by Jägers to hold loose ball ammunition. Powder-horns, usually slung along the shoulder-belt by a flask-cord, were carried by light troops who did not always use prepared cartridge. Brass match-cases, sometimes attached to grenadiers' shoulder-belts, were purely decorative due to the obsolescence of the grenade.

The haversack was simply a fabric bag, slung over one shoulder, to contain food and spare equipment. Water-canteens varied in pattern; Britain used a wooden design resembling a shallow barrel. With no official issue, French troops carried a variety of canteens, gourds, barrels, metal flasks or glass bottles in wickerwork covers. Other items of personal equipment included spare headgear (the French Imperial Guard carried theirs in ticken covers, strapped to the knapsack), with plumes often enclosed in oilskin and tied around the sabre-scabbard by the cap-cords on campaign. If necessary, knapsacks could be replaced by a blanket-bundle held together with straps, or by rolling its contents into the greatcoat and slinging the resulting tube over one shoulder, when it became a considerable protection against sabre-cuts. In addition to 'official' equipment, most soldiers on campaign accumulated a quantity of 'personal' impedimenta.

Leather-work was usually 'buff', usually pipeclayed for parade, though glazed or painted leather was also used, black being favoured by many Jäger and light infantry corps. When a sabre and bayonet were carried, both were usually held in a combined 'frog', but when the bayonet was carried alone its scabbard could be affixed to the cartridge-box belt (as carried by French fusiliers, for example), eliminating the need for a second shoulder-belt. The shoulder-belt plate was an invariable fitting on British equipment, but rarely-used in others; its contemporary name was 'breastplate', which should not be confused with the modern name for the cuirass.

Cavalry troopers wore an ammunition-pouch at the rear of the shoulder-belt, and often a second belt over the same shoulder to support the carbine. In the early years of the Napoleonic Wars the sabre was often suspended from a shoulder-belt, but this gave way to a waist-belt with slings, at times supporting a bayonet-scabbard as well. The sabretache, initially a satchel slung from the waist-belt, became purely ornamental though during the Napoleonic Wars it was still used for holding papers, pen and ink and even acting as a writing-desk for officers. Cavalrymen also carried such items as spare horseshoes and nails, sponges, combs, corn- and nose-bags, watering-bridle and grooming-brushes, and much of their personal equipment in the valise on the saddle; Frederick Johnson of the British 6th Dragoons in 1815, for example, carried a 'Writing Roll', two shirts, flannel waistcoat, nightcap, pair of stockings, pair of overalls, knife and fork, and a leather roll holding a comb, razor and tooth-brush, all in his 'Velleice'.[155]

Officers' equipment, more elaborate and extensive than that of their men, was usually carried on waggons or mules. Apart from such exotics as patent folding beds, candelabra, porcelain and the like (occasionally taken on campaign) a typical waggon-load was that belonging to Major Dickson of the Royal Artillery in February 1810: '1 large chest, 2 portmanteaux, 1 carpet bag with liquor

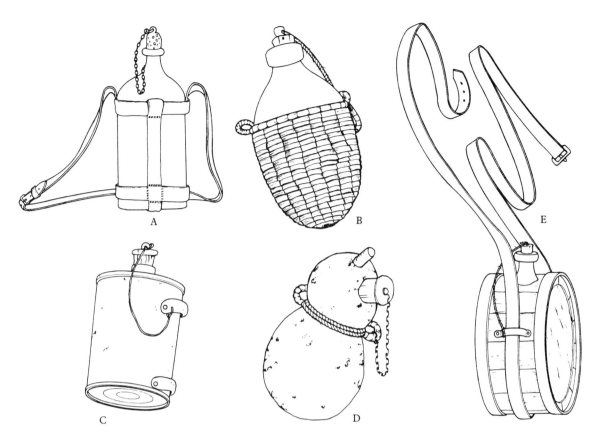

Fig. 88. Types of Waterbottle. A. Non-regulation glass bottle in a leather frame; B. Non-regulation glass bottle in a wickerwork case; C. Tin water bottle; D. Gourd; E. British regulation canteen of barrel construction.

canteens, 2 canteen baskets, 1 cot and bedding, 2 camp-kettles, 1 tent with poles, 1 sword, 1 cheese in bag, 1 box with papers, 1 bag with papers and orderly books.'[156] 'Canteens' of this type varied from the 'curious and ingenious contrivance' containing cooking utensils, breakfast- and dinner-services, lamps and candlesticks all in a portmanteau,[157] to a box holding tea, sugar, brandy, a tin kettle-cum-teapot, two cups and saucers, two spoons, two forks, two metal plates and a soup-tureen, 'which on fortunate occasions acted as a punch-bowl.'[158] Senior officers might take dressing- and writing-cases, marquees, tables, chairs and even livestock on campaign: in the Peninsular War Major-General Lowry Cole was followed by a dozen goats, a cow, thirty-six sheep and a shepherd!

Despite Wellington's rescinding in 1809 of an order which instructed officers to carry knapsacks, to lessen fatigue and increase mobility, many British officers (particularly those in the forefront of campaign) carried equipment similar to that of their men, like the officers of other armies, often including a large haversack which according to Kincaid of the 95th:

'... is a sort of dumb waiter ... a well regulated one ought never to be without ... a couple of biscuit, a sausage, a little tea and sugar, a knife, fork and spoon, a tin cup (which answers to the names of *tea-cup, soup-plate, wine-glass* and *tumbler*), a pair of socks, a piece of soap, a tooth-brush, towel, and comb, and half a dozen cigars.'[159]

BOOTS

Footwear was one of the most vital pieces of equipment; generals often took more care to see that their army was well-shod than well-fed. Adequate boots was a question which obsessed Napoleon, who issued detailed

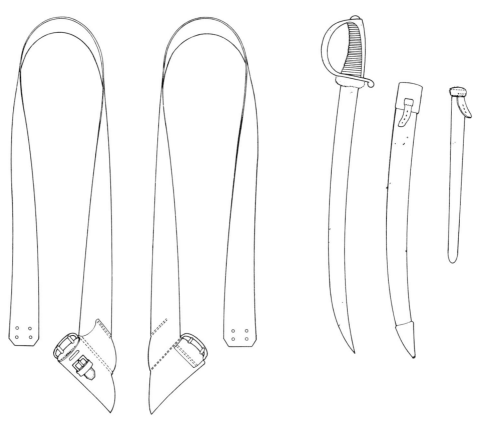

Fig. 89. French Sabre-Briquet showing front and back views of the belt, sabre scabbard and bayonet scabbard. Note the woollen washer below the hilt intended to prevent the blade rusting in the scabbard.

orders before embarking on a campaign, for example in 1806:

'Every detachment ... should start, each man with a pair of shoes, besides two pairs in his knapsack. At Mayence they will receive another pair to replace that worn on the march. At Magdeburg they will receive a new pair ... so that every man may reach his corps with a pair of shoes on his feet and a pair in his knapsack';[160] in this one campaign (1806–07) 587,008 pairs of shoes and 16,948 of boots were issued to the French army, plus 397,000 pairs sent from France.[161]

Nevertheless, armies frequently staggered through a campaign with bare feet, slowing down the rate of movement and cohesion on the march. The issued boots might never be replaced or might be manufactured by unscrupulous contractors using glue instead of stitching, so that they soon fell apart; or they might be replaced out of necessity by requisitioned civilian footwear (sandals in the Peninsula, fur winter boots in Russia), or even 'home-made' items fashioned by regimental cobblers; there were cases in the Peninsula when the situation was so critical that pieces of raw hide were sewn around the feet, remaining in situ until they dropped off! Only occasionally was 'native' footwear an advantage; for example, Spanish sandals were preferable to boots for climbing the Pyrenees, and were often more comfortable.

The term 'shoe' was used in contemporary parlance to describe the low infantry boot; 'boot' implied the high cavalry styles. Except that top-boots made walking difficult, cavalry footwear had little tactical significance, whereas deficient infantry footwear could affect the outcome of a battle. The typical British infantry shoe was the same shape for both feet, the soldier being told to wear them alternately to equalize the wear. They had no lace-holes; the soldier had to punch his own. An issue of two pairs (plus extra soles and heels for which the man paid 4s. annually) a year took no account of the rigours of cam-

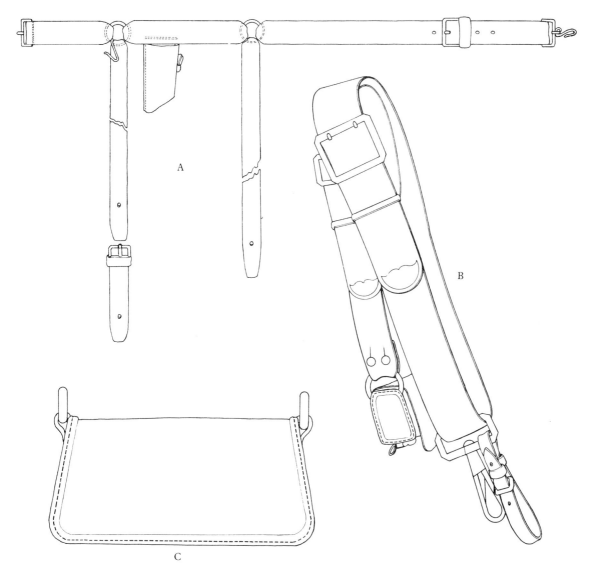

Fig. 90.   A. French light cavalry waistbelt with bayonet frog; B. French cavalry shoulder belts and carbine swivel; C. French cavalry pouch.

paign, and unless a free issue of shoes was authorized by a kindly general the soldier had to pay for any replacements over and above his two pairs a year. Despite widespread corpse-robbing, however, torn blankets and strips of hide wrapped around the feet provided the footwear of many armies often for months on end.

BODY-ARMOUR

A relic of medieval warfare, the cuirass (breast- and back-plates) was worn by the heavy cavalry of a number of armies; in France the first general issue was made in 1802, though the 7th Cavalry (ex-Cuirassiers du Roi of the Ancien Régime) had worn them before. The French pattern consisted of a heavy iron breastplate and a lighter backplate, joined together by shoulder-straps and secured by a waist-belt buckled at the front and bolted to the backplate. The shoulder-straps constituted an extra protection, being made of overlapped brass scales or occasionally chain or leather. Two later patterns of cuirass ('Mk II' after 1806, 'Mk III' in 1809) differed only

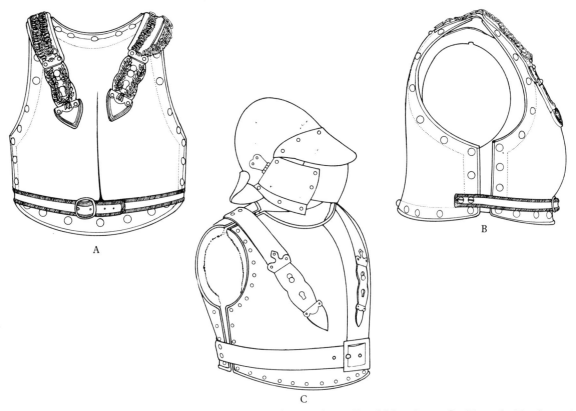

Fig. 91. A. French officers' cuirass, 1812, front view; B. Side view; C. French Engineers' Trench armour.

marginally, though officers' cuirasses were more decorative, with gilded rivets and ornamental straps. From 1810 French carabiniers wore similar cuirasses, covered with thin brass sheeting (copper-plated for officers). Protecting the jacket from wear, the cuirass-lining or 'cuffs' was scarlet for cuirassiers and light blue for carabiniers, of cloth with white lace edging for troopers and silver lace for officers. The usual German cuirass consisted of a front-plate alone, with cross-straps on the wearer's back, the front often enamelled black (as worn by Austria and Russia).

In combat the cuirass was proof against long-range musketry but was of most value in mêlée. The breastplate would turn a sabre or lance, though the unarmoured back of German cavalry was a desperate disadvantage; at Eckmühl, when French and Austrian cuirassiers met, the unarmoured Austrian backs resulted in most uneven casualties: the proportion of Austrian killed and wounded respectively amounted to thirteen and eight

for each Frenchman.[162] A cuirass could be a severe disadvantage when the rider was unhorsed, however, Wellington remarking at Waterloo how unhorsed Frenchmen were unable to rise, struggling like 'turned turtles'.

Cavalry helmets cannot really be considered 'armour': even the French iron cuirassier helmets and the German boiled-leather types would not stop a hefty sword-cut. Heavier armour – helmets, breastplates and sometimes thigh-plates – were worn by some engineers when working in range of the enemy. Antique Turkish helmets and mail-coats were worn by some Asiatic tribesmen of the Russian army and the mamelukes in Egypt, but were of little use against firearms. A further protection was the ubiquitous rolled cloak or greatcoat, worn bandolier-fashion by both cavalry and infantry, giving considerable protection against the cut to the left shoulder, the principal stroke of a cutting weapon. The order to 'roll cloaks' came to be regarded by the French cavalry as a sign that action was imminent.

'FOREIGN' EQUIPMENT

Apart from enormous quantities of captured *matériel* used by many nations, huge amounts were supplied by Britain to various allied nations throughout the Revolutionary and Napoleonic Wars. Some idea of the magnitude of these supplies can be gathered from a list made by Lord Londonderry, describing equipment supplied to Prussia, Russia and Sweden prior to the 1813–14 campaign:

218 cannon with carriages, ammunition and attendant waggons; 124,119 stand of arms, 18,231,000 rounds of ball-ammunition and 23,000 barrels of powder and flints; 34,443 swords and lances, 624 drums, bugles and cavalry standards; 150,000 complete uniforms including greatcoats, cloaks, etc.; 187,000 yards of cloth, 175,796 boots and spare leather, 114,000 blankets, 58,000 linen shirts and drawers, 87,190 pairs of gaiters, 69,624 pairs of stockings, 90,000 sets of accoutrements, 63,457 knapsacks, 14,820 saddles and blankets, 100,000 caps and feathers, 22,000 forage-caps, 14,000 stocks, 140,000 shoe-brushes, combs and blacking-balls, 3,000 gloves, 20,000 pickers, brushes, sponges, etc., 5,000 flannel shirts, caps and trousers, 14,000 sheets, 5,000 haversacks and canteens, 702,000 lbs of biscuit and flour, 691,360 lbs beef and pork, 28,625 gallons of brandy and rum, plus tents, carts, medical equipment and hospital-stores.[163]

From this it is obvious that many nations throughout the Napoleonic Wars used not only items of their own manufacture, but vast quantities of weapons and equipment of foreign pattern also.

HAIRSTYLES

The powdered 'queue' (pigtail) of the eighteenth century lingered well into the Napoleonic Wars; originally to keep long hair out of the eyes, it had become an archaic ornament, its preparation described by John Shipp (1797).

'A large piece of candle-grease was applied first to the sides of my head, and then to the long hair behind. After this, the same operation was gone through with nasty, stinking soap ... A large pad, or bag, filled with sand, was poked into the back of my neck, the hair twisted tightly round it, and the whole tied with a leather thong ... the skin of my face was pulled so tight by the bag ... that it was impossible so much as to wink an eyelid....'[164]

In British service a General Order of 20 July 1808 was received with great delight:

'His Majesty has been graciously pleased to dispense with the use of queues ... the commanding officers of regiments will take care that the men's hair is cut close in their necks in the neatest and most uniform manner, and that their heads are kept perfectly clean by combing, brushing, and frequently washing them....'

Other styles of hair-dressing included that favoured by hussars (especially French), of a queue and braided side-tresses or 'cadenettes', as described by a hussar of the Béon Legion: the hair was parted down the middle of the head, the tresses plaited and tied around the end with ribbon, or strips of lead from a flattened musket-ball, and treated with pomade or candle-grease. They actually protected the cheeks from sabre-cuts. In some armies officers were allowed to wear false queues of horsehair or whalebone, sometimes attached to the collar; similar cosmetic decoration included the painting-on of moustaches in burnt cork for recruits too young to grow their own, in those corps in which moustaches were compulsory. 'Sideboards', when permitted, were usually allowed to extend no lower than the bottom of the ear.

Though beards were traditionally the distinguishing feature of pioneers, moustaches, beards and long hair were not uncommon on campaign, some British officers wearing 'whiskers' even in England, as the mark of a veteran campaigner. Other hair-dressing included that of the cossacks noted by Countess Schwerin, of plastering their hair with gun-oil, whilst the famous traveller Dr Clarke noted that *all* Russians, aristocracy and serfs, kept their hair 'universally in a state not to be described ... only divested of vermin when they frequent the bath!'[165]

HORSES AND SADDLERY

Adequate training was necessary to produce a

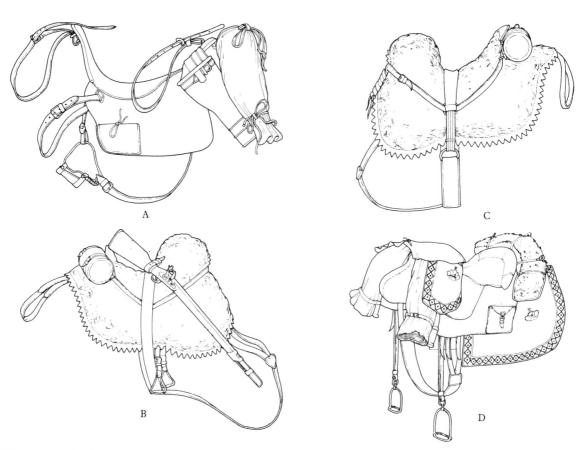

Fig. 92. A. French 'Hungarian' pattern saddle, 1812; B. French light cavalry shabraque, showing method of attaching carbine; C. Other side of same saddle; D. Austrian heavy cavalry horse-furniture.

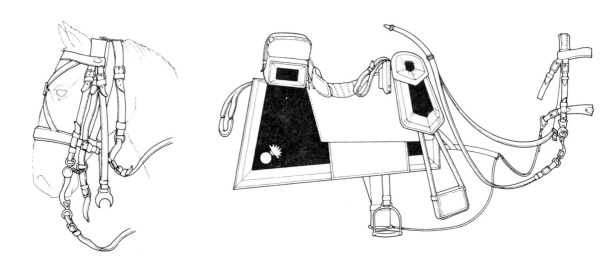

Fig. 93. Left: French light cavalry bridle. Right: French heavy cavalry horse-furniture.

suitable cavalry horse; as Le Marchant wrote in his *Rules and Regulations* (1796):

'... a dragoon and his horse should be so formed to each other to act as one body; for which purpose the rider should make himself acquainted with the temper and powers of his animal, so that by judicious management, the horse may be rendered docile, and execute readily whatever may be expected of him ... It is alone by temper and perseverance, not by severity, that vice is to be conquered....'[166]

Contemporary horsemen believed that certain breeds were more easily trained, an old Peninsular officer writing: 'The superior breeding of the English horses renders them more unsteady than the half cart-horse of the Frenchman';[167] hence, by implication, one reason for the lack of control of British charges.

Horses varied in size according to their duties: the heavy cavalry required strong, large mounts, and the light cavalry smaller, faster horses with stamina for more protracted fast movement than the heavy type. The French heavy cavalry preferred Norman or Flemish mounts, great weight-carriers but heavy and slow: a 'charge' executed at Eckmühl after a long day was unable to move faster than a trot, whilst Marbot found a cuirassier horse incapable of travelling at the speed required of an A.D.C. In the 1806 campaign the Prussian and Saxon cavalry horses were superior to many of the French, so Napoleon re-mounted a large part of his cavalry on captured horses. Despite the often poor-quality mounts used by many French cavalry (particularly in Spain), most regiments took pains to acquire the best available, colonels being allowed to purchase remounts locally when available. This allowed the fashionable practice of mounting squadrons on horses of the same colour; in 1803, for example, the 20th Chasseurs à Cheval had black horses for the 1st Sqdn, bay for the 2nd, chestnut for the 3rd and grey for the 4th, a practice copied by several armies. Similarly, whole regiments could be mounted on horses of the same colour, for example the black of the Grenadiers à Cheval of the French Imperial Guard.

The quality of British horses has often been remarked upon; certainly, the heavyweight and lightweight 'hunter' was superior to most others, despite the large fodder-consumption of the heavyweight, but frequently the British cavalry received mounts which were totally unsuitable: in July 1809, for example, the 14th Light Dragoons received sixty-one remounts,

'... I may almost say Cart Horses from the Irish Commissariat Corps. What makes this more ridiculous is that they are chiefly Horses that have been *cast* in *England* as being unserviceable for the *Heavy Dragoons!*'[168]

It is interesting to note the number of horses used by a cavalry regiment: the 14th Light Dragoons from 1808 to 1814 received 1,384 mounts plus 381 from other units; bought thirteen Spanish horses and captured sixty-three, a total of 1,821, of which only 278 returned to England. Officers purchased their own horses, receiving an often-inadequate fixed compensation of £35 for those lost. The quality of Spanish and Portuguese horses was often infamous; in 1808 Col. William Robe claimed that for artillery duty, any old, 'cast' animals from England were better than the best Iberian horses, ill-proportioned and lacking in strength. So short were the Spanish and Portuguese armies that, for example, the Spanish 1st Chasseurs mustered only 185 horses for 577 men in June 1808.

Fodder-consumption varied. The British daily ration consisted of 14 lbs of hay or straw, 12 lbs of oats, or 10 lbs of barley or Indian corn; in January 1810 this was reduced to 10 lbs of hay and 12 lbs of barley or Indian corn; 'green forage', when issued, was 28 lbs. Often on campaign *any* edible material was consumed (on the retreat from Burgos horses are recorded as eating their own harness and even limber-box lids), from corn-flour cakes eaten normally by Portuguese peasants, to the German Legion troops who shared their own bread-ration with their horses, which maintained a better condition than the mounts of their British comrades, whose unsavoury habit was to sell part of their horse's forage to buy alcohol for themselves.

A hard campaign with little forage could reduce whole brigades to pitiable wrecks, the best English horses being particularly vulnerable, being unused to such conditions, as Sir Robert Wilson noted:

'English horses can never serve abroad in English condition ... at least as long as the English cavalry are nurtured to require warm stables, luxurious beds, etc. – as long as efficiency abroad is sacrificed to appearance at home....'[169]

The Russian cavalry mounts were ideally suited for campaigning, Wilson writing that:

'Their heavy-horses are matchless for an [sic] union of size, strength, activity, and hardiness; they have the bulk of the British cart-horse, but have too much blood to be coarse,'[170] whilst the ill-conditioned cossack ponies, 'mean in shape and slouching in motion' were so rugged as to travel 'incalculable journeys, and remain exposed to heat or cold, day or night, without manifesting any sense of inconvenience,'[171] '... can walk at the rate of five miles an hour with ease, or dispute the race with the swiftest....'[172]

A wide variety of saddlery was used by different nations, most conforming to the same basic construction. The saddle was made of wood and/or leather, secured by a leather or woven girth passing under the horse's belly, and straps around the horse's breast and a 'crupper' around the tail; stirrups, either iron or brass, were sometimes ornamented and equipped with a socket on the right stirrup in which to rest the butt of a lance. Pistol-holsters were attached to the front of the saddle, at either side, covered by cloth 'holster-caps' in some cases. Bridles were varied in pattern, sometimes including cross-straps over the horse's fore-head, and sometimes (as on the French 'Hungarian' bridle) with an ornamental metal crescent hanging under the horse's throat. Harness-plates, worn on the breast and sometimes fore-head, usually bore regimental devices. Over the saddle was placed the 'shabraque', an ornamental blanket in regimental colouring, or in many cases a sheepskin, or half-sheepskin and half-shabraque. On campaign plain shabraques were used, or were removed completely. A blanket was usually placed under the saddle and the rider's equipment – rolled cloak at the front and valise or portmanteau at the back – was strapped over the shabraque (the cloak could also be carried underneath). Extra pouches contained such items as grooming-equipment, picket-rope (which could be attached to the bridle) and horseshoes, the latter sometimes carried in the second holster of regiments armed with only one pistol each. Though the carbine could be carried slung from the spring-clip on the rider's shoulder-belt, many saddles included a tube or 'boot' in which the muzzle (or butt) of the carbine could be placed, with a loop higher up to secure the stock (or barrel).

Among unusual saddlery was that of the cossacks: as Wilson reported,

'They have only a snaffle bridle on their horses for the convenience of feeding at all times, and even in the presence of the enemy ... Their activity is too incessant to admit of long stops for regular feeding....'[173] and according to Sir R. Ker Porter, 'An uncouth saddle is bound on the horse ... like a doubled pillow, under which is a square piece of oil cloth painted in various colours.'[174]

FLAGS AND STANDARDS

Originally serving to identify bodies of troops in the days before the evolution of uniforms, flags and standards were primarily used in the Napoleonic Wars for reasons of morale.

Infantry flags, or 'Colours', were large and rectangular (the British size was 6 ft 6 ins by 6 ft, on a 9 ft 10 in. pike); cavalry carried rectangular 'standards' or swallow-tailed 'guidons', much smaller and frequently not taken on campaign. Though a number of standard motifs existed for each army, flags invariably bore distinctive regimental devices or lettering either embroidered or painted, the standard of painting often being surprisingly crude.

Republican France boasted many designs of flag, often based upon the national red, white and blue and bearing the Phrygian cap and fasces, though some, particularly those of the National Guard, more closely resembled the elaborate patterns of the seventeenth century. In 1797 a regulation pattern was adopted by the demi-brigades, but not until 1804 were the legendary 'Eagles' issued. Unique among military heraldry, the 'Eagles' relegated the flag to a decorative extra, the real symbol being the 12-inch high, gilt sculpted eagle atop the pike. The actual flags

Fig. 94. Left: *Eagle of the French 84th Line Regiment, with an honour award plate, the only case of such an award known.* Right: *Eagle of the 8th Line Regiment taken by the 87th Regiment at Barrosa.*

were small, only 80 cm. square, originally comprising a white diamond with alternate red and blue triangles at the corners, with gold embroidery on one side reading: 'L'EMPEREUR/DES FRANÇAIS/AU – eme REGIMENT/D'INFANTERIE (ARTILLERIE, etc.)/DE LIGNE', and the reverse: 'VALEUR/ET DISCIPLINE/1er (2 eme, etc.) BATAILLON.' Due to the number lost in action it was ordered in 1808 that Eagles should be carried by 1st Battalions only. In 1812 a tricolour design was issued, with battle-honour instead of the 'Valeur et Discipline', and in 1815 some units received a plainer type, devoid of almost all decoration save lettering. A few ancient flags were carried – the Vistula Legion, for example, used those of the old Polish Legion at least until 1812 – and satellite nations used similar patterns to the French but in their own colouring – red, white and green for the Kingdom of Italy, for example.

Prussia and Russia used a similar motif – the national eagle – placed centrally on a coloured flag bearing diagonal or vertical bars or 'waves' of a contrasting colour. Each Prussian musketeer battalion had two flags, but fusiliers none (except the Guard Fusiliers, granted flags in 1814); each Russian battalion had a 'white' flag and a 'coloured' flag, the 'white' ones withdrawn in 1813. Three Russian patterns (1800, 1803, 1813) and the 'Colours of St George' (honour-flags bearing details of the award) were carried simultaneously, there being no automatic replacement of 'old' flags upon the advent of a new pattern.

British infantry battalions carried a 'King's Colour', and a 'Regimental Colour', the former a large Union flag and the latter of the facing-colour with a small Union in the top corner nearest the pole (units with black or white facings had large St George's crosses on the Regimental Colour). Both Colours carried regimental devices, title and battle-honours, usually a shield, escutcheon or circlet with a 'Union' wreath around. Cavalry standards were allocated at one per two troops, the first or 'King's' crimson and the remainder of the facing-colour, both bearing regimental

Fig. 95. '*Eagle*'-*bearer of the Grenadiers of Napoleon's Imperial Guard. Print after Charlet.*

devices and/or the 'Union' badge of rose, thistle or shamrock.

Other states – Austria for example – took their flag-designs from the national coat-of-arms; some were small, like those of the Duchy of Warsaw, whose flags had ornamental eagle-heads in French fashion.

'Colour parties' were established to protect the regimental flags, consisting of a subaltern ('ensign') who carried the flag, and a number of experienced N.C.O.s as escort; after 1808 the French flag-bearer was designated 'Premier Porte-Aigle' and his two senior N.C.O.s 'Deuxième' and 'Troisième', carrying half-pikes bearing a small pennon, red and white respectively, lettered 'NAPOLEON' on one side and the regimental number on the other. Similar appointments existed in most armies, the rank of 'Colour-Sergeant' being introduced into British service in 1813

as a reward for deserving N.C.O.s. As the automatic target for enemy fire, appointment to the colour-party was often an unwelcome honour, as Sergeant Lawrence of the British 40th recorded when ordered to the Colours at Waterloo:

'Though used to warfare as any one, this was a job I did not like. There had been before me that day *fourteen* sergeants killed or wounded around them, and both staff and colours were almost cut to pieces.'[175]

In the field the practical value of Colours was to act as a rallying-point, lifted high to indicate through the chaos where a broken unit should re-form. For more pedestrian uses such as the marking of camping-grounds, small marker-flags or 'camp colours' were used. In inclement weather all flags might be 'cased', rolled around the pole and enclosed in an oilskin tube; in French service the flag was often removed completely, leaving just the metal eagle as the symbol. For morale, however, flags were paramount, symbolizing a mystical bond between the regiment, its sovereign and sometimes religion as well; the measure of victory was calculated by the number of flags captured, and the loss of a flag was the worst disgrace which could befall a unit.

Consequently, the most bitter fights occurred around the possession of flags. For example, the defence of the Colours of the British 1/3rd Foot (Buffs) after the regiment was scattered by cavalry at Albuera. The Regimental Colour was carried by 16-year-old Ensign Edward Thomas, who raised his flag to rally his company, of whom only two men out of sixty-three survived. Thomas answered a call to surrender his Colour with: 'Only with my life'; the French took both. The bearer of the King's Colour, Ensign Charles Walsh, fell wounded, and Lieutenant Matthew Latham seized it. Alone and surrounded he clung to the flag despite terrible injuries including a severed left arm and a disfiguring blow to the face. Pierced by a dozen lance-thrusts and trampled upon, he managed to tear the Colour from its pike and conceal it beneath his body, from where it was recovered after the battle; miraculously, Latham survived. Such was the value placed upon regimental flags; in fact even today two

Fig. 96. Rampon defending the colours of the 32è Demi-Brigade *at Montelegino, 10 April 1796. After Berthon.*

British regiments – Blues & Royals and Royal Scots Dragoon Guards – wear arm- and cap-badges respectively commemorating the capture of French Eagles at Waterloo!

145. Ross-Lewin, H., *With the 32nd in the Peninsular and other Campaigns* (ed. J. Wardrell), Dublin, 1904.
146. Wellington to Lt-Col. Torrens, 6 November 1811; 'Despatches', VIII, pp. 371–2.
147. Napoleon to Joseph, 22 December 1808; 'Napoleon's Correspondence with King Joseph', I, p. 384.
148. Warre, p. 191.
149. Wellington to Marquess Wellesley, 8 August 1809; 'Despatches', V, pp. 11–12.
150. Phipps, R. W., *The Armies of the First French Republic* (1926–39); quoted in Rogers, *Napoleon's Army*, p. 64.
151. Sir John Burgoyne, 'Military Opinions of Field-Marshal Burgoyne', 1839, p. 465, quoted in 'Journal', Society for Army Historical Research, Vol. XLVII, p. 11.
152. Cooper, *Rough Notes*, pp. 80–81.
153. Sir John Burgoyne, *Life and Correspondence of Field-Marshal Burgoyne* (ed. Lt-Col. Hon. G. Wrottesley, London, 1873), I, p. 255, quoted in Brett-James, *Life in Wellington's Army*, p. 117.
154. 'Militaris', 'On the Equipment of the British Infantry', *United Service Journal*, 1831, II, p. 204.
155. Quoted in 'Journal', Society for Army Historical Research, Vol. XXXV, p. 176.
156. Quoted in Brett-James, *Life in Wellington's Army*, p. 70.
157. J. G. Smith, *The English Army in France*, London, 1831, II, pp. 198–9; quoted in Brett-James, *Life in Wellington's Army*, p. 71.
158. Blakeney, pp. 209–10.
159. Kincaid, p. 23.
160. Napoleon, *Correspondence*, No. 11413.
161. Quoted in Petrie, *Napoleon's Campaign in Poland*, p. 24.
162. Marbot, I, p. 300.
163. Londonderry, *The War in Germany and France*, p. 366.
164. Shipp, p. 14.
165. Quoted in *Royal Military Chronicle*, 1812.
166. Quoted in Rogers, *Mounted Troops*, p. 155.
167. *United Service Journal*, 1831, II, p. 62.
168. Capt. Henry Neville, 1 July 1809, quoted in Rogers, *Mounted Troops*, p. 165.
169. Wilson, 'Brief Remarks'; see Rogers, *Napoleon's Army*, p. 42.
170. Ibid.; see *Royal Military Chronicle*, 1812, p. 204.
171. Porter, pp. 131–4.
172. Wilson, 'Brief Remarks', p. 27.
173. Ibid.
174. Porter, p. 134.
175. Lawrence, p. 239.

Fig. 97.   Enrolment of volunteers in France 1792. Print after A. Vinchon.

Fig. 98.   A common aspect of the soldier's life: drill and inspection. Print published by J. Wheble, 1798.

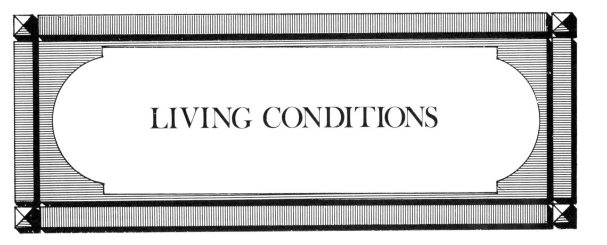

LIVING CONDITIONS

RECRUITING

Though many nations relied upon some form of impressment, mass-conscription was rarely considered. France passed the 'Réquisition' law in 1793, authorizing a 'levée en masse' by making all males between the ages of eighteen and thirty-five liable for military service for the duration of hostilities, though the term 'conscription' was not used until September 1798 when the Conscription Law divided the available manpower into five classes by age and marital status. These were subject to call-up by annual classes, Napoleon fixing the proportion of each class to be selected after 1805, selection within the class by lot; thereafter it was usual to anticipate the annual conscriptions. In 1809, for example, 100,000 of the 1809 class were called, plus 20,000 of 1806, 30,000 of 1807 and even some from 1810's class. Thus by 1813 many conscripts were boys of fifteen and sixteen years of age (the 'Marie-Louises'); in that year 400,000 recruits were under twenty-one and 147,000 a little older. The conscription system was naturally unpopular and produced the 'réfractaires' who went into hiding to avoid military service; of the 936,000 called up in 1813–14 probably less than 120,000 ever served.

Russia's conscription was a 'levy' on the number of 'souls' entered on the tax-roll, the population being so large that a levy of one per 500 would produce 32,000 recruits. In some years there were no levies, but there were three in 1813, each of five men per hundred 'souls'. Duration of enlistment was twenty-five years. Prussia's mass-conscription was imposed in 1813 to raise the Landwehr, including all able-bodied men between seventeen and twenty-four. Other nations, like Spain, only used conscription to make up the numbers not covered by voluntary enlistment; their system, the 'Quinta' (originally taking every fifth man) gave exemption to all artisans and middle-class, the bulk of the levied troops selected by ballot from the agricultural labourers.

The only major power to rely totally upon voluntary enlistment was Britain, hence Wellington's oft-misquoted 'scum of the earth' remark: recruits came only from the lower orders of society or those driven to enlistment from penury. To form an army like the French, Wellington wrote,

'... we must compose our army of soldiers drawn from all classes of the population ... from the good and the middling, as well in rank as in education, as from the bad, and not, as we in particular do, from the bad only'; nevertheless, '... it is really wonderful that we should have made them the fine fellows they are.'[176]

Britain's only 'conscription' was a ballot-system for service in the militia, which could be avoided by paying for a substitute. In 1803, another scheme, the 'Army of Reserve', raised a 'regular' force by ballot but was restricted to service in the British Isles and intended to provide volunteers for the regular army without depleting the militia. The plan was a failure, the Army of Reserve consisting largely of substitutes who would have enlisted in the militia or regulars in any case, and was abandoned when the second year's ballot, intended to raise 29,000 men, brought in only 7,683 and 3,041 deserted! From 1805, militia-men were allowed and encouraged to volunteer into the regular army, providing a much higher calibre of recruit than before; hence the high quality of Wellington's Peninsula army when compared to that before volunteering from the militia was sanctioned.

PROMOTION

Military education was limited, despite a number of military colleges producing trained subalterns; for example, only 3.9 per cent of British first-commission officers came from the Royal Military College (established 1802),[177] though the artillery and engineer officers of most nations received the specialist training their duties demanded. 'Influence' – patronage by influential individuals – whilst rife in many German states, accounted for a smaller number of commissions than might be imagined; in 1809, for example, the British army contained only 140 peers or sons of peers.

For promotion, 'seniority' was prevalent in many armies: promotion in chronological order of length of service irrespective of ability, producing ancient senior officers and stifling young talent. 'Purchase', the buying of advancement, whilst producing anomalies like seven-year old ensigns and a rise from ensign to lt.-colonel in nine months (Andrew Gammell, ensign 24 December 1793, lt-col. 18 September 1794), was in British service later controlled to ensure officers were sufficiently experienced before buying another step, and after all produced comparatively youthful commanders like Wellington. Only about one-fifth of British officers in the Peninsula were 'purchase' men.

Promotion from the ranks was more unusual, but no less than 5.42 per cent. of British officers had risen that way, plus 4.5 per cent. who had served as 'volunteers' – i.e. fought as enlisted men until a vacancy for a subaltern occurred. There was much more scope for advancement in the egalitarian French army; in 1805 fully half the com-missioned officers had risen from the ranks. The officer-training schools produced many, but it is interesting to note that of Napoleon's marshals, Berthier, Davoût, Grouchy, Keller-mann, Macdonald, Marmont, Pérignon, Sérurier and Soult had all been commissioned under the Ancien Régime.

Instruction and discipline began with the non-commissioned officers, who were doubly important in armies (like the Russian) in which the officers were indolent and poorly-educated. The selection of N.C.O.s was far from easy, for although a man might be promoted for some act of valour he might be incapable of performing his duty; in the British army, for example, some privates were promoted and 'reduced' four or five times. One of Wellington's comments concerned the N.C.O.s of the Guards, who 'regularly got drunk once a day, by eight in the evening, and got to bed soon after – but they always took care to do first what they were bid.'[178]

DISCIPLINE

Methods of enforcing discipline varied between armies, and between regiments; some were so good that a word of chastisement from an officer was sufficient, whilst others had to be transformed into virtual penal battalions.

Punishment was frequently barbaric. For serious crimes, a popular system in German armies was the 'horse', a triangular-section box with the point uppermost, upon which the culprit was sat with a leg on each side, each leg often weighted with muskets. Flogging was the staple British form of correction, with as many as 1,000 lashes (usually in instalments) being not uncommon. Less-severe punishments included 'running the gauntlet'; and capital punishment was meted out by firing-squad or (for looting) the gallows. The different levels of correction consisted of company 'court', regimental courts-martial (with a maximum sentence of 300 lashes in British service) or, for more serious crimes, general courts-martial.

For minor infringements the N.C.O.s and officers in many armies were allowed to strike the culprit; foreign observers related with distaste how prevalent was this practice in the Russian army, junior officers frequently be-

Fig. 99.   Two of the troubles commonly endured by soldiers. Top: *The exhaustion of the march.* Bottom: *The nervous expectation of combat: an artillery battery awaits in reserve. Prints after Albrecht Adam, showing the Russian campaign of 1812.*

labouring their poor, uncomplaining and faithful soldiers without mercy, despite Barclay de Tolly's 'Code of Infantry Service' (1811) which stressed that officers must 'refrain from dealing out punishment ... when you are teaching you should reserve chastisement only for occasions of carelessness, though even here you must proceed with moderation and prudence.'[179]

Contrasting to this brutal treatment was the British 'Regulations for the Rifle Corps':

'Every superior ... shall give his orders in the language of moderation and of regard to the feelings of the individual under his command; abuse, bad language and blows being positively forbid.'[180]

Few regiments adopted so enlightened a code, and barbarous though the punishments were, they were little-resented by the men who accepted that every regiment contained a hard core of criminals; indeed, one who was himself flogged wrote of his ordeal:

'Perhaps it is a good thing for me as could then have happened, as it prevented me from committing greater crimes, which must at last have brought me to my ruin.'[181] As in so many other cases, the mentality of the early nineteenth century is scarcely reconcilable with that of the last quarter of the twentieth.

ACCOMMODATION

Permanent barracks originated only in the nineteenth century, though fortified places had always included accommodation for the garrison. The usual system of quartering in the eighteenth century was the 'billet', the compulsory appropriation of parts of civilian dwellings, some nations assigning their troops to inns and lodging-houses, paying for rent and food, whilst others imposed upon unwilling civilians; unscrupulous innkeepers could make a handsome profit by accepting full payment and feeding their guests with offal. Permanent barracks, where they existed, were often insanitary, airless buildings with no facilities at all, 'beds' often consisting of planks with (sometimes) straw mattresses, two or three men to a bed; 'married quarters' where such existed were usually sections of the barrack-room enclosed by blanket-partitions. In fact, in good weather it was

often more pleasant to bivouac in the open than suffer the smoke-filled barrack-rooms.

The most rudimentary bivouac was the soldier's blanket or greatcoat, the latter sometimes used as a sleeping-bag by inserting the legs into the sleeves; other sleeping-bags could be made by sewing two sacks together. A more elaborate shelter, often constructed at the end of every day's march, was a 'booth' or lean-to made from tree-branches and covered with straw or ferns. Officers often carried tarred canvas, waterproof mattresses into which dry leaves or straw could be stuffed; those lacking such luxuries could build a 'bedstead' of branches, covered with straw, lying on top about nine inches from the ground to avoid rising damp; a more bizarre version was built by the French 26th Light Infantry for their colonel after Austerlitz: '... a number of Russian corpses, face to the ground ... a layer of hay on top....'[182]

Tents varied from enormous, multi-roomed edifices in which an officer could live in style, surrounded by bed, table, chairs, desks and dinner-services. Officers' tents tended to decrease in size according to the occupant's rank, subalterns usually sharing with two or three others. Designs included 'marquis tents' (marquees),[183] originally of canvas lined with ticken, with a 'porch' attached; Adye lists the standard marquee with a 7-foot ridgepole and a weight of 1 cwt 17 lbs, but many were larger and in semi-permanent camps could include stone-built chimneys. 'Bell'-tents were conical, with a nine-foot pole and weighing 43 lbs;[184] designed to hold twelve men, three per company were issued to the British army in 1813, with at least twenty men to each, so that 'none could turn without the general consent, and the word "turn" given.'[185] 'Private tents' held five men, Adye's 'Common Infantry Tent' listed as having a seven-foot ridgepole and a weight of 27 lbs.[186] 'Fly'-tents with an extended 'roof' were similar. 'Laboratory tents' were used for the making of munitions, Adye's dimensions being an eighteen-foot ridgepole, $14\frac{1}{2}$-foot high and weighing 3 cwt 24 lbs.[187]

Despite tented 'encampments' for home service, the use of tents on campaign was restricted by difficulties of transportation. Those issued by Britain in 1813 were prone to

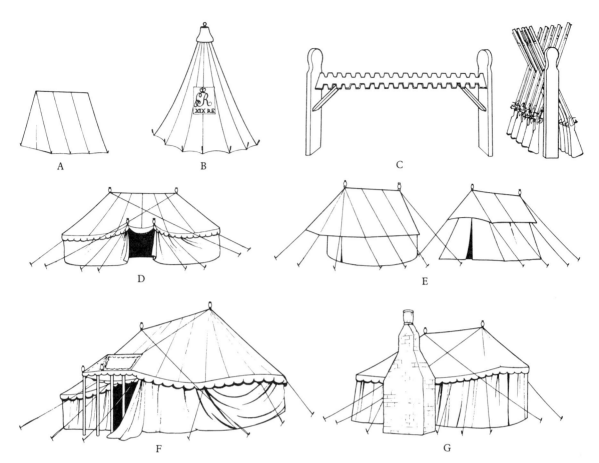

Fig. 100. Various tents. A. 'Private Tent'; B. Bell tent, 1801; C. Horse for supporting firelocks; D. Tent 'chiefly calculated for Subalterns'; E. 'Fly Tents'; F. Field officers' 'Marquis'; G. 'Marquis' with chimney.

blowing away in high winds and collapsing like 'clammy winding-sheets'[188] in wet weather. Prior to these tents, Britain had copied the Portuguese, whose military blankets had loops at the corners which allowed them to be assembled into three- or two-man shelters; Wellington ordered that British blankets should be similarly adapted. France was so reluctant to use tents (apart from those belonging to officers) that quantities of captured Prussian tents were cut up for bandages.

The French, however, excelled in the construction of huts, camps resembling little wooden towns complete with thatched or tiled roofs, glazed windows and even gardens, every hut with its tables, chairs and cooking utensils. Those at Nivelle were found by the British to have 'their green blinds over their little lattice windows; their neat little fire-

places, bedsteads of green boughs, shelves for their prog, and arm-racks, so like the natty Frenchman in camp.'[189] The British built similar huts, constructed of 'Two upright posts, about seven feet high, with forked ends ... planted in the ground about fifteen feet asunder. On these was placed a ridge-pole, or roof-tree, against which other poles were placed on each side in a slanting position, so as to form the frame of a roof. The whole was then covered with pine branches, or heath, broom, or straw. One end was closed up with poles placed nearly close together, and stuffed in the joins with grass or moss. The other end, which was left open at the entrance, had for a door a moveable screen of wicker-work.'[190] One such hut built by the British 51st in the Bois de Boulogne in 1815 was so large that it was named 'The British Hotel'! Even more substantial dwellings were constructed by the

Fig. 101. Left Above: *Austrian troops in camp. Print after J. A. Klein.*

Fig. 102. Left Below: *Cossacks in bivouac. Print after J. A. Klein.*

Fig. 103. Above: *A typical scene from Napoleon's campaigns: the Emperor works amid the bivouac of the Guard Grenadiers. Print after Raffet.*

Highlanders, trenched and with adequate drainage, and roofed 'more substantially than many of our Highland bothies....'[191]

But even veteran bivouackers could not alleviate all the miseries of campaigning; they had to be philosophical, like Charles Napier:

'I make no apologies for the dirt of this note; for flead, bugged, centipeded, beetled, lizarded and earwigged, cleanliness is known to me only by name. Moreover, a furze-bush makes a bad table for writing on, and a worse chair, when breeches are nearly worn out with glory, oh! oh!'[192]

CAMP-FOLLOWERS

A train of civilian 'camp-followers' trailed behind every army. Some were employed by the army – waggon-drivers and muleteers of the commissariat, the latter sometimes brigands in disguise (particularly during the Peninsular War when each British battalion employed about twenty or thirty). Other non-establishment personnel were the servants and grooms employed by some officers, in addition to the batman usually allocated from the ranks.

Many wives followed an army, including some officers' ladies who became as famous

Fig. 104.   A cavalry camp in the field: Italian dragoons in the Russian campaign of 1812. (Print after Albrecht Adam).

as their husbands, like Mrs Dalbiac and Juana Smith who accompanied the British in the Peninsula. In British service, six wives per company (plus children) were allowed to accompany their husbands overseas, a number inevitably swelled as unofficial 'wives' were accumulated en route. They undertook the company's washing, cooking, etc., and were so prized that any widow could expect a dozen proposals of marriage before her deceased husband was even buried. The hardships borne by these women on campaign, particularly in retreat like those to Corunna and from Moscow, are difficult to comprehend; devoid of official assistance, their plight was desperate. Camp-followers posed a strategic problem, blocking roads and impeding movement, plundering and disrupting discipline. Active Provost-Marshal or not, the camp-followers 'stuck to the army like bricks.'[193]

Sutlers often accompanied an army, selling food, alcohol and tobacco from carts or muleback. In French service they included 'vivandières' or 'cantinières', women attached to particular units of which their husband was often a member, often distinguished by quasi-military uniform and a spirit-barrel slung over the shoulder. They often followed their regiments into action, encouraging, helping the wounded and handing out cups of brandy gratis, saying, like those of the 4th Line and 26th Light Infantry at Austerlitz, 'Pay me tomorrow.' Inevitably some were killed, like Marie Tête-du-bois of the 1st Grenadiers of the Imperial Guard at Waterloo, whose regiment erected a simple wooden cross bearing the inscription: '. . . dead on the

Fig. 105.   French prisoners of war with a Hungarian guard (right). Print after J. A. Klein.

field of honour ... Passerby, whoever you may be, salute Maria,'[194] a fitting tribute to all female camp-followers whose tribulations have gone unrecognized by all except those with whom they marched.

A few women actually fought in the Napoleonic Wars, some enlisting as men to follow a husband or sweetheart and some, like Madame de Bennes, to fight for a cause. This aristocratic French lady enlisted, *not* disguised as a man, in the Damas Legion, an émigré unit in British service, 'in defence of her religion and her King'[195] and to avenge her husband, killed by Republicans in 1793. After several campaigns she was captured at Quiberon, ordered to be shot, but escaped to England to fight again! Other female 'soldiers' – a few civilian volunteer companies – ostensibly trained with arms, using the occasion simply to exhibit their elegant costume 'à la Amazone'; dresses styled on military uniforms were highly fashionable for a time, until the novelty wore off.

DESERTION

Desertion was the bane of every army. Some rogues enlisted and deserted regularly simply to collect enlistment-bounties; in 1787 a British deserter was hanged for absconding and re-enlisting forty-nine times. On campaign enormous numbers would slip away after a defeat or during harsh service, a favourite trick being to accompany wounded men to the rear, as many as ten or a dozen men helping each casualty to the dressing-station, and only re-joining their unit after the battle. Others deserted to become brigands, like the notorious Frenchman 'Marshal Stockpot' who led a multi-national gang during the Peninsular War until caught and shot.

There was little political defection without orders from higher command (though whole regiments deserted en masse at times, for example the 2nd Nassau Regiment and Frankfurt Battalion which marched over to the British in 1813), though there was a steady trickle of impressed Germans leaving the French army. William Warre saw one such group, captured at Jena and conscripted into French service, deserting to the British in May 1810:

'... remarkably fine men ... but they complain of never being paid, and that the French treat them like canaille. Nor have they enough to eat ... they told me they had rather serve us than the enemies of their country....'[196]

Conscripted troops were usually more prone to desertion than volunteers, for example the thousand impressed peasants and convicts sent from Naples to Spain in 1810, half deserting even before reaching the Pyrenees. The greatest desertion was amongst the inferior types of 'foreign corps', like the Chasseurs Britanniques of the British army, an émigré unit diluted by ill-assorted foreigners who fought well but could not be trusted with 'outpost' duty due to their partiality for desertion. A Court-Martial of October 1812 was held on eighteen Chasseurs who had deserted en masse, sixteen Italians, a Swiss and a Croat. Others were seen in the French ranks at San Marcial, still wearing British uniform. The Brunswick Oels Jägers, also in British service, deserted so frequently that Leach of the 95th claimed that the British had but a lease on them, whilst Costello records how General Craufurd addressed them:

'... if any of those gentlemen have a wish to go over to the enemy, let them express it, and I will give my word of honour I will grant them a pass to that effect instantly, for we are better off without such.'[197]

The iniquitous practice of enlisting prisoners-of-war (who usually changed sides at the first opportunity) was used by many armies, from the British enlisted in the French 'Irish Legion', to the Russo-German Legion formed by Russia from German prisoners, to the so-called 'emigrés' enlisted by Britain during the Revolutionary Wars as being preferable to a protracted stay in prison-camp.

Though desertion was, in some armies, more the rule than the exception (for example the Spanish and Neapolitan), G. R. Gleig of the British 85th gave an interesting reason to account for a proportion of desertions: superstition. He believed the desertion-rate was higher when single sentries were posted near a corpse: 'I don't care for living men, but, for Godsake, sir, don't keep me beside *him*' as one remarked.[198]

REINFORCEMENTS

Different methods of reinforcement were used by various armies. France possessed a comparatively sophisticated system for supplying drafts of conscripts, illustrated by the order issued by Napoleon in November 1806 to Marshal Kellermann, commander of the Reserve Army (training-units and dépôt battalions), requesting between 8,000 and 10,000 conscripts.

Eight provisional battalions were formed, each around a company of a third battalion of a regiment of the Grande Armée, to which nucleus conscripts of eight to ten days' training were added, their training continuing en route to the army during which march they were organized into companies, battalions and provisional regiments. On arrival the provisional units were broken up and the men drafted as required, a practice which ensured that every unit maintained a hard corps of experienced troops. During the 1806–07 campaign Kellermann despatched 73,624 men and 9,559 horses, in addition to 78,832 men and 9,747 horses from regimental depôts. The estimated time required to train an adequate soldier was an optimistic one month.

The alternative system of reinforcing, as practised by the British for example, was less effective: throughout the Peninsular War a steady flow of new battalions replaced those depleted by campaigning, some regiments being thus totally inexperienced, prompting correspondence like the following from

Wellington in June 1813:

'The new regiments are, as usual, the worst of all. The –th —— —— are a disgrace to the name of soldier, in action as well as elsewhere; and I propose to draft their horses from them, and to send the men to England, if I cannot get the better of them in any other manner.'[199]

Reinforcements to serving battalions travelled separately from Britain, varying between a handful to 100 men in the charge of inexperienced subalterns who frequently had difficulty in delivering their drafts. One young officer was court-martialled for delivering only twenty-nine out of forty-one men, and another whose twenty men had sold fourteen of their blankets.

Units becoming so weak as to be unable to act in the field were sometimes formed with other such into a 'provisional battalion'; several were used by the British in the Peninsula. France used similar provisional units in Spain for convoy-escort, taking a squad from several corps to avoid seriously depleting any one. Stragglers and recovered invalids could similarly be formed into provisional units until they re-joined their own corps; for example the British 2nd Battalion of Detachments which fought at Talavera had one company of 92nd Highlanders and others from the 42nd, 79th, 91st and 95th Rifles. Some provisional units became permanent, for example, the French 13th Cuirassiers, originally the 1st Provisional Heavy Cavalry consisting of detachments from the 1st, 2nd and 3rd Cuirassiers and 1st and 2nd Carabiniers.

PRISONERS-OF-WAR

Prisoners-of-war were accommodated in camps erected for the purpose, prisons or occasionally 'hulks', decrepit ships moored permanently offshore and inevitably foul. There were other ways, however, which relieved the captors of the duty of providing guards. Prisoners could be encouraged to change sides, a doubtful policy but one used by a number of nations. Secondly, prisoners could be released on 'parole', allowing them to be sent home if they gave their word of honour not to serve against their captors for a specified period. An example of parole-breaking occurred in the Vendée, when the paroled French Army of Mayence was sent to suppress the Vendéan rebels who claimed alliance with the captors of the 'Mayençais', the conditions of parole being that they should not take the field against any Allied troops; the Republicans claimed that the Vendéans were internal rebels, against whom the parole did not apply. The Vendéans themselves, unable to accommodate prisoners, released all they took on parole, shaving the prisoners' heads to indicate their parole and to signify that they could expect death if captured a second time. Prisoners could be redeemed, or released from parole, by 'exchange', the mutual agreement to swap man for man and rank for rank.

MUSIC

Music played an important part in Napoleonic warfare, most significantly for the transmission of orders in the field by infantry drum and cavalry trumpet. It was the most vital for light infantry, where troops in skirmish order might be out of range of voice or signalling-whistles. Various types of light infantry 'bugle' were used, including hunting-horns, large 'waldhorns' by Germans and even animal-horns. Cooper's manual (1806) claimed that 'A good bugle may be heard at the distance of three miles,'[200] and though Cooper included drum-calls in his book light infantry invariably used the handier bugle. A wide range of calls existed, not only the essential 'Advance', 'Retreat', 'Halt', 'Cease Firing', etc., but such detailed instructions as 'Run', 'Fire', 'Extend', 'Close', 'Lie Down', 'Call in Skirmishers', etc., as well as ordinary calls like 'Rouse', 'Drill', 'Fatigue', and 'Officers' Dinner'.

Regimental bands were usually regarded as separate from the drums and fifes, ranging in members from five to fifty-odd, with non-combatants or even civilians hired by the battalion commander in some armies. Instruments included keyless trumpets, French horns, keyless harmony-horns and trombones (the latter often with gargoyle-heads) among the brass, clarinettes, hautbois, huge bassoons and curved 'serpents' among the woodwinds; plus fifes, flutes and a number of percussion

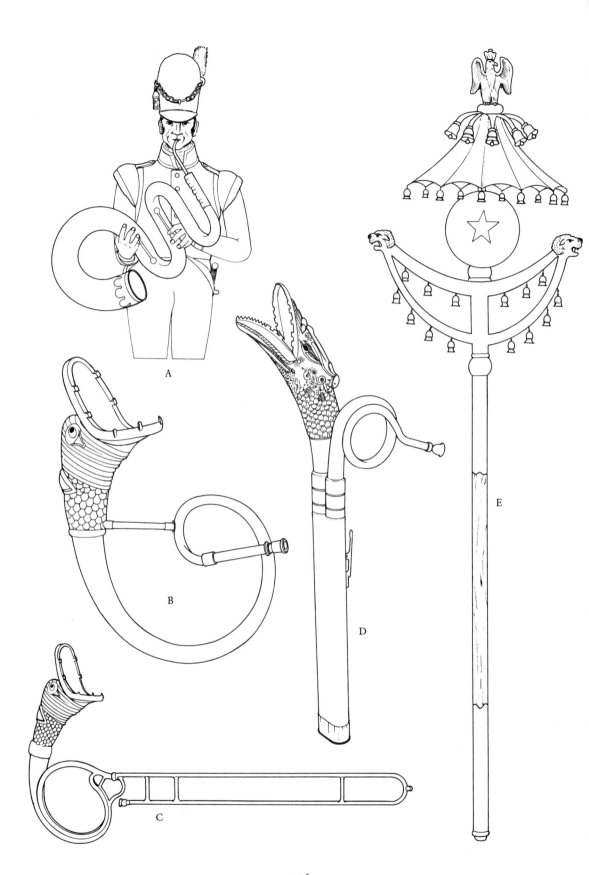

A

B

C

D

E

instruments ranging from side-drums to 'base' drums (wider than the modern type), kettle-drums (large ones for mounted bands), tambourines, cymbals and 'jingling johnnies' or 'chapeaux chinois', ornamental poles hung with bells which tinkled when shaken or when the upper section was rotated by a handle. The three latter instruments were often played by negroes dressed in outlandish oriental costume. Instruments like fifes and triangles were sometimes played by small children, though the popular idea of the 'drummer boy' is not exactly true: many, particularly French, were adults and seasoned campaigners.

'Military music' reached a peak in France, Napoleon encouraging its playing as a morale-booster; for example he gave LeBrun and Rouget de Lisle the daunting task of composing 'a hymn based on a familiar tune like that of the "Marseillaise" or the "Chant du Départ" which must contain sentiments for any and all circumstances of war.'[201] French bands played their troops along the march and right into action, drummers often suffering severe losses beating out the 'Pas de Charge' (known as 'Old Trousers' to the British). Indeed, drum-majors like Sénot of the Imperial Guard became more famous than many generals!

British bands were usually less involved in the fighting than the French, the musicians sometimes helping to evacuate casualties, but only rarely (like the 48th's band at Talavera) having to join in the fighting. In general their music was less 'martial' than that of the French, though 'The British Grenadiers' and 'Rule Britannia' were always popular. 'The Downfall of Paris' was a universal favourite, the tune originally the anarchist 'Ça Ira' of the French Revolution, banned by Napoleon but popular with Prussian, Austrian and Russian bands. Traditionally its first non-French performance was at Famars (1793) when the colonel of the British 14th exhorted his musicians to copy what the French were playing so that they might be beaten 'to their own damned tune.'[202] With 'La Carmagnole' and 'La Marseillaise', 'Ça Ira' was the most popular battle-song of the Revolution. Other tunes were 'borrowed': the British 31st played a catchy French tune known as 'Bonaparte's March' after they recruited two French deserters into their band in 1813, and similarly 'Le Sentinel': written by an Austrian, popular with the French and adopted by the British in the Peninsula.

As well as providing appropriate music for solemn occasions (the most moving of all perhaps the playing by the British 79th of 'To the Land of the Leal' as the cortège of the popular Spanish general La Romana passed through Cartaxo in 1811), the regimental band's main function was as a morale-booster. In battle it could fire the blood (Coignet thought the French Imperial Guard band at Austerlitz 'enough to make a paralytic move forward',[203] and perhaps distract the men from their likely fate; at Geldermalsen (1795) Lord Cathcart is reputed to have shouted to the British 28th just as they came under fire: 'Where is your band, sir? Now is the time for it to play.'[204] At Tarifa (1811) the Irish 87th repelled a French attack with their band playing behind them, first the rousing 'Garryowen' (later immortalized as Custer's signature-tune) and, as the attack was repelled, 'St Patrick's Day'. More menacing was the tune played by the Liddesdale volunteers as they marched to face the reported 'invasion' in 1804, an intimidating song from reiving days:

> 'Oh wha daur meddle wi' me?
> An' wha daur meddle wi' me?
> My name is wee Jock Elliott,
> An' wha daur meddle wi' me?'[205]

German bands accompanied singing, on the march, in bivouac, and in action. British observers wrote with delight about German music: 'They were marching in columns ... and the men in front singing choruses of the most pleasing description ... there can be no doubt of its beneficial influence ...';[206]

Fig. 106. Musical instruments. A. Serpent; B. Bucin; C. Trombone with Bucin head; D. Bassoon; E. Jingling Johnny or 'Chapeau Chinois'.

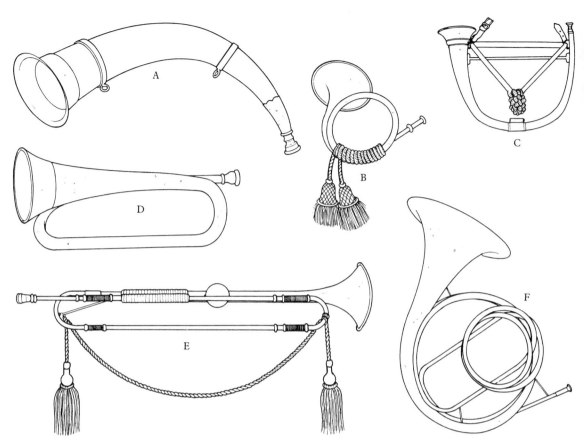

Fig. 107. Bugles and horns. A. British Rifle horn of cow-horn and silver; B. French horn;
C. Prussian horn; D. Light Infantry bugle; E. Cavalry trumpet; F. Harmony horn.

'It was not the least delightful of our pleasures to listen to the glees of the German riflemen....'[207] Both bands and singers – particularly those of the King's German Legion – were far more proficient than those of other nations. A great favourite was the stirring 'Ein Schifflein sah ich fahren' ('I saw a small ship sailing'), later given French words and as 'La Parisienne' becoming the song of the 1830 Revolution and being adopted by the Foreign Legion. The Germans also sang in action; for example, the Prussians raised Luther's 'A Mighty Fortress is Our God' as they pushed into the blazing shambles of Plançenoit, whilst an officer of the Allied army at Leipsig remembered how his men marched into action signing 'Heil dir im Siegerkrantz!', the old Prussian national anthem sung to the tune of 'God Save the Queen'. The unit came under shell-fire, but '... this hostile greeting only made us sing louder our hymn of war and the Fatherland....'[208]

Singing cheered other nations as well; at Barrosa Col. Browne heartened his provisional battalion with a solo rendition of 'Heart of Oak', and at Waterloo an anonymous Scot sang 'Bruce's address', appropriately modified: 'See approach Napoleon's pow'r.'[209] The Spanish marched to a half-song, half-chant, lead-singers beginning and the remainder joining in the chorus. 'A la guerra, Espagñoles' and the many anti-French

Fig. 109. Right: *British hussar trumpeters. Contemporary print*

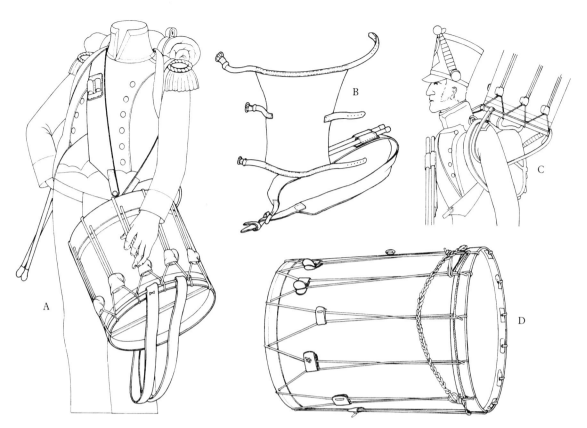

Fig. 108. Drums. A. French drummer showing the method of carriage; B. Drum belt and apron; C. Method of slinging drum on the march; D. British bass drum.

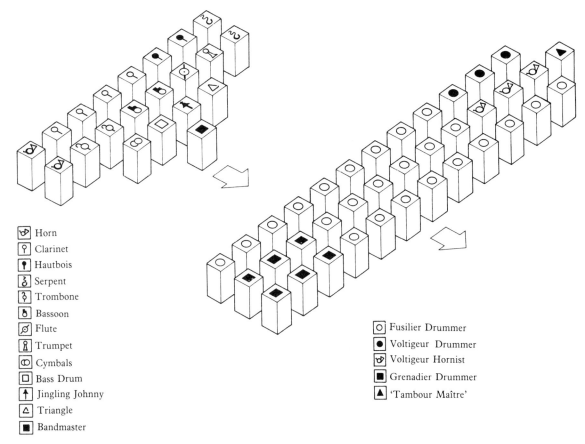

Horn
Clarinet
Hautbois
Serpent
Trombone
Bassoon
Flute
Trumpet
Cymbals
Bass Drum
Jingling Johnny
Triangle
Bandmaster

Fusilier Drummer
Voltigeur Drummer
Voltigeur Hornist
Grenadier Drummer
'Tambour Maître'

Fig. 110. Left: *Diagram of the layout of a French 20 piece military band.*
Right: *Diagram of the corps of drums of a three battalion French Infantry regiment drilling as a body.*

songs or 'cancioneiros' were popular, including one incorporating the catch-phrases of their allies and enemies:

> 'Viva los Ingleses que dicen
> God damn you.
> Mueran los que dicen
> Sacré nom de Dieu.'[210]

Portuguese bands accompanied their men in song, most popularly 'Vencer o morir' ('Conquer or Die').

Highland bagpipers probably had more morale-effect than all other bands put together. Not carried on official regimental strength, pipers were privately-engaged to fulfil their traditional honour of playing their clansmen into action, and thus scorned the status of regimental bandsmen, one referring to a drummer: 'Shall a little rascal that beats upon a sheepskin take the right hand of me

that am a musician?'[211] Consequently, many feats of heroism were performed by pipers, like George Clark of the 71st, wounded at Vimiero but continuing to play saying: 'Deil ha' my saul if ye shall want music!';[212] or John McLauchlan of the 74th, who played his pipes over the wall of Badajos and fell at Vittoria; or Kenneth Mackay of the 79th who walked *outside* a square at Waterloo playing 'Cogad na sith' ('Peace or War'). Pipe-music inflamed the Highlanders on going into action; surely the most appropriate battle-music in history was 'Hey Johnny Cope, are ye waukin' yet?' as the French were turned out of their beds at Arroyo dos Molinos (the song was later modified to name the surprised French general – 'Hey Monsieur Gérard, are ye waukin' yet?').[213] And at Maya 'The haughs of Cromdale' caused the 92nd to charge a much-superior French force who '... panic-struck at their audacity wheeled about and ran.'[214] At the Cape of Good Hope in 1806, Highlanders not only played the pipes but even danced a reel, causing both the English and the retiring enemy to regard them with 'utter astonishment.'[215]

Totally different was the music played by naval landing-parties; at San Sebastian British 'tars' in the trenches fiddled 'Heart of Oak', answering each French shell with 'Jack's Alive'! A good regimental band was invaluable for recruiting purposes, but in the field and under fire it could raise morale to an amazing level, be it 'La Marseillaise' or 'Chanson de l'Oignon', 'Heart of Oak' or 'The Young May Moon'. As Robert E. Lee was to remark, 'Without music we wouldn't have any army.'

Musicians usually wore uniforms more costly and distinctive than their pedestrian fellows, often 'reversed colours' (jackets of the regimental facing-colour), though these attracted too much attention from the enemy; such practices were therefore officially forbidden by Britain in 1812, an order which had but little effect.

176. Quoted in Glover, *Wellington's Army*, p. 24.
177. This and following statistics from Glover, *Wellington's Army*, pp. 37–9.
178. Stanhope, *Conversations with the Duke of Wellington*, p. 18, quoted in Oman, *Wellington's Army*, p. 217.
179. Quoted in Duffy, *Borodino*, p. 42.
180. Quoted in Glover, *Wellington's Army*, p. 75.
181. Stevenson, Sergt. J., *Twenty-One Years in the British Foot Guards*, London, 1830; quoted in Glover, *Wellington's Army*, p. 69.
182. *Souvenirs de Guerre du Général Baron Pouget*, Paris, 1895; quoted in Duffy, *Austerlitz*, p. 67.
183. Grose, II, p. 233.
184. Adye, pp. 262–3.
185. Cooper, *Rough Notes*, p. 146.
186. Adye, p. 262.
187. Ibid.
188. Lt-Col. Gurwood, quoted in Brett-James, *Life in Wellington's Army*, p. 94.
189. Bell, pp. 99–100.
190. Leslie, p. 83.
191. Sergt. Anton: Fitchett, pp. 248–9.
192. Napier, *Life of C. J. Napier*, I, p. 164.
193. Bell, I, pp. 74–5.
194. Lachouque and Brown, p. 483.
195. *London Chronicle*, 10 December 1795.
196. Warre, pp. 120–21.
197. Costello, pp. 46–7.
198. Gleig, pp. 106–7.
199. Wellington to Earl Bathurst, 29 June 1813; 'Despatches', X, p. 473.
200. Cooper, p. 98.
201. Quoted in Winstock, p. 142.
202. Quoted ibid., pp. 106–7.
203. Coignet, p. 124.
204. Sir H. Murray, *Memoir of Capt. A. S. Murray*, 1859, p. 51.
205. Sir Walter Scott, *The Antiquary*, notes, p. 378, Routledge Kenilworth edn., n.d.
206. Anon, *Memoirs of the late War*, 1831, p. 245; quoted in Winstock, p. 142.
207. Quoted in Winstock, p. 141.
208. Lieut. Kretzchmer, quoted in Brett-James, *Europe Against Napoleon*, pp. 182–3.
209. Hope, p. 423.
210. Quoted in Winstock, p. 145.
211. Quoted ibid., p. 137.
212. Lt-Col. L. B. Oatts, *Proud Heritage*, Nelson, London, 1952, I, p. 72.
213. A. Clerk, *Memoir of Col. John Cameron*, 1858, p. 51.
214. Hope, p. 179.
215. Quoted in Winstock, pp. 139–40.

Fig. 111.   Skirmishing: French grenadiers drive off cavalry. Print after Horace Vernet.

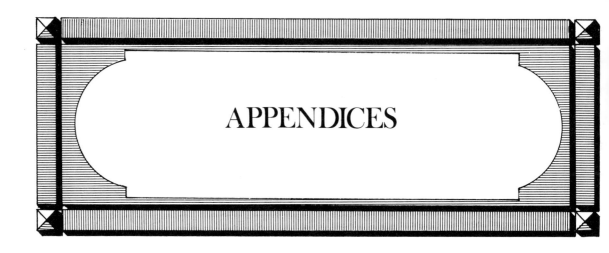

APPENDICES

THE REVOLUTIONARY CALENDAR

Western Europe used the Gregorian Calendar throughout the Napoleonic Wars (the Julian Calendar was used in Russia until 1917; in 1812, for example, it was twelve days behind the Gregorian); but France introduced the Revolutionary Calendar in 1792, re-naming the months and numbering the years 'I', 'II' etc. from the birth of the Republic. Years ran from September to August, months being:

Vendémiaire	(September)
Brumaire	(October)
Frimaire	(November)
Nivôse	(December)
Pluvôise	(January)
Ventôse	(February)
Germinal	(March)
Floréal	(April)
Prairial	(May)
Messidor	(June)
Thermidor	(July)
Fructidor	(August)

The years were numbered:

I	1792–93
II	1793–94
III	1794–95
IV	1795–96
V	1796–97
VI	1797–98
VII	1798–99
VIII	1799–1800
IX	1800–01
X	1801–02
XI	1802–03
XII	1803–04
XIII	1804–05
XIV	1805; the Gregorian Calendar was reinstated in 1806.

UNITS OF MEASUREMENT

Adye lists the different measurements for the term 'pace':[216]

France and England: $2\frac{1}{2}$ feet per pace.
Five French royal feet = one geometrical pace

$$= 6.102 \text{ English feet}$$
$$= 5.6719 \text{ Rhineland feet.}$$

One Toise = 6.395 English feet.

And different measurements for the term 'mile':[217]

One English mile	= 868	geometrical paces	
One Swedish ,,	= 5,761	,,	,,
One Swiss ,,	= 4,512	,,	,,
One Danish ,,	= 4,071	,,	,,
One German ,,	= 4,000	,,	,,
One Dutch ,,	= 3,158	,,	,,
One French league	= 2,400	,,	,,
One Spanish ,,	= 2,286	,,	,,
One Scottish ,,	= 1,500	,,	,,
One Italian mile	= 1,000	,,	,,
One Russian verst	= 575	,,	,,

ARTILLERY TABLES

The following tables are extracted from Adye, in which manual many more comprehensive details of specification and performance can be found.

I. *Ranges of Brass Guns with one shot, 1793.*

| | Charge | | Point- | | To first graze of shot (yds) | | | |
Nature	lbs	ozs	blank	1°	2°	3°	4°	5°
Heavy 24-pdr	8	0	473	781	1,032	1,405	1,585	1,710
Medium 24-pdr	8	0	488	757	1,103	1,425	1,557	1,745
Light 24-pdr	3	0	162	364	606	722		1,390
Medium 12-pdr	4	0		705	973	1,189		
Light 12-pdr	3	0		601	816	1,063		
Desagulier 6-pdr	2	0		646	966	1,325		
Six-feet 6-pdr	2	0		683	948	1,327		
Medium 6-pdr	2	0		775	1,003	1,444		
Reduced 6-pdr	2	0		642	976	1,150		
Five-feet 6-pdr	1	8		587	825	950		
Four ft 6 ins 6-pdr	1	8		628	804	991		
Desagulier 3-pdr	1	0		679	883	918		

2. *Ranges of French Brass Field Guns in French weights and measures.*

| | Elevation | | |
Nature	Deg.	Min.	Range in Toises
12-pdr (4 lbs charge)	—	58	300
	1	3	350
	1	39	400
	1	49	450
	1	56	480
8-pdr (2½ lbs charge)	1	24	350
	1	51	400
	2	8	450
	2	24	480
4-pdr (1½ lbs charge)	—	58	250
	1	20	300
	1	40	350
	2	0	400
	2	20	450
	2	40	480

3. *Ranges with a heavy 5½-inch howitzer, 1793.*

Elevation (degrees)	Range to first graze (yds) (2-lb charge)	Range to first graze (yds) (3-lb charge)	Elevation (degrees)	Range to first graze (yds) (2-lb charge)	Range to first graze (yds) (3-lb charge)
1	453	479	7	1,449	1,577
2	595	722	8	1,355	1,721
3	666	921	9	1,585	1,801
4	847	1,000	10	1,853	1,791
5	957	1,325	11	1,793	
6	1,173	1,530	12	1,686	

Extreme range from 1,400 to 1,900 yards (2-lb charge), 1,400 to 2,000 (3-lb charge)

Note: 'The Germans do not name their shells from the diameter of the bore which receives them, but from the weight of a stone ball that fits the same bore as the shell. Thus a 7 lbs howitzer admits a stone ball of that weight; the shell for this weighs 15 lbs and answers to the English 5½ inch. The 30 lbs howitzer shell weighs 60 lbs. and is rather more than 8 inches in diameter.'[218]

4. *Ranges with Land Service Mortars at 45° elevation.*

Nature	Charge	Range (yds)
13-inch iron	14 ozs	245
,, ,,	8 lbs 0 ozs	2,706
,, brass	2 lbs 2 ozs	862
,, ,,	4 lbs 8 ozs	1,324
10-inch iron	8 ozs	235
,, ,,	4 lbs 8 ozs	2,536
,, brass	1 lb 10 ozs	823
,, ,,	2 lbs 8 ozs	1,215
8-inch iron	5 ozs	225
,, ,,	1 lb 9 ozs	1,720
,, brass	10 ozs 8 dr	580
,, ,,	17 ozs 8 dr	1,062
5½-inch ,,	1 oz 8 dr	155
,, ,,	6 oz 0 dr	1,175

5. *Charges for Field Guns.*

Nature	Charge for roundshot (lbs)	Charge for canister (lbs)
Medium and heavy 12-pdrs	4	3½
Light 12-pdrs	3	3
Desagulier 6-pdr	2½	2
Medium 6-pdr	2	2
Light 6-pdr	1½	1¼
Heavy 3-pdr	1	1
Light 3-pdr	12 ozs	—

'The charge for battering guns is ⅓ the weight of the round shot, for round shot, and ¼ of it for case shot ... By experiments made at Woolwich in March, 1801, it is recommended ... on service, the charges of field ordnance with round shot, shall be reduced to the usual quantities for case shot.'[219]

6. *Marks on powder barrels.*

'The different sorts of powder are distinguished by the following marks on the heads of the barrels.

No. ½ Cylinder
L G

No. 2 Cylinder
S G

No. 3 Cylinder
F G

} – Marked in Red: denotes powder entirely made of the cylinder charcoal and is that which is now always used on service.

S A   –   The dust from No. 3.
R A   –   For rifle arms.
L G   –   in white ... being a mixed powder, is not so uniform as the other and is
therefore generally used in filling shells.

L G or F G   –   in blue, is powder made of pit-coal.
R S   –   in yellow, is restoved.'[220]

7.   *Composition of match.*

'The slow match used by the English is made by contract: one yard of it will burn about
8 hours. The French slow match is usually made by soaking light twisted white-rope for
3 days in a strong lye. It burns about 3 feet in 6 hours.

'Slow match was made at Gibraltar, during the last siege, in the following manner: eight
ounces of saltpetre were put into a gallon of water, and just made to boil over a slow fire;
strong blue paper was then wetted with the liquor, and hung to dry. When dry, each sheet
was rolled up tight, and the outward edge pasted down, to prevent its opening; half a sheet,
thus prepared, will burn 3 hours.
'Quick Match Compositions:

Worsted Match		*Cotton Match*	
Worsted	10 oz	Cotton	1 lb 12 oz
Mealed powder	10 lbs	Saltpetre	1 lb 8 oz
Spirits of wine	3 pints	Mealed Powder	10 lbs
Water	3 pints	Spirits of wine	2 quarts
Isinglass	$\frac{1}{2}$ pint	Water	3 pints

'Note – The French have lately made their slow match by soaking the rope in a solution of
sugar of lead and rain water: in the proportion of $\frac{3}{4}$ of an ounce of sugar of lead to one pint
of water: and this they esteem as preferable to the old sort.'[221]

ARTILLERY TACTICS, AFTER ADYE

'The artillery of the park is generally divided into brigades of 4 or 6 pieces, and a reserve, according to the force and extent of the front of an army. The reserve must be composed of about 1/6th of the park, and must be placed behind the first line. If the front of the army be extensive, the reserve must be divided.

'The following are the principal rules for the movements and positions of the brigades of artillery:

'In a defensive position, the guns of the largest caliber must be posted in those points, from whence the enemy can be discovered at the greatest distance, and from which may be seen the whole extent of his front.

'In an offensive position, the weakest points of the line must be strengthened by the largest calibers, and the most distant from the enemy; those heights on which the army is advancing

may rest its flanks, be secured by them, and from which the enemy may be fired upon obliquely.

'The guns should be placed as much as possible under cover; this is easily done upon heights, by keeping them so far back that the muzzles are only to be seen over them: by proper attention many situations may be found of which advantage may be taken for this purpose, such as banks, ditches, &c. every where to be met with.

'A battery in the field should never be discovered by the enemy till the very moment it is to open. The guns may be masked by being a little retired; or by being covered by troops, particularly cavalry.

'To enable the commanding officer of artillery to choose the proper positions for his field batteries, he should of course be made acquainted, with the effect intended to be produced; with the troops that are to be supported; that he may place his artillery so as to support, but not incommode the infantry; nor take up such positions with his guns, as would be more advantageously occupied by the line. That he may not place his batteries too soon, nor too much exposed; that he may cover his front and his flanks, by taking advantage of the ground; and that he may not venture too far out of the protection of the troops, unless some very decided effect is to be obtained thereby.

'The guns must be so placed as to produce a cross fire upon the position of the enemy, and upon all the ground which he must pass over in an attack.

'They must be separated into many small batteries, to divide the fire of the enemy; while the fire from all these batteries, may at any time be united to produce a decided effect against any particular points.

'These points are the débouchés of the enemy, the heads of their columns, and the weakest points in the front. In an attack of the enemy's position, the cross fire of the guns must become direct, before it can impede the advance of the troops; and must annoy the enemy's positions nearest to the point attacked, when it is no longer safe to continue the fire upon that point itself.

'The shot from artillery should always take an enemy in the direction of its greatest dimension; it should therefore take a line obliquely or in flank; but a column in front.

'The artillery should never be placed in such a situation, that it can be taken by an enemy's battery obliquely, or in flank, or in the rear; unless a position under these circumstances, offers every prospect of producing a most decided effect, before the guns can be destroyed or placed hors de combat.

'The most elevated positions are not the best for artillery, the greatest effects may be produced from a height of 30 or 40 yards at a distance of about 600; and about 16 yards of height to 200 of distance.

'Positions in the rear of the line are bad for artillery, because they alarm the troops, and offer a double object to the fire of the enemy.

'Positions which are not likely to be shifted, but from whence an effect may be produced during the whole of an action, are to be preferred; and in such positions a low breastwork of 2 or 3 feet high may be thrown up, to cover the carriages.

'Artillery should never fire against artillery, unless the enemy's troops are covered, and his artillery exposed; or unless your troops suffer more from the fire of his guns, than his troops do from yours.

'Never abandon your guns till the last extremity. The last discharges are the most destructive; they may perhaps be your salvation, and crown you with glory.'[222]

216. Adye, p. 210.
217. Ibid., pp. 189–90.
218. Ibid., p. 252.
219. Ibid., p. 81.

220. Ibid., pp. 164–5.
221. Ibid., pp. 177–8.
222. Ibid., pp. 24–7.

BIBLIOGRAPHY

A large proportion of the books which have been written about the Napoleonic Wars have some bearing, however slight, upon the subject of weapons and equipment and their employment in action. The bibliography below lists some of the most significant concerning weapons and armies, but does not include those concerned primarily with uniforms and organisation; for these, bibliographies may be found in the author's *Napoleonic Source Book* (London 1990) and in the reprints by Arms & Armour Press of *Uniforms of the Peninsular War* (1995), *Uniforms of Napoleon's Russian Campaign* (1995) and *Uniforms of Waterloo* (1996). Also included below are those works mentioned in the footnotes. Wherever possible, English-language editions have been listed.

Adye, R.W., *The Bombardier and Pocket Gunner*, 2nd rev. edn., London 1802.

Anon., *A Manual for Volunteer Corps of Cavalry*, London 1803.

Anon., *A Manual for Volunteer Corps of Infantry*, London 1803.

Anon., *An Elucidation of Several Parts of His Majesty's Regulations for the Formations and Movements of Cavalry*, London 1808.

Anon., *Instructions and Regulations for the Formations and Movements of the Cavalry*, London 1803.

Anon., *Rules and Regulations for the Formation, Field-Exercise and Movements of His Majesty's Forces*, London 1792, rev. edn. 1798 (Sir David Dundas' drill).

Anon., *The Artillery Officer's Assistant*, Madras 1848

Anon., *The British Military Library or Journal, comprehending a Complete Body of Military Knowledge*, London 1799–1801.

Bailey, D. W., *British Military Longarms 1715-1865*, London 1986.

Baker, E., *Remarks on Rifle Guns*, 11th edn., London 1835.

Beaufroy, Capt. H. *Scloppetaria, or Considerations on the Nature and Use of Rifled Barrel Guns*, London 1808, r/p Richmond 1971. (Written under the *nom-de-plume* of 'A Corporal of Riflemen'.)

Bell, Maj.Gen. Sir George, *Rough Notes by an Old Soldier*, London 1867.

Blackmore, H. L. *British Military Firearms*, London 1961.

Blakeney, R., *A Boy in the Peninsular War*, ed. J. Sturgis, London 1899.

Bragge, W. *Peninsular Portrait: The Letters of Capt. William Bragge*, ed. S.A. Cassels, London 1963.

Brett-James, A. *Europe against Napoleon*, London 1970.

——, *Life in Wellington's Army*, London 1972.

——, *Wellington at War 1794-1815*, London 1961.

——, *1812*, London 1966.

Bugeaud, Marshal R.T., *Aperçus sur quelques détails de la guerre*, Paris 1846.

Chambers, Lt.Col. G. L., *Bussaco*, London 1910.

Chandler, D. G., *Dictionary of the Napoleonic Wars*, London 1979.

——, *The Campaigns of Napoleon*, London 1967. (Most significant modern study.)

Coignet, J.-R., *The Note-Books of Captain Coignet, Soldier of the Empire*, intro. Hon. Sir John Fortescue, London 1929.

Congreve, Sir William, *Details of the Rocket System*, London 1814.

Cooper, J. S. *Rough Notes of Seven Campaigns in Portugal, Spain, France and America*, Carlisle 1869, r/p 1914.

Cooper, Capt. T.. H., *A Practical Guide for the Light Infantry Officer*, London 1806, r/p London 1970.

Costello, E., *Memoirs of Edward Costello*, London 1857; r/p as *The Peninsular and Waterloo Campaigns: Edward Costello*, ed. A. Brett-James, London 1967

Darling, A. D., *Red Coat and Brown Bess*, Ottawa 1970.

Duffy, C., *Austerlitz*, London 1977.

——, *Borodino and the War of 1812*, London 1972.

——, *Fire and Stone: the Science of Fortress Warfare 1660–1860*, Newton Abbot 1975.

Dupuy, R . E ., and Dupuy, T . N ., *Encyclopedia of Military History*, London 1970.

Elting, Col. J. R., *Swords around a Throne: Napoleon's Grande Armée*, London 1989.(Very important modern study.)

Esposito, Brig.Gen. V. J., and Elting, Col. J. R., *A Military History and Atlas of the Napoleonic Wars*, London 1964. (Excellent collection of maps.)

Fitchett, W. H. *Wellington's Men*, London 1900.

Ffoulkes, C., and Hopkinson, E. C., *Sword, Lance and Bayonet*, Cambridge 1938, r/p New York 1967.

Gleig, Rev . G . R ., *The Subaltern*, Edinburgh 1872.

Glover, M., *The Peninsular War*, Newton Abbot 1974.

——, *Warfare in the Age of Bonaparte*, London 1980.

——, *Wellington as Military Commander*, London 1968.

——, *Wellington's Army in the Peninsula 1808–14*, Newton Abbot 1977.

Glover, R., *Peninsular Preparation: The Reform of the British Army 1795–1809*, Cambridge 1963.

Gooding, S. J., *An Introduction to British Artillery in North America*, Ottawa 1972.

Griffith, P., *Forward into Battle: Fighting Tactics from Waterloo to Vietnam*, Chichester 1981.

Griffith, P., *French Artillery*, London 1976.

Grose, F., *Military Antiquities*, London 1801.

Gross, Baron, *Duties of an Officer in the Field, and Principally of Light Troops*, London 1801.

Hanger, Col. G., *Reflections on the Menaced Invasion*, London 1804.

——, *To All Sportsmen*, London 1814.

Haythornthwaite, P. J. *Napoleon's Military Machine*, Tunbridge Wells 1988.

——, *The Armies of Wellington*, London 1994.

——, *The Napoleonic Source Book*, London 1990.

——, *Wellington's Military Machine*, Tunbridge Wells 1989.

Henegan, R., *Seven Years' Campaigning in the Peninsula and the Netherlands from 1808 to 1815*, London 1846.

Hicks, Maj. J. E., *French Military Weapons 1717–1938*, New Milford, Connecticut, 1964.

Hogg, I.V., *A History of Artillery*, London 1974.

Holmquist, B. M., and Gripstad, B., *Swedish Weaponry Since 1630*, Royal Army Museum, Sweden, 1982.

Hope, Lieut. J., *Military Memoirs of an Infantry Officer 1809–16*, London 1833.

Hughes, Maj.Gen. B. P., *British Smoothbore Artillery*, Harrisburg, Pennsylvania, 1969.

——, *Firepower: Weapons Effectiveness on the Battlefield 1630–1850*, London 1974.

——, *Open Fire: Artillery Tactics from Marlborough to Wellington*, Chichester 1983.

James, C., *The Regimental Companion*, London 1804.

Jones, Maj.Gen. Sir J. T.., *Journal of the Sieges carried on by the Army under the Duke of Wellington in Spain between the Years 1811 and 1814*, London 1846.

Kincaid, Sir John, *Adventures in the Rifle Brigade*, London 1830, and *Random Shots from* a *Rifleman*, London 1835, r/p in combined edn., London 1908.

Lachouque, H., and Brown, A. S. K., *The Anatomy of Glory*, London 1962. (History of Napoleon's Imperial Guard, with many contemporary illustrations.)

Lawrence, W., *The Autobiography of Sergeant William Lawrence,* ed. G. N. Bankes, London 1886, r/p Cambridge 1987.

Lavin, J. D., *A History of Spanish Firearms*, London 1965.

Le Mesurier, H., *A System for the British Commissariat*, London 1796; r/p as an appendix in R. Glover, *Peninsular Preparation.*

Leach, J., *Rough Sketches in the Life of an Old Soldier*, London 1831, r/p London 1986.

Leslie, Col., *Military Journal of Col. Leslie of Balquhain*, Aberdeen 1887.

Londonderry, Lieut.Gen. Marquess of, *Narrative of the Peninsular War*, London 1826.

——, *Narrative of the War in Germany and France in 1813 and 1814*, London 1830.

Macdonald, Capt. R. J., *History of the Dress of the Royal Artillery*, London 1899.

Marbot, A.-M., *The Memoirs of Baron de Marbot*, trans. A. J. Butler, London 1913.

Mason, R. O., *Pro Aris et Focis: Considerations of the Reasons that exist for Reviving the use of the Long Bow with the Pike*, London 1798, r/p with intro. by E. G. Heath, London 1970.

Mercer, Gen. A. C., *Journal of the Waterloo Campaign*, Edinburgh and London 1870.

Mollo, J., *Military Fashion*, London 1972.

Muller, W., *Elements of the Science of War*, London 1811.

Napier, W. F. P., *History of the War in the Peninsula*, London 1832–40.

——, *Life and Opinions of General Sir Charles Napier*, London 1857.

Napoleon, *The Confidential Correspondence of Napoleon Bonaparte with his Brother Joseph*, London 1855.

Nosworthy, B., *Battle Tactics of Napoleon and his Enemies*, London 1995.

Oman, Sir Charles, *History of the Peninsular War*, Oxford 1902–30.

Oman, Sir Charles, *Wellington's Army 1809–14*, London 1912.

Ottenfeld, R. von, and Teuber, O., *Die Oesterreichische Armee*, Vienna 1895.

Pakenham, T.., *The Year of Liberty: The Great Irish Rebellion of 1798*, London 1969.

Parquin, C., *Napoleon's Army: Charles Parquin*, ed. B. T.. Jones, London 1969.

Pasley, C. W., *Course of Military Instruction*, London 1817.

Peterson, H. L., *Round Shot and Rammers*, Harrisburg, Pennsylvania, 1969.

Petrie, F. L., *Napoleon and the Archduke Charles*, London 1909.

——, *Napoleon at Bay*, London 1914.

——, *Napoleon's Campaign in Poland 1806–1807*, London 1901.

——, *Napoleon's Conquest of Prussia 1806*, London 1907.

Porter, Sir Robert Ker, *Travelling Sketches in Russia and Sweden*, London 1808.

Priest, G., *The Brown Bess Bayonet 1720–1860*, Norwich 1986.

Quennevat, J. C., *Atlas de la Grande Armée*, Paris 1966.

——, *Les Vrais Soldats de Napoléon*, Paris 1968.

Richardson, R. G., *Larrey: Surgeon to Napoleon's Imperial Guard*, London 1974.

Robson, B., *Swords of the British Army*, London 1975.

Rogers, Col. H. C. B. *Napoleon's Army*, London 1974.

——, *The Mounted Troops of the British Army*, London 1959.

——, *Weapons of the British Soldier*, London 1960.

——, *Wellington's Army*, London 1979.

Ross, M. *Banners of the King: The War of the Vendée 1793*, London 1975.

Rothenberg, G. E., *Napoleon's Great Adversaries: The Archduke Charles and the Austrian Army 1792–1814*, London 1982.

——, *The Art of War in the Age of Napoleon*, London 1977.

Rousselot, L., *L'Armée Française*. (Series of plates.)

Rowlandson, T.., *Loyal Volunteers of London & Environs*, London 1799, r/p London 1972.

Shipp, J., *The Path of Glory*, ed. C. J. Stranks, London 1969.

Simmons, G., *A British Rifle Man*, ed. Lt. Col. W. Verner, London 1899.

Sutcliffe, S., *Martello Towers*, Newton Abbot 1972.

Tomkinson, Lt.Col. W., *Diary of a Cavalry Officer*, ed. J. Tomkinson, London 1895.

Tylden, Maj. G., *Horses and Saddlery*, London 1965.

United Service Journal. Published in the several decades after the end of the Napoleonic Wars, later as *Colburn's United Service Magazine*, this contains a number of articles concerning the utility and employment of various weapons, written by veterans of the Napoleonic Wars.

Verner, Lt.Col. W., *History and Campaigns of the Rifle Brigade 1809–13*, London 1919.

Wagner, E. *Cut and Thrust Weapons*, London 1967.

Warre, Sir William, *Letters from the Peninsula*, ed. E. Warre, London 1909.

Weller, J., *Wellington at Waterloo*, London 1967.

——, *Wellington in the Peninsula*, London 1962.

Wellington, Duke of, *Dispatches of Field Marshal the Duke of Wellington*, ed. J. Gurwood, London 1834–38.

——, *Supplementary Despatches and Memoranda of Field Marshal the Duke of Wellington*, ed. 2nd Duke of Wellington, London 1858–72.

Whately, R., *Historic Doubts Relative to Napoleon Bonaparte*, London 1819, 9th rev. edn. 1849.

Wilkinson-Latham, R. *British Artillery on Land and Sea 1790-1820*, Newton Abbot 1973.

——, *Swords and Bayonets*, London 1973.

——, *Swords in Colour*, Poole 1977.

Wilson, Sir Robert, *Brief Remarks on the Character and Composition of the Russian Army, and a Sketch of the Campaigns in Poland in the Years 1806 and 1807*, London 1810.

——, *General Wilson's Journal 1812–14*, ed. A. Brett-James, London 1964.

——, *Narrative of Events during the Invasion of Russia by Napoleon Bonaparte, and the Retreat of the French Army*, ed. Rev. H. Randolph, London 1860.

——, *Private Diaries of Travels . . . with the European Armies in the Campaigns of 1812, 1813, 1814*, ed. Rev. H. Randolph, London 1861.

Winstock, L., *Songs and Music of the Redcoats*, London 1970.

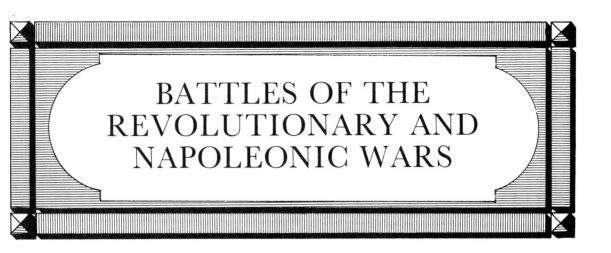

BATTLES OF THE REVOLUTIONARY AND NAPOLEONIC WARS

Note: In the following list, the names of commanders are sometimes those of generals in overall command, rather than actual battlefield commanders.

Date	Battle	Victors	Defeated
1792			
20 September	Valmy	French (Dumouriez/ Kellermann)	Austro-Prussians (Brunswick)
6 November	Jemappes	French (Dumouriez)	Austrians (Albert of Saxe-Teschen)
1793			
18 March	Neerwinden	Austrians (Saxe-Coburg)	French (Dumouriez)
21–23 May	Valenciennes	Austrians (Saxe-Coburg)	French (Custine)
6 September	Hondschoote	French (Houchard)	Anglo-Hanoverians (York)
13 September	Menin	French (Houchard)	Netherlandish (Orange)
15–16 October	Wattignies	French (Jourdan)	Austrians (Saxe-Coburg)
28–30 November	Kaiserslautern	Prussians (Brunswick)	French (Hoche)
22 December	Fröschwiller	French (Hoche)	Prussians (Brunswick)
26 December	Geisberg	French (Hoche)	Austrians (Wurmser)
1794			
24 April	Villers-en-Cauchies	Anglo-Austrians (Ott)	French
18 May	Tourcoing	French (Souham)	Allies (Saxe-Coburg)
26 June	Fleurus	French (Jourdan)	Allies (Saxe-Coburg)
1795			
16–20 July	Quiberon	French (Hoche)	French royalists/British (Puisaye and d'Hervilly)
29 October	Mainz	Austrians (Clerfayt)	French (Pichegru)
24 November	Loano	French (Massena)	Austro-Piedmontese (Wallis)
1796			
12 April	Montenotte	French (Bonaparte)	Austrians (Beaulieu)
14 April	Millesimo	French (Augereau)	Austro-Piedmontese (Provera)

1796 *continued*

14–15 April	Dego	French (Bonaparte)	Austrians (Beaulieu)
16–17 April	Ceva	Austro-Piedmontese (Colli)	French (Augereau)
21 April	Mondovi	French (Bonaparte)	Piedmontese (Colli)
8 May	Fombio	French (Bonaparte)	Austrians (Beaulieu)
10 May	Lodi	French (Bonaparte)	Austrians (Beaulieu)
30 May	Borghetto	French (Bonaparte)	Austrians (Beaulieu)
16 June	Wetzlar	Austrians (Charles)	French (Jourdan)
9 July	Malsch	*Inconclusive encounter between French (Moreau) and Austrians (Charles)*	
3 August	Lonato	French (Bonaparte)	Austrians (Quasdanovich)
5 August	Castiglione	French (Bonaparte)	Austrians (Wurmser)
24 August	Amberg	Austrians (Charles)	French (Jourdan)
24 August	Friedberg	French (Moreau)	Austrians (Latour)
3 September	Würzburg	Austrians (Charles)	French (Jourdan)
4 September	Roveredo	French (Massena)	Austrians (Davidovich)
8 September	Bassano	French (Bonaparte)	Austrians (Wurmser)
12 November	Caldiero	Austrians (Alvintzy)	French (Bonaparte)
15–17 November	Arcola	French (Bonaparte)	Austrians (Alvintzy)

1797

14 January	Rivoli	French (Bonaparte)	Austrians (Alvintzy)
23 March	Malborghetto	French (Massena)	Austrians (Charles)
18 April	Neuweid (or Lahn)	French (Hoche)	Austrians (Werneck)

1798

2 July	Alexandria	French (Bonaparte)	Egyptians (Coraim)
21 July	Pyramids	French (Bonaparte)	Egyptians (Murad and Ibrahim)
27 August	Castlebar	French (Humbert)	British (Lake)
5 September	Collooney	French (Humbert)	British (Vereker)
8 September	Ballinamuck	British (Cornwallis)	French (Humbert)

1799

19 February	El Arish	French (Bonaparte)	Ottoman (Ibrahim Aga)
7 March	Jaffa	French (Bonaparte)	Ottoman (Abou-Saad)
18 March–20 May	Acre (siege)	Ottoman (Djezzar)	French (Bonaparte)
21 March	Ostrach	Austrians (Charles)	French (Jourdan)
25 March	Stockach	Austrians (Charles)	French (Jourdan)
5 April	Magnano	Austrians (Kray)	French (Schérer)
17 April	Mount Tabor	French (Bonaparte)	Ottoman (Achmed)
27 April	Cassano	Austro-Russians (Suvarov)	French (Moreau)
4–7 June	Zürich	Austrians (Charles)	French (Massena)
17–19 July	Trebbia	Austro-Russians (Suvarov)	French (Macdonald)
25 July	Aboukir	French (Bonaparte)	Ottoman (Mustapha)
14 August	Zürich	Austrians (Charles)	French (Massena)
15 August	Novi	Austro-Russians (Suvarov)	French (Joubert)
19 September	Bergen-op-Zoom	French (Brune)	Anglo-Russians (York)
25 September	Zürich	French (Massena)	Allies (Korsakov)
2 October	Bergen-op-Zoom	Anglo-Russians (York)	French (Brune)
6 October	Castricum	French (Brune)	Anglo-Russians (York)
4 November	Genoa	Austrians (Melas)	French (Championnet)

1800

20 March	Heliopolis	French (Kléber)	Ottoman (Vizier)
3 May	Stockach	French (Moreau)	Austrians (Kray)
5 May	Möskirch	French (Moreau)	Austrians (Kray)
16 May	Ulm	French (Moreau)	Austrians (Kray)
9 June	Montebello	French (Lannes)	Austrians (Ott)
14 June	Marengo	French (Bonaparte)	Austrians (Melas)
19 June	Höchstadt	French (Moreau)	Austrians (Kray)
3 December	Hohenlinden	French (Moreau)	Austrians (John)

1801

20 March	Alexandria	British (Abercromby)	French (Menou)

1805

11 October	Haslach	French (Dupont)	Austrians (Mack)
14 October	Elchingen	French (Ney)	Austrians (Werneck/Riesch)
17 October	Ulm (capitulation)	French (Napoleon)	Austrians (Mack)
30 October	Caldiero	French (Massena)	Austrians (Charles)
8 November	Zell	French (Davout/Marmont)	Austrians (Merveldt)
11 November	Dürrenstein	French (Mortier)	Russians (Miloradovich/ Dokhturov)
16 November	Oberhollabrünn (or Hollabrünn)	French (Napoleon)	Russians (Bagration)
2 December	Austerlitz	French (Napoleon)	Austro-Russians (Kutuzov)

1806

8 January	Cape Town	British (Baird)	Franco-Dutch (Janssens)
6 July	Maida	British (Stuart)	French (Reynier)
9 October	Schleiz	French (Bernadotte)	Saxons (Tauenzein)
10 October	Saalfeld	French (Lannes)	Prussians (Louis)
14 October	Jena	French (Napoleon)	Prussians (Hohenlohe)
14 October	Auerstädt	French (Davout)	Prussians (Brunswick)
6 November	Lübeck	French (Soult/Bernadotte)	Prussians (Blücher)
26 December	Pultusk	*Indecisive encounter between French (Lannes) and Russians (Bennigsen)*	
26 December	Golymin	*Indecisive encounter between French (Murat) and Russians (Gallitzin)*	

1807

25 January	Mohrungen	French (Bernadotte)	Russians (Markov)
7–8 February	Eylau	French (Napoleon)	Russians (Bennigsen)
10 June	Heilsberg	French (Napoleon)	Russians (Bennigsen)
14 June	Friedland	French (Napoleon)	Russians (Bennigsen)
29 August	Kjöge (or Roskilde)	British (Wellesley)	Danish (Castenskiold)
2–5 September	Copenhagen	British (Cathcart)	Danish (Peimann)

1808

15 June–17 August	Saragossa	Spanish (Palafox)	French (Verdier)
14 July	Medina del Rio Seco	French (Bessières)	Spanish (Cuesta/Blake)
19 July	Baylen	Spanish (Castaños)	French (Dupont)
17 August	Roliça (or Roleia)	British (Wellesley)	French (Delaborde)

173

1808 *continued*

Date	Battle		
21 August	Vimeiro	British (Wellesley)	French (Junot)
23 November	Tudela	French (Lannes)	Spanish (Castaños)
30 November	Somosierra	French (Napoleon)	Spanish (San Juan)
20 December–20 February 1809	Saragossa	French (Lannes)	Spanish (Palafox)
21 December	Sahagun	British (Paget)	French (Debelle)
29 December	Benevente	British (Paget)	French (Lefebvre-Desnouëttes)

1809

Date	Battle		
16 January	Corunna	British (Moore)	French (Soult)
28 March	Medellin	French (Victor)	Spanish (Cuesta)
16 April	Sacile	Austrians (John)	French (Eugène)
19 April	Tengen	French (Davout)	Austrians (Hohenzollern)
19–20 April	Abensberg	French (Napoleon)	Austrians (Charles)
21 April	Landeshut	French (Napoleon)	Austrians (Hiller)
22 April	Eckmühl (or Eggmühl)	French (Davout/Lannes)	Austrians (Charles)
23 April	Ratisbon	French (Napoleon)	Austrians (Charles)
3 May	Ebersberg	French (Massena)	Austrians (Hiller)
12 May	Oporto	British (Wellesley)	French (Soult)
21–22 May	Aspern-Essling	Austrians (Charles)	French (Napoleon)
14 June	Raab	French (Eugène)	Austrians (John)
5–6 July	Wagram	French (Napoleon)	Austrians (Charles)
10 July	Znaim	*Inconclusive encounter between French (Napoleon) and Austrians (Charles)*	
28 July	Talavera	British (Wellesley)	French (Victor)
19 November	Oçana	French (Soult)	Spanish (Areizago)

1810

Date	Battle		
27 September	Busaco	Anglo-Portuguese (Wellington)	French (Massena)

1811

Date	Battle		
4 March	Barrosa (or Chiclana)	British (Graham)	French (Victor)
3 April	Sabugal	Anglo-Portuguese (Wellington)	French (Reynier)
5 May	Fuentes de Oñoro	Anglo-Portuguese (Wellington)	French (Massena)
16 May	Albuera	Anglo-Portuguese/ Spanish (Beresford)	French (Soult)
25 May	Usagre	British (Lumley)	French (Latour-Maubourg)
25 September	El Bodon	Anglo-Portuguese (Picton)	French (Montbrun)
28 October	Arroyo dos Molinos	Anglo-Portuguese (Hill)	French (Girard)

1812

Date	Battle		
9 January	Valencia	French (Suchet)	Spanish (Blake)
19 January	Ciudad Rodrigo	Anglo-Portuguese (Wellington)	French (Barrié)
6 April	Badajoz	Anglo-Portuguese (Wellington)	French (Philippon)

1812 continued

22 July	Salamanca	Anglo-Portuguese (Wellington)	French (Marmont)
28 July	Vitebsk	French (Napoleon)	Russians (Barclay de Tolly)
8 August	Inkovo	*Inconclusive encounter between French (Sébastiani) and Russians (Platov)*	
17 August	Smolensk	French (Napoleon)	Russians (Barclay de Tolly)
17–18 August	Polotsk	French (Oudinot/St. Cyr)	Russians (Wittgenstein)
19 August	Valutino	French (Napoleon)	Russians (Barclay de Tolly)
7 September	Borodino (or 'The Moscowa')	French (Napoleon)	Russians (Kutuzov)
18 October	Vinkovo	Russians (Bagration)	French (Murat)
24 October	Maloyaroslavets	French (Eugène)	Russians (Kutuzov)
3 November	Fiodoroivskoy	French (Davout)	Russians (Miloradovich)
14 November	Polotsk	French (Victor)	Russians (Wittgenstein)
16–17 November	Krasnyi	French (Napoleon)	Russians (Kutuzov)
26-28 November	Berezina	French (Napoleon)	Russians (Chichagov/ Wittgenstein)
28 November	Loshnitsa	French (Oudinot)	Russians (Chichagov)

1813

1 May	Poserna	French (Ney)	Allies (Winzingerode)
2 May	Lützen	French (Napoleon)	Allies (Wittgenstein)
20–21 May	Bautzen	French (Napoleon)	Allies (Wittgenstein)
21 June	Vittoria	Anglo-Portuguese (Wellington)	French (Joseph/Jourdan)
25 July	Maya	Anglo-Portuguese (Wellington)	French (Soult)
25 July	Roncesvalles	Anglo-Portuguese (Wellington)	French (Soult)
28–30 July	Sorauren	Anglo-Portuguese (Wellington)	French (Soult)
23 August	Grossbeeren	Allies (Bernadotte)	French (Oudinot)
26 August	Katzbach	Allies (Blücher)	French (Macdonald)
26 August	Pirna	French (Vandamme)	Allies (Eugene of Württemberg)
26–27 August	Dresden	French (Napoleon)	Allies (Schwarzenberg)
30 August	Kulm-Priesten	Allies (Ostermann-Tolstoy/ Kleist)	French (Vandamme)
31 August	San Sebastian	Anglo-Portuguese (Wellington)	French (Rey)
31 August	San Marcial	Anglo-Portuguese (Wellington)	French (Soult)
6 September	Dennewitz	Allies (Bernadotte)	French (Ney)
7 October	Vera	Anglo-Portuguese/Spanish (Wellington)	French (Taupin)
12 October	Colditz	French (Murat)	Allies (Schwarzenberg)
14 October	Liebertwolkwitz	*Inconclusive encounter between French (Murat) and Allies*	
16–19 October	Leipzig	Allies (Schwarzenberg/ Bernadotte/Blücher)	French (Napoleon)
30–31 October	Hanau	French (Napoleon)	Bavarians (Wrede)
9 November	St. Jean de Luz	Anglo-Portuguese (Hope)	French (Soult)
10 November	Nivelle	Anglo-Portuguese (Wellington)	French (Soult)

1813 *continued*

9–12 December	Nive	Anglo-Portuguese (Wellington)	French (Soult)
13 December	St. Pierre	Anglo-Portuguese (Hill)	French (Soult)

1814

29 January	Brienne	French (Napoleon)	Allies (Blücher)
30 January	La Rothière	French (Napoleon)	Allies (Blücher)
10 February	Champaubert	French (Napoleon)	Russians (Olssufiev)
11 February	Montmirail	French (Napoleon)	Allies (Yorck/Sacken)
12 February	Château-Thierry	French (Napoleon)	Allies (Yorck)
14 February	Vauchamps	French (Napoleon)	Allies(Blücher)
17 February	Valjouan	French (Grouchy/Gérard)	Allies (Wrede)
18 February	Montereau	French (Napoleon)	Allies (Schwarzenberg)
27 February	Bar-sur-Aube	Allies (Wittgenstein/Wrede)	French (Oudinot)
27 February	Orthez	Anglo-Portuguese (Wellington)	French (Soult)
7 March	Craonne	French (Napoleon)	Allies (Blücher)
9–10 March	Lâon	Allies (Blücher)	French (Napoleon)
13 March	Rheims	French (Napoleon)	Allies (St.-Priest)
17 March	Fismes	Allies (Blücher)	French (Marmont)
20–21 March	Arcis-sur-Aube	Allies (Schwarzenberg)	French (Napoleon)
25 March	La Fère-Champenoise	Allies (Schwarzenberg)	French (Marmont/Mortier)
30 March	Paris (or Montmartre)	Allies (Schwarzenberg)	French (Marmont)
10 April	Toulouse	Anglo-Portuguese (Wellington)	French (Soult)
14 April	Bayonne	Anglo-Portuguese (Hope)	French (Thouvenot)

1815

2 May	Tolentino	Austrians (Bianchi)	Italians (Murat)
16 June	Quatre Bras	Anglo-Allied (Wellington)	French (Ney)
16 June	Ligny	French (Napoleon)	Prussians (Blücher)
18 June	Wavre	*Inconclusive engagement between French (Grouchy) and Prussians (Thielmann)*	
18 June	Waterloo	Anglo-Allied (Wellington) and Prussians (Blücher)	French (Napoleon)

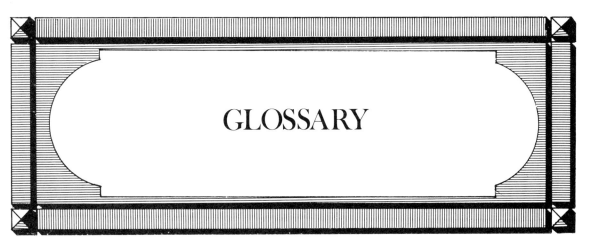

GLOSSARY

Words and terms listed in this glossary include many in common usage during the Napoleonic Wars, and those which had a different meaning at that time from what they have today. Words in languages other than English are listed only in those cases where the precise military definition might not be found in a modern dictionary.

Foreign words are indicated by a letter in parentheses:
(F) French
(G) German
(S) Spanish
(Port.) Portuguese
(Pol.) Polish
(R) Russian

Abatis – barricade of felled trees.

Adjoint (F) – Assistant-Adjutant-General.

Aide-de-Camp (orig. F) – Junior staff officer attached to marshal or general.

Aiguillette (orig. F) – Braided cord shoulder-decoration.

Amalgame (F) – Tactical amalgamation of regular and volunteer units.

Ammuzette – Large-bore firearm or 'wall piece'.

Arm (of service) – cavalry, infantry, artillery, etc.

Arme blanche (F) – a) cavalry sabres; b) generic term for cavalry.

Artillerie volante (F) – fast horse artillery, all gunners being mounted.

Association – early term for local volunteer company.

Ataman (R) – cossack senior officer.

Athwart – Method of wearing a bicorn hat with corners at the sides.

Atiradore (Port.) – sharpshooter of caçadores.

Avant-train (F) – limber.

Ball (as in 'ball ammunition') – musket-ball or musket-cartridge.

Banquette (orig. F) – firing-step behind a parapet.

Barrelled sash – Hussar girdle with lace 'barrels'.

Barbette (orig. F) – a cannon was 'en barbette' when able to fire over a parapet without using an embrasure.

Barret (G) – large, floppy field cap.

Bashkir (R) – Asiatic light cavalryman.

Bastion – a) four-sided fortification; b) design of lace on a uniform, following the same shape.

Batardeau (orig. F) – dam to retain water in a fortress-ditch.

Battalion company – 'centre' company of an infantry battalion.

Battery – orig. a gun-emplacement; later became synonymous with a company of six or eight fieldpieces.

Belly-box – cartridge-box worn at the front of the waist-belt (archaic).

Bengal lights – type of carcass composed of saltpetre, sulphur, and red orpiment.

Blacking ball – blackening agent for equipment.

Blouse (F) – smock-type garment.

Bomb – Mortar-shell; loosely applied to all explosive projectiles.

Bombardier – junior N.C.O. of artillery.

Bonnet (orig. F) – triangular fortification placed in front of a ravelin.

Bonnet de police (F) – undress cap.

Brassard – cloth arm-band.

Breastplate – small badge worn on the shoulder-belt.

Breastwork – parapet for the protection of troops.

Bricole (F) – rope or strap used for man-handling a cannon; a cannon fired 'en bricole' when the shot struck a sloping revetment.

Brigade – a) tactical formation of two or more battalions; b) British artillery battery.

Brigadier (F) – sergeant.

Briquet (F) – infantry sabre.

Brown Bess – nickname applied to Long Land Pattern musket and subsequent patterns.

Busby – fur hussar cap (not in common use at this date).

Butin (F) – colloquialism for personal kit, orig. 'booty'.

Cabinet (F) – Napoleon's personal household.

Caçadore (Port.) – rifleman (lit. 'hunter').

Cadenettes (F) – tresses of plaited hair hanging from the temples.

Cahouk (F) – mameluke head-dress.

Caisson (F) – ammunition-waggon.

Canister – artillery ammunition comprising lead balls in a tin.

Cantinière (F) – female sutleress.

Cap – general term for any military head-dress.

Caponnière (orig. F) – a) a covered communication-trench from an enceinte to a detached work; b) a casemated fortification projecting across a ditch for delivering flanking-fire.

Capsquare – metal plate securing the trunnions of a cannon to the carriage.

Captain-lieutenant – British commissioned rank (archaic).

Captain-general (S) – commanding general (of a province, etc.).

Carabinier (F) – a) type of heavy cavalry; b) grenadier of light infantry.

Carbine – short cavalry musket.

Carcass (also carcase) – incendiary or illumination-device (usually a shell but term also applied to tar-barrels, etc.).

Carnets (F) – Notebooks kept by Napoleon to record details of units.

Carriage – wooden framework supporting a cannon-barrel.

Carronade – large-calibre, short-range cannon.

Cartouche (F) – cartridge-box.

Cascabel – knob at the sealed end of a cannon-barrel.

Casemate – chamber in a fortress-wall.

Case-shot – canister.

Cavalier – raised battery, usually inside a bastion.

Cazador (S) – as 'caçadore'.

Cazador a caballo (S) – as 'chasseur à cheval'.

Centre company – 'battalion company'.

Chapeau chinois (F) – lit. 'Chinese hat': see 'jingling johnny'.

Charoual (F) – mameluke trousers.

Chase – segment of cannon-barrel between chase-girdle and muzzle.

Chasseur (F) – lit. 'hunter': light troops.

Chasseur à cheval (F) – light cavalry.

Chasseur à pied (F) – light infantry.

Chasseur-carabinier (F) – Westphalian Guard rifleman.

Chef de Bataillon (F) – battalion-commander.

Chef de musique (F) – bandmaster.

Chef de péloton (F) – platoon-leader.

Chef d'escadron (F) – cavalry squadron-commander.

Chemin des Rondes (F) – sentry-walk around the top of a revetment.

Cheval-de-frise (orig. F) – barricade made of stake- or blade-studded beams.

Chevau-léger (F) – light cavalry.

Chevau-léger-lancier (F) light cavalry armed with lance.

Chinese light – illumination-device composed of nitre, sulphur, antimony and orpiment.

Chock – see 'quoin'.

Chosen man – corporal (archaic; used by British 95th Rifles until c. 1805).

Citadel – four- or five-sided strongpoint in a fortress defence.

Clash pans – cymbals.

Clinometer – instrument for measuring the incline on which a cannon stands.

Club – hair-dressing in the form of a short queue.

Cockade – rosette of national colours worn on head-dress.

Coehorn (also Coehoorn) – mortar named after its designer.

Coffret (F) – ammunition-chest.

Cohort (F) – formation of National Guard (orig. Roman).

Colback (also colpack) (F) – fur hussar cap.

Colour-sergeant – British senior N.C.O. rank instituted 1813.

Commissaire ordinaire (F) – assistant-commissary.

Commissaire ordonnateur (F) – commissary-in-chief.

Commissary – supply-officer.

Company – small unit of infantry, cavalry or artillery.

Conducteur (F) – artillery-driver.

Cordon (orig. F) – rounded coping-stones surmounting a revetment.

Cornet – cavalry second-lieutenant.

Corps – a) tactical unit comprising several divisions; b) term used to indicate any unit of troops from detached companies up to brigade.

Corps d'observation (F) – detached formation protecting lines of communication, watching enemy, etc.

Cossack (R) – generic term for Caucasian irregular cavalry; from Turkish 'quzzaq' = freebooter.

Counterscarp – slope or retaining-wall on outer side of a ditch.

Countersign – password.

Covered way (also covert-way) – infantry fire-step along a ditch.

Crapaud – British nickname for French soldiers.

Cravat (F) – a) swatch of material on top of a standard-pole; b) pompom encircling a sword-blade at the juncture of blade and hilt.

Crochet (F) – miniature parallel trench.

Crownwork – fortification composed of two small bastions with two long branches at either side.

Cuirass (F) – breastplate.

Cuirassier (F) – armoured heavy cavalry.

Czapka (also Czapska, Shapska, Tchapka, etc.) (Pol.) – square-topped cap.

Degen (G) – straight-bladed infantry sword.

Demi-brigade (F) – unit comprised of part-regulars and part-volunteers.

Demi-lune (F) – see 'ravelin'.

Dents de loup (F) – cloth 'wolf-teeth' edging to a shabraque.

Desagulier – light fieldpiece named after designer.

Detachments – (as in Btn of D—.): composite unit formed of stragglers.

Diechselpferd (G) – wheel-horse.

Dispart – Half the difference between the diameter of a gun-barrel at the base-ring and at the swell of the muzzle; generally 1/56th of the length.

Division – a) tactical formation of several brigades; b) two companies of a battalion, drawn up in line, three ranks deep; c) two fieldpieces with attendant vehicles; d) section of General Staff.

Dolman – tail-less, braided jacket.

Dolphin – lifting-handle on a cannon-barrel.

Draft – system of breaking up a unit, transferring personnel to other corps.

Dragon (F) – dragoon.

Dragoon – medium cavalry; orig. mounted infantry.

Dragoon Guard – British heavy cavalry.

Dumpling – short-barrelled pistol.

Eclaireur (F) – cavalry-scout.

Ecoute (orig. F) – small mine-gallery.

Embrasure – opening in a parapet to allow gunfire through the wall.

Enceinte (F) – fortress-wall or perimeter.

Enfilade – fire from a flank, raking the entire length of the formation.

Ensign – infantry second-lieutenant.

Envelope – continuous enceinte.

Epaulement (orig. F) – breastwork.

Esplanade – open space between a citadel and the nearest buildings.

Espontoon – see 'spontoon'.

Etat-Major (F) – staff.

Evolution – drill-movement.

Expense magazine – small magazine placed near a battery.

Facings – coloured distinctions on a uniform (collar, cuffs, etc.).

Fahnenträger (G) – infantry colour-bearer.

Fahnrich (G) – aspirant officer serving in the ranks.

Fantassin (F) – infantryman.

Farrier – cavalry pioneer or one who cares for unit's horses.

Faschinenmesser (G) – bill-hook or machete.

Fascine – bundle of brushwood used in fortification.

Fausse-braye (orig. F) – low outer rampart, usually earthen.

Feld Lazaretten (G) – field hospital.

Feldmütze (G) – field-cap.

Feld-Postillione (G) – courier.

Felloe (also Felly) – curved wooden segment forming part of the outer ring of an artillery wheel.

Fencible – home-defence unit corresponding to regular army.

Fermelet (F) – mameluke waistcoat.

Feuerwerker (G) – artillery N.C.O.

Feuerwerkscompagnie (G) – artillery rocket-corps (Austrian).

Fire Ball – illumination device comprising rosin, sulphur, alum powder, starch, saltpetre, mealed powder and linseed oil.

Firelock – flintlock musket.

Fixed ammunition – artillery projectile with wooden 'sabot' affixed.

Flank company – grenadiers and light infantry of a line battalion.

Flanquers (F) – light infantry, particularly of Middle Guard.

Flèche (F) – lit. arrow; arrow-shaped earthworks.

Fliegendes Lazarett (G) – mobile hospital.

Flügel-Adjutant (G) – A.D.C.

Flügelhorn (G) – hunting-horn.

Flügelmütze (G) – mirliton cap.

Fly – rapidly-moving infantry waggon.

Flying artillery – horse-artillery.

Fore-and-aft – method of wearing a bicorn hat with corners at back and front.

Foreign corps – all non-British units of British army.

Forlorn hope – first storming-party into a breach.

Fourgon (F) – heavy transport-waggon.

Fourrier (F) – cavalry quartermaster-sergeant.

Fraises (orig. F) – storm-poles.

Freikorps (G) – independent companies.

Freiwilligenjäger (G) – rifle companies of middle-class volunteers serving as N.C.O and officer-training units.

Frizzen – part of a flintlock from which the flint strikes sparks.

Frog – leather belt-fitting from which a scabbard is suspended.

Fugelman – (G., lit. 'file-leader'): a soldier who stood in front of a company during drill, from whom the others took their time.

Fuhrwesen (G) – train.

Furniture – metal fittings on a musket.

Fusil – light musket (F) any musket.

Fusil dépareillé (F) – Republican term describing a composite musket made from spare bits of many different patterns.

Fusil d'honneur (F) – presentation-musket awarded for outstanding service.

Fusilier – (F) line infantry 'centre' company; (G) as before or light infantry; (B) title of three line regiments (7th, 21st & 23rd), orig. one armed with a fusil.

Fusiliers-Chasseurs (F) – unit of Imperial Guard infantry.

Fusiliers-Grenadiers (F) – unit of Imperial Guard infantry.

Gabion (orig. F) – earth-filled wickerwork basket used in fortification.

Gabion farci (F) – gabion rolled in front of a sapper to shield him from enemy fire.

Gala (G) – 'gala uniform' = parade-dress.

Gallery – largest type of mine-tunnel.

Galloper – light, shafted fieldpiece without a limber.

Garde du Corps (G) – French term used by many German armies for heavy bodyguard cavalry.

Gardes d'honneur (F) – light bodyguard cavalry; also escort units of individual cities.

Garland – wooden framework to hold round-shot in a neat pile.

Gendarme (F) – orig. any armed man, but by this time implying troops engaged in security or provost rôle.

Général de Brigade, de Division, etc. (F) – General of Brigade, Division, etc.; title not automatically accorded to commanders of these formations.

Generalquartiermeister (G) – chief of staff.

Glacis (orig. F) – slope descending from a fortification.

Goddam (F) – French nickname given to British troops from their constant use of that expression; dates from Hundred Years War.

Gorget (orig. F) – decorative crescent-shaped plaque worn by officers around the neck; symbol of commissioned rank and a relic of medieval armour.

Grand-Quartier-Général (F) – general head-quarters.

Grasshoppers (F) – French nickname given to British riflemen.

Grenadier – élite infantry, orig. those armed with hand grenades.

Grenadier à Cheval (F) – Imperial Guard Horse Grenadier.

Grognard (F) – lit. 'grumbler'; nickname of French Guard infantry.

Grosse-bottes (F) – lit. 'big boots'; nickname of French Guard Horse Grenadiers.

Guard ('Garde' F & G) – orig. royal body-guard; term implied veteran élite troops.

Guerite (orig. F) – sentry-box sited on ramparts; loosely applied to sentry-boxes in general.

Guerrilla (S) – irregular patriot-fighter.

Guides (F) – light cavalry, orig. escorts.

Guidon (orig. F) – cavalry standard.

Gun-metal – usually described 'brass' guns, generally eight to ten parts tin to 100 parts copper.

Habit-veste (F) – jacket.

Halberd – pole-arm with axe-head used by colour-escorts of some armies.

Half-brigade – (F) see 'demi-brigade'; (B) half an artillery battery.

Half-moon – see 'demi-lune'.

Half-pay – an officer receiving half-pay was one who held a commission but had no employment.

Handicraft – enlisted man employed in a trade, e.g. regimental cobbler.

Handlanger (G) – artillery labourer.

Handspike – lever used to manoeuvre a cannon.

Handwerker (G) – artillery artificer.

Hat company – 'battalion company', i.e. those wearing hats, not flank company head-dress (grenadier bearskins or light infantry caps).

Haversack – fabric bag used for carrying food, etc.

Helmet-cap – usually applied to a fur-crested 'round hat' made to resemble a 'Tarleton'.

Hessian boots – decorative boots, below knee-length, often trimmed with lace.

Hetman (R) – cossack general.

Hirschfänger (G) – wide-bladed, machete-like sword.

Hornwork – fortification consisting of a bastion front and two branches at the sides.

Horse – cavalry (archaic).

Housings – horse-furniture.

Howitzer – short-barrelled cannon designed for high-angle fire.

Hussar (B) ('Hussard' F, 'Husar' G) – light cavalry, styled on Hungarian light horse.

Infirmier-brancardier (F) – stretcher-bearer.

Insurrection (G) – Hungarian and Croation home-defence organizations.

Intendant (F) – commissary.

Invalids – soldiers unfit for active service, used for garrison duty.

Jäger (G) – lit. 'huntsman'; light troops.

Jäger zu Fuss (G) – light infantry.

Jäger zu Pferd (G) – light cavalry, mounted rifles.

Jingling Johnny – musical instrument comprising bells hung from an ornamental pole.

'Junta' forces (S) – regiments raised by authority of provisional regional governments in Spain during Peninsular War.

Kalmuk (also kalmuck, calmuk, etc.) (R) – Asiatic light cavalry.

Kasket (G) – helmet; usually applied to leather helmets (excluding shakos).

Kiwer (R) – concave-topped shako adopted by Russia in 1812.

Knapsack – infantry pack.

Kollet (G) – short-tailed tunic.

Konfederatka (Pol.) – early type of czapka.

Krankenträger (G) – stretcher-bearer.

Krümper (G) – Prussian reservist trained in 1808–12 period.

Kurtka (Pol.) – lancer-jacket.

Laboratory – room (in fortress) or tent (in field) where powder was made up into cartridges.

Lancer (F 'lancier') – light cavalryman armed with a lance.

Landsturm (G) – home-defence militia.

Landwehr (G) – second-line 'levée en masse' or militia.

Legion (F 'légion') – orig. a self-contained

unit comprising infantry, cavalry, artillery, transport etc.; term often used indiscriminately but some examples of original use in Napoleonic Wars – e.g. Brunswick 'Black Legion', etc.

Leib (G) – Lifeguard or Guard unit (e.g. 'Leib-Battalion' etc.).

Lentille (F) flat woollen disc worn on shako instead of pompom.

Levée en masse (orig. F) – mass-conscription.

Light Bobs – British nickname for light infantry.

Light dragoons – light cavalry.

Light infantry (F 'infanterie légère') – orig. fast-moving skirmishers, but in practice sometimes little different from line troops.

Limber – two-wheeled carriage connecting cannon with gun-team.

Line – term describing ordinary infantry, cavalry etc.; meaning 'infantry of the line of battle', etc.

Linstock (also linkstock) – pike holding slow-match.

Litewka (G) – thigh-length tunic.

Local Militia – British part-time home-defence force formed 1808.

Loophole – small hole punched in a wall to allow defenders to fire through.

Lunette (orig. F) – a) triangular fortification on or beyond a glacis; b) small fortification sited to one side of a ravelin.

Magazine – a) storage-place for munitions; b) supplementary container for musket-ammunition carried by the individual soldier.

Mameluke – Egyptian cavalry, some incorporated in the French Imperial Guard.

Mantlet – wheeled wooden screen protecting the diggers at the head of a sap.

Mine – a) subterranean gallery in which an explosive charge was placed to bring down a fortification; b) the explosive charge required to accomplish (a).

Maréchal de Camp (F) – major-general.

Maréchal-des-logis (F) – senior N.C.O. (quartermaster).

Marie-Louises (F) – nickname for young conscripts of the 1813–14 period.

Marine (F 'marin') – troops raised for service aboard ship.

Match – impregnated burning-cord for igniting cannon, etc.

Match-case – metal cylinder worn on grenadiers' cross-belts, orig. to ignite hand-grenades; purely decorative by this period.

Marquis – large tent, now 'marquee'.

Masse de manoeuvre (F) – part of French army entrusted with enveloping attacks.

Masse primaire (F) – main part of French army engaged in main theatre of battle.

Masse secondaire (F) – secondary part of French army engaged in subsidiary sector of battle.

Merlon – solid parapet between two embrasures.

Military shoe – term describing footwear which even James' 'Regimental Companion' (1804) was 'at a loss to understand'; probably alluded to shape.

Militia – home-defence force.

Mirliton (F) – hussar-cap with flying 'wing'.

Mother Shipton – British tall 'round hat' named after famous Yorkshire witch.

Music – regimental band.

Musketeer (G) – 'centre' companies of line infantry.

Musketoon – light musket.

National Guard (F 'Garde Nationale') – home-defence units.

Nid d'hirondelles (F) – see 'swallows' nest'.

Necessaries – issued items of personal kit.

Normal (G) – title given to units formed from selected personnel.

Oberjäger (G) – Jäger N.C.O.

Old Trousers – British nickname for the French drum-call 'Pas de Charge'.

Opolchenie (R) – militia.

Ordenanca (Port.) – levée en masse militia.

Ordinär (G) – term describing field batteries.

Ordre mixte (F) – attack-formation comprising both columns and lines.

Ouvriers (F) – artisans, labour battns.

Palisade – fence of pointed wooden stakes.

Pallasch (G) – straight-bladed heavy cavalry sabre.

Parados – a rearward parapet.

Parallel – siege-trench running parallel to enemy fortifications.

Parapet – wall or earthen bank on the forward

edge of a fortification or siege-work, protecting troops behind.

Park – artillery reserve.

Parole – a) system of releasing prisoners of war; b) password.

Partida (S) – guerrilla band; regularized strength from 2 Dec. 1808 of 100 infantry or fifty cavalry, a regulation generally disregarded.

Partisan – guerrilla.

Pelisse (orig. F) – furred hussar jacket; also applied to officers' braided frock-coats.

Péloton (F) – platoon.

Pennon – lance-flag.

Petard – explosive device for blowing in a door; almost redundant by this time.

Petit Quartier Général (F) – lit. 'small H.Q.': staff which accompanied Napoleon whenever he went on horseback.

Pickers – wire needle used for clearing musket touch-hole.

Piece – any cannon (orig. 'fieldpiece').

Pioneer (F 'pionier') – regimental artificer or carpenter.

Piquet (also 'picquet') – infantry outpost or sentinel.

Place of Arms – enlargement of covered way of a fortress where troops could be assembled for sorties.

Plastron – coloured chest-panel on a jacket.

Pokalem (F) – undress-cap worn 1812–15.

Pomatum – hair-dressing.

Pontonier (F) – pontoon-constructor.

Pontoon – mobile bridge of boats.

Porte-Aigle (F) – colour-bearer.

Post – outpost, sentinel.

Prepared ammunition – ball and propellant in a cartridge.

Present – to 'present' (fire) = to take aim.

Prolonge (F) – rope attaching cannon to team to obviate repeated unlimbering.

Provisional Cavalry – similar to British Fencible Cavalry.

Provisional regiments – composite units formed from detachments.

Pupilles (F) – cadets.

Queue – a) pigtail-hairstyle; b) tobacco-plug shaped like a queue.

Quoin – wooden block used for elevating a cannon-barrel.

Rampart – earthen or masonry wall forming main part of fortress-defence.

Rangers – orig. describing fast-moving light infantry.

Raquettes (F) – 'flounders' or knots on end of cap-cords.

Raupenhelm (G) – crested helmet, e.g. Bavarian.

Ravelin (also raveline) – triangular detached fortification in front of a fortress-wall.

Redan – 'V'-shaped fortification.

Redoubt – detached fortification, or a redan placed in a bastion.

Reinforces – reinforcing-bands on a cannon-barrel.

Retrenchment – interior defence of a fortress.

Revetment – retaining-wall of a fortification.

Rifles – infantry armed with rifled muskets.

Roller – neck-cloth.

Rotte (G) – basic three-man unit for cavalry manoeuvre.

Round hat – short 'topper', often with wide or turned-up brim.

Running ball – musket-charge without wadding.

Sabot – wooden shoe on 'fixed ammunition'.

Sabre – cavalry sword; (F) a cavalryman, e.g. 'a regiment of 800 sabres'.

Sabretache – decorated leather case hung from sword-belt.

Sap – narrow siege-trench.

Sap faggot – eight-inch thick fascine, three feet long.

Sap roller – see 'gabion farci'.

Sapper – orig. one who dug saps; later generic term for engineer.

Saucissons (F) – lit. 'sausages': long, thin fascines.

Scarp – outer slope of a rampart.

Schirmütze (G) – peaked cloth cap.

Schützen (G) – riflemen.

Sea Fencibles – British home-defence naval volunteers based in sea-ports.

Sentinel (also 'centinel') – sentry; also archaic term for private soldier.

Serpent – woodwind musical instrument.

Shabraque – ornamental horse-furniture.

Shako (also 'chaco') – cylindrical head-dress, peaked.

Shell-jacket – orig. a sleeveless over-jacket.

Shoulder-knot – early term for epaulette or fringed shoulder-strap.

Shoulder-scale – epaulette constructed of overlapping metal scales.

Slow-match – see 'match'.

Spadroon – light, straight-bladed sword.

Spatterdash – long gaiters.

Spencer (F) – short-tailed jacket.

Spontoon – short or half-pike.

Stamm-regiment (G) – regular unit acting as depôt or cadre for reserve regiment.

Standartenträger (G) – cavalry standard-bearer.

Steel – frizzen.

Stock – leather or fabric strip worn around the neck.

Storm-poles – palisade planted on a scarp, projecting horizontally or slightly downwards.

Stovepipe – cylindrical shako.

Subdivision – British artillery formation: one gun, crew and waggon.

Substitute – militiamen paid to serve in place of one selected by ballot.

Suffocating Pots – sulphur/nitre composition, when ignited causing distress to the enemy, or used for fumigation.

Sugar-loaf – any tall, cylindrical head-dress – 'round hat' or shako.

Suprevest (F) – cloth 'over-jacket' cut in the shape of a cuirass, worn by German and Russian bodyguard units.

Swallows' nest – large 'wing' enveloping top of shoulder.

Sweeps – nickname of British 95th Rifles.

Tambour (F) – a) a drum; b) a drummer; c) a small, palisaded fortification.

Tarleton – fur-crested leather helmet, named after General Banastre Tarleton.

Tartar (R) – Asiatic light cavalry.

Tenaille (orig. F) – small fortification in a ditch in front of a wall.

Tenaillon (orig. F) – small fortification on one side of a ravelin.

Tenue de route (F) – marching-order.

Terreplein (orig. F) – wide upper part of a rampart.

Tête de colonne (F) – lit. 'head of column': term describing colour-party, musicians, pioneers etc.

Timonier (F) – wheel-horse.

Tin helmet – lightweight, tropical cavalry helmet.

Tirailleur (F) – sharpshooter.

Tirailleur-grenadier (F) – Imperial Guard light infantry.

Toise (F) – old French unit of measurement, = 6.395 English feet; used for measuring fortifications.

Toug (F) – mameluke standard – horsehair tail on a pole.

Tow Rows – British nickname for grenadiers.

Train – troops responsible for driving transport, artillery etc.

Trench fascine – fascine from four to six feet long, four to nine inches thick.

Triangle – framework constructed from spontoons to which a prisoner was tied for flogging.

Trou de loup (F) – see 'wolf pit'.

Trucks – small, solid artillery-carriage wheels.

Trunnions – lugs projecting from a cannon-barrel, fitting on to the carriage.

Truppentrain (G) – train detachments assigned to line units.

Turban – ornamental cloth strip around a helmet.

Turkish bells – Jingling Johnny.

Turkish music – musical instruments of oriental origin – jingling johnny, cymbals, tambourine, kettle-drum etc.

Turnback – turned-back section of coat-tail.

Uhlan (G) – lancer (orig. Turkish 'oghlan' = 'child').

Unicorn – light Russian howitzer (also 'licorn').

Unlaced – an 'unlaced' regiment was one of which the officers' uniforms had no metallic lace decoration.

Vandyke (also 'vandyck') – zigzag lace edge along a shabraque, etc.

Vedette – cavalry scout.

Velite (F) – trainees; light infantry (orig. Roman light troops).

Vent – touch-hole in a cannon-barrel.

Veterans – old or semi-invalid soldiers fit only for garrison duty except in emergencies.

Vivandière (F) – female sutleress.

Voisko (R) – cossack tribal regiment.

Volley-gun – multi-barrelled firearm, all chambers igniting simultaneously.

Voltigeur (F) – lit. 'vaulter'; light infantry companies of line battalions.

Volunteers – a) part-time home-defence troops; b) young men serving as enlisted men in hope of winning a commission.

Wachtmeister (G) – artillery or cavalry sergeant-major.

Wadmiltilt – waterproof tarpaulin made of woollen material, retaining natural oils of sheep.

Waldhorn (G) – hunting-horn.

Wall-piece – large-calibre musket mounted on fortress-wall (F 'mousquet à chevalet').

Waterdeck – waterproof, painted canvas saddle-cover.

Water fascine – fascine six feet long, one to two feet thick, weighted with stone to make it sink into wet or marshy ground.

Watering-cap – cylindrical shako (usually with folding peak) worn by cavalry in undress.

White Light – see 'Chinese light'.

Wing – shell-like epaulette worn by flank companies and light cavalry.

Wolf-pit – cone-shaped pit used as anti-personnel trap, usually six feet deep and four to five feet wide at the surface.

Wolf-teeth – zigzag cloth edge to a shabraque.

Worm – corkscrew-device for extracting unfired charge from barrel.

Wurst Wagen (G) – lit. 'sausage-waggon'; artillery transport or caisson with padded seat on top.

Yalek (F) – mameluke jacket.

Yeomanry – British volunteer cavalry.

Zigzags – approach-trenches in siege-works.

Zimmermann (G) – pioneer.

Züg (G) – platoon.

Zügführer (G) – file-leader.

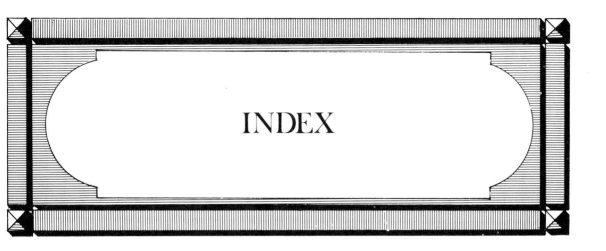

INDEX

Page numbers in italics refer to illustrations; e.g. *106*